# Headgear of Hitler's Germany

## Vol. 1: Heer · Kriegsmarine · Luftwaffe

## Vol. 1: Heer · Kriegsmarine · Luftwaffe

# Headgear of Hitler's Germany

By Jill Halcomb
and Wilhelm P. B. R. Saris
with Otto Spronk

**1st EDITION**

**Copyright 1989 by Jill Halcomb**

**ISBN No. 0-912138-41-6**

**Designed by Roger James Bender and Roger Waterman**

**Type Set by Perez Productions**

**Published by R. James Bender Publishing, P.O. Box 23456, San Jose, California, 95153**

**Printed in the United States of America**

# ACKNOWLEDGEMENTS

The abundance of documentation, film footage, photographs and artifacts which survive the Third Reich is, at times, amazing. Perhaps no other nation has ever bequeathed so much detailed information to historians. There are some major voids of data, of course, but in comparison to other empires which have come and gone, for its short lifespan, the Third Reich is an extremely well documented entity.

A great deal of credit must go to those persons who collected and preserved documents and photographs, long before collecting had reached its present popularity. These individuals were actively accumulating and preserving each bit of history that crossed their path. This book and those volumes to follow are the result of their years of dedication to the conservation of information and artifacts of the period. I refer to many persons world-wide who have spent years cataloging and sorting data, but specifically to Wilhelm P.B.R. Saris, The Netherlands, who so graciously provided an enormous and sometimes overwhelming amount of documentation, as well as photographs and drawings of insignia. He and Otto Spronk, The Hague, should be highly commended for the tremendous amount of data and work they have devoted to this series. One cannot express the importance of their assistance adequately. It is to them that this book is dedicated.

John M. Coy, James J. Boulton and Len Champion likewise generously contributed many excellent photographs from their extensive collections. Others provided photographs and documentation from their libraries, providing the sort of input so necessary to the research and production of any book. They are listed in alphabetical order:

| | |
|---|---|
| Leo van Aerle | Jack Buske |
| John R. Angolia | Francis Catella |
| Kim Alstott | Derek Chapman |
| F. Patt Anthony | Josef Charita |
| E. John Bagale | Stan Cook |
| Terence Baldwin | C.R. Davis |
| Jürgen Bandau | David Delich |
| Kurt Barickman | Dieter Deuster |
| Roger Bender | Ray Embree Jr. |
| Klaus D. Benseler | Alfred Ex |
| Robert Bernard | Gentry Ferrell |
| Pete Bilheimer | Rita Fleishhmann |
| Flugkapitän a.D. Karl Born | Horst Fleming |
| Anton Breuker | William J. Floyd |

Don Frailey
Hartwig Friedrich
Paul Geers
Mark Griffith
Bud Hasher
Jack Hatter
Arie Hendriks
Harry Hinds
John F. Holden
Heinz v. Hungen
Jay Jeandron
Anthony Jenssen
LTC (ret.) Thomas M. Johnson
Jim Jones
Jan de Jonge
Clem Kelly
Tim Knight
Richard Korpanty
H. Kruesel
Ron Kwan
Benno Ladwig
Ken Lazier
David Littlejohn
Ingo Löhken
Richard Long
Robert McCarthy
Niall Malcolm
Gordon Mandley
Ron Manion
Andrew Mollo
Richard Mundhenk
Harper Noehren
Heinz Nowarra
Karl Ortmann
Klaus D. Patzwall
Peter Pauwels
Brent Price
H.B. Ramke
Bill Rentz
George Petersen
Dipl. Ing. Karl Ries
Horst Rivier

Pieter Roelse
Tony Rowland
Gerhard Rudloff
Gordon L. Rulong
Eberh. Schmidt
Oskar Schönweitz
Carl Schultheis
Richard Schulze-Kossens
Willi Schumacher
Carlton J. Schwab
Bob Sevier
Mike Shaner
Tom Shutt
Helga Sichermann-
  Spielhagen
René Smeets
Ed Stadnicki
Peter Stahl
Roger S. Steffen
Emily Caldwell Stewart
Joe Stone
Hugh Page Taylor
Alain Taugourdeau
Hans Tessaro
Frank D. Thayer, Jr.
Robert J. Thiege
Mikel Thorne
Robert J. Treend
C. Gary Triggs
Ulric of England
Jan Vincx
Andrew W. Walker
Gary L. Walker
Roger Waterman
Jerry Weiblen
Otto Weidinger
Gordon Williamson
Kit Wilson
Steve Wolfe
Josef Zienert
Ray Zyla

## Institutions and Archives
Bayerische Armeemuseum
Bibliotek der Universität
  Heidelberg

Bibliothek für Zeitgeschichte,
  ehem. Weltkriegsbücherei

Bundesarchiv-Militärarchiv,
  Freiburg
Bundesarchiv, Koblenz
Bund Oberland
Deutsches Museum, München
ECPA
Hochschul-und
  Landesbibliothek, München
Instituut voor Oorlogs-
  dokumentatie, Amsterdam
Landesbibliothek Darmstadt
National Archives,
  Washington, D.C.

Preussischer Kulturbesitz
Preussische Staatsbibliothek,
  Berlin
Stadtarchiv, Frankfurt
Stadtarchiv, Lüdenscheid
Stahlhelm-Archiv
Wehrbereichskommando III,
  Zentralbibliothek d.
  Bundeswehr, Düsseldorf
Wehrgeschichtliches Ausb.
Zentrum Marineschule
  Mürwick

## PUBLISHER'S ACKNOWLEDGEMENTS

During the difficult years of research associated with this project I have seen an era of international cooperation unmatched in this hobby. I have also witnessed an incredible exhibition of dedication and effort to constantly improve the final product. The authors waded through over 50,000 pages of documents, regulations, periodicals and newspapers, and have accurately translated more than 2000 pages of information. This continual research has expanded the original concept of a single volume to cover all military, political and civil headgear of the Third Reich to a multi-volume series of at least three books.

My special thanks must go to Otto Spronk who supplied hundreds of rare photographs for the project. He patiently awaited specific requests from the authors, and when received, he would go on 24 hour rampages searching his massive negative files and then spend countless hours in the dark room developing the needed prints. I wish to also thank George Petersen who, although he has no time for a decent night's sleep, carefully went through the book and made numerous contributions to accuracy and photographic input. Our mutual friend, Ed Owen, lent his expertise with a camera to photograph many rare items from the Petersen collection as well as others on the east coast.

I have had the pleasure to "network" with numerous collectors and researchers during the project, many of whom I call "friend." They have opened their collections to us and have provided us with additional input, so necessary to the research and success of any book. They are listed under "Authors' Acknowledgements." To them and those above, I can only say "Thank You" for a job well done.

Roger James Bender

# FOREWORD

**■■■■**

In the years since the end of the great conflict we know as World War II, there has been an interest, either for diversion or investment, in obtaining mementos or souvenirs of the largest scale war we hope to have ever seen. A popular category of such collectibles has been Third Reich regalia, perhaps because of its abundance, diversity and colorful nature. Reference guides were needed for potential hobbyists, as well as for historians, researchers or those merely interested in understanding the significance of objects presented to them. A number of pamphlets, articles and books have been published in the U.S. with varying degrees of accuracy. Among reasons for the weaknesses might have been that pertinent regulations were only available in the German language or that there was a prevalence of hearsay information. Over time, the language barrier has become less significant as the sphere of collectors has come to include those either fluent in German or resourceful enough to seek assistance with translation. Rumor and speculation still have to be avoided, of course.

It should be said that while definite intentions were stated in published regulations, the potential exists for encountering numerous variations. The collector should not allow differences in style, however, from that which is regarded as regulation, to justify acceptance of a fraudulent item. With the increase in popularity of Third Reich collectibles, their value has risen to the point that it has become worthwhile for the unscrupulous to produce facsimiles of nearly every conceivable relic of the time of Hitler's regime. This unfortunate situation discourages many would-be and veteran collectors. But, a great deal can be learned by comparing original and reproduction items - with the application of some common sense.

Among reference works intended as guides to identification, there have been few devoted to the study of headgear worn before and during World War II by people in the military and civilian organizations of the Third Reich. This series of books, then, helps fill a void in the collection of reference materials by presenting an exhaustively researched interpretation of the documentation which survives.

In this first volume, the three main military brances are considered, beginning with some background information regarding the derivation of the caps of the 1930s and 1940s. This is the first time a book has presented thoroughly researched data regarding the heritage and tradition preceding the development of the Third Reich headgear it describes.

I am sure this series will help you in your study, and I hope that you will, as I do, anxiously await the remainder of books in the set.

Jack Hatter
Warminster, Pennsylvania

# TABLE OF CONTENTS

# 1

# REICHSHEER/HEER

## Service/Visored Cap (Dienstmütze/Schirmmütze)

The visored cap worn by the German Army underwent several changes during the period 1919-1945. By a decree of March 6, 1919, Reichspräsident Friedrich Ebert was authorized to disband the army and to form a provisional Reichswehr (the armed forces collectively) for the new German Republic, structured from the Reichsheer and Reichsmarine. Enlistment was voluntary and was limited to 100,000 men. This Reichswehr was formally instituted by law (Wehrgesetz) on March 23, 1921.[1]

On May 5, 1919, initial uniform regulations were issued,[2] which were to be the first in a series of changes and modifications of the uniform worn by the armed forces. From these alterations would evolve the familiar uniform visored cap, the Schirmmütze, associated with the Third Reich.

### 1919-1927

The visored cap (Klappmütze) of this period featured a field-grey top with a 4cm wide field-grey band; very often the color of it being somewhat darker than the cap top (though not as dark as on those caps produced later). It was piped around the crown seam and above and below the band in the appropriate Waffenfarbe (branch-of-service color). Officers and men wore a black lacquered leather chin strap[3] above the black lacquered leather visor. It was not until February 1927 that cap cords, in silver or bullion wire weave, or gold plating, were introduced for wear by the officer ranks.[4] Officers below the rank of General wore Waffenfarbe piping on their caps; generals' caps were piped in gilt aluminum wire.[5]

---

[1]*Die Deutsche Reichswehr--Das Deutsche Reichsheer. May 9, 1930, p. 22.*
[2]*Die Deutsche Reichswehr in neuen Uniformen. 1920, p. 20.*
[3]*Heeresverordnungblatt (HVBI.). "Bekleidung und Ausrüstung des Reichsheeres," Nr. 77, Jahrgang 2. Berlin: December 20, 1920, p. 1014.*
[4]*Ibid. "II Änderung an der Uniform der Generale," Nr. 18, Jahrgang 9, Berlin: August 1, 1927, pp. 92-95f.*
[5]*Ibid., p. 92.*

This enlisted man wears the standard German Army visored cap, c. 1914. Note that both the state and national cockades are worn. This photo clearly shows the "Gibralter" sleeve band.

Gustav Noske (left) during a speech for the elections of the Nationalversammlung, January 1919. The enlisted man at his left wears a variation chin strap on his visored cap.

Von Seeckt (l) and von Hindenburg (r) during the autumn maneuvers of the Reichswehr in Mecklenburg, 1925. Von Seeckt wears his Dienstmütze according to the 1919 regulations.

O. Spronk

O. Spronk

Generalleutnant Wilhelm Heye (l) and Erich von Witzleben (r) are shown in a pre-1927 photo as both are still wearing leather chin straps.

# Insignia

## a) Cockades

In 1919, the metal black/white/red Reichskokarde (national tri-color) was worn secured to the center of the cap band. This, in turn, was encircled by a rather thin stamped white metal oakleaf wreath (officers could purchase this wreath hand-embroidered in silver bullion wire if they desired). In the center of the cap top was positioned another cockade (Landmannschaftsabzeichen), this one in the appropriate Landesfarben (state colors) from which the wearer originated.[6]

### State Cockade Colors (Landesfarben)

| | |
|---|---|
| Anhalt | Red/green/white |
| Baden | Yellow/red/yellow |
| Bayern | White/blue |
| Braunschweig | Blue/yellow |
| Bremen | Red/white |
| Hamburg | White/red |
| Hessen | Red/white |
| Lippe | Yellow/red |
| Lübeck | White/red |
| Mecklenburg | Blue/yellow/red |
| Oldenburg | Blue/red |
| Preussen | Black/white |
| Sachsen | White/green |
| Schaumburg-Lippe | White/red/blue |
| Thüringen | White/red |
| Württemberg | Black/red[7] |

These colors were worn by the following:

a. Kommando-Behörden (headquarters of divisions or larger units), and Truppenteilen;

b. Regimental, battalion, and detachment staffs wore the colors of the state that had the greatest portion of strength of garrisoned mounted/standing units;

1. The colors of Preussen: The staffs of Infanterie-Regimenter Nr. 6, 12, 16, 17, and 18; the III. Bataillon des Infanterie-Regiment Nr. 18; the Reiter-Regimenter Nr. 14 and 16 and Artillerie-Regiment Nr. 5;*

*In 1932 the colors for the Prussian Artillerie-Regiment Nr. 5 were changed to those of Württemberg. (HVBl. "Landesfarben," Nr. 395, Jahrgang 1932, p. 137.)

2. The colors of Sachsen: The staffs of Artillerie-Regiment Nr. 4, the Fahr-Abteilung Nr. 4, and Kraftfahrabteilung Nr. 4;

3. The colors of Württemberg: The staffs of Reiter-Regiment Nr. 18, Pionier-Bataillon Nr. 5, Nachrichten-Abteilung Nr. 5, Kraftfahr-Abteilung Nr. 5 and Fahr-Abteilung Nr. 5;

---

[6]*Die Deutsche Reichswehr--Das Deutsche Reichsheer*, May 9, 1930, p. 32.
[7]*Ibid.*, p. 22.

Generalleutnant Wilhelm Heye talking to Generalleutnant Reinhardt (l) during the maneuvers of the Gruppenkommando 2 in 1927. Heye wears the gold cap cords per the 1927 regulations, while Reinhardt still wears the old-style leather chin strap.

(Below) NCOs in training with an officer explaining tactics in 1932. All are still wearing the Reichsadlerkokarde.

**4.** The colors of Hessen: The staff of Infanterie-Regiment Nr. 15.

Members of the Reichswehr ministry, inspectors, armaments schools, etc., wore the colors of their last detachment. In the event that these persons had not previously served in a unit, they wore their state colors.[8]

### Form II
### Reichs-(Adler-) Kokarde

Documentation dated September 29, 1919 gave notice that the Reichskokarde, formerly worn in the colors of black/white/red, would be replaced by a gold-colored oval, on which was displayed a black eagle of the German Republic.[9] In March 1933 Reichspräsident Paul von Hindenburg took a very popular step by reinstating the black/white/red national cockade, the colors of Imperial Germany, to the headdress of the armed forces.

J.R. Angolia

The Reichsadlerkokarde and oakleaf wreath in metal. The first type wreath was used until approximately 1936.

This NCO wears the Reichsadlerkokarde with black Imperial eagle on gold.

The Reichsadlerkokarde in metal and hand-embroidered oakleaf wreath on dark green cloth.

O. Spronk

[8]*Ibid.*, p. 33.
[9]*Die Uniformen der Deutschen Armee*, "Änderung der Kokarde," Sept. 29, 1919, p. 2.

Formerly a Landeskokarde in cloth had been worn on the Bergmütze (mountain cap), but a day after the black/white/red cockade was restored, it was announced that only the national cockade was to be worn on the Bergmütze.[10]

## Form III

By 1934 the construction of the national cockade for wear on the visored cap, mountain cap as well as the field cap for officers and officials was as follows:

a. Base: 1.0mm fluted, black lacquered and pressed Vulkanfiber, having a diameter of 23mm.

b. Roundel: "Neusilber" (copper 62-65 hundredths, nickel 13-14 hundredths and zinc 21-25 hundredths), 0.5mm thick in galvanized silver, then polished and covered with clear lacquer. Two pins or clips on the reverse fastened the roundel to the Vulkanfiber base; two longer pins fastened the cockade to the cap. A red piece of felt was placed under the top silver portion before the cockade was assembled, thus showing the center of the finished cockade to have a red "bull's eye."

c. For men and non-commissioned officers: The metal roundel was attached to the Vulkanfiber base by four pins. The center of the base was perforated to accommodate an eyelet (Öse) by which the cockade could be secured to the cap by a cotter pin or ring.[11]

In May 1935, the construction of the national cockade was modified. The fluted Vulkanfiber base was replaced by one made of aluminum (painted black), 0.8mm thick and 5mm high, tapered and hollow pressed. The metal inner portion remained unchanged; however, by late 1935 only two of the four

This photo, taken from an F.W. Assmann-Katalog, shows several types of cockades used by the army.

retaining pins remained.[12] The purpose of the changes of May 1935 were simply so that the cockade would be the correct size in proportion to the redesigned oakleaf wreath, which was thicker than the old-style wreath and slightly vaulted[13] (4x6.2cm and manufactured in white metal). Reserve-and Landwehroffiziere, Offiziere (W) der Reserve and Landwehr (W), der aktiven Offiziere (W) und Sanitäts- und Veterinäroffiziere der Reserve wore a similar

[10]HVBl. "Reichsflagge, Reichskokarde und landmannschaftliches Abzeichen," March 15, 1933, p. 39.

[11]Anzugordnung für das Reichsheer. H. Dv. 122, Abschnitt A. Berlin: November 14, 1934, pp. 118-119.

[12]HVBl. "Reichskokarde." Nr. 215, Jahrgang 1935, p. 70.

[13]Ibid. "Beschreibung und Abnahmevorschrift der Reichskokarde für die Feldmütze der Offiziere, sowie für Schirm- und Bergmütze." Jahrgang 1935, pp. 70-71.

cockade on their headdress, but with the addition of a silver-white Iron Cross[14] (the so-called "Landwehr" or "Maltese" cross). Use of this cockade was discontinued in June 1936.[15]

John Coy

Early Landwehr visored cap piped in crimson. Note the Maltese cross in the center of the cockade.

The use of "Neusilber" in the cockade was prohibited by an order issued in November 1935. Thereafter, only light metal (aluminum) was to be used in the manufacturing of not only the cockade, but the wreath and national emblem as well.[16] Parts formerly manufactured in gilded brass were now made of gold anodized aluminum.

By 1937 the base could also be made from pressed black cardboard. The size of the silver roundel varied from 4 to 5mm. No changes of significance took place after 1937.[17]

## National Emblem

After Hitler had obtained the offices of both Reichskanzler and then Reichspräsident, he decreed that the swastika (Hakenkreuz) emblem of the National Socialist Party appear on the uniforms of the armed forces. It was

[14]Ibid. "Uniformen der Reserve- und Landwehroffiziere, usw." Nr. 289, June 12, 1935, p. 100.

[15]HVBl. Nr. 573, Jahrgang 1936, p. 225.

[16]Ibid. "Abzeichen, usw." Nr. 674, Jahrgang 1935, p. 237.

[17]Catalogue F.W. Assmann & Söhne. Lüdenscheid: Ausgabe 1937, p. 2.

worn in varying forms of the combination of an eagle and swastika. The new insignia was officially adopted by an order dated October 30, 1935,[18] but a memo issued by Reichswehrminister Generaloberst von Blomberg a year earlier had already stated that all members of the Wehrmacht were to wear the ". . . Hoheitszeichen der NSDAP an der Dienstmütze . . ." (national emblem of the Party on the visored cap)." It said, furthermore, that the national emblem was to be worn above the national cockade, in the position formerly occupied by the Landeskokarde.[19]

The first model national emblem featured an eagle with outstretched wings, its head facing to its left, clutching a wreath of oakleaves, encircling an embossed swastika. This national emblem measured approximately 4.3 x 2.8cm, and was to be worn on the front of the visored cap top by both officers and men (officers and, with special permission from a senior officer, enlisted men could also wear the national emblem embroidered in silver bullion wire upon a field-grey (later dark blue-green) cloth backing by 1937). By 1943 general officers could purchase the hand-embroidered national emblem in gilt wire, worked upon the aforementioned backings. The first model national emblem had a shorter wingspan and was less refined than its successor. This second model was already being produced in 1935 by the firms of Giesse & Schmidt Metallwarenfabrik in Ruhla (Thüringen) and Emil Jüttner. The second national emblem was larger than the first model, measuring approximately 6.4 x 2.5cm, and was more detailed. Both the first and second model national emblems were to be worn affixed to the cap top 1cm from the upper cap band piping.[20] The national emblem was manufactured of "Neusilber" and was in silver finish for the army (army generals did not wear gilt cap insignia at this time).

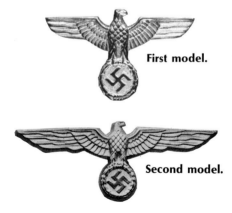

First model.

Second model.

[18]Davis, Brian Leigh. *German Army Uniforms and Insignia, 1933-1945*, p. 10.
[19]HVBl. "Hoheitszeichen," Nr. 326, Jahrgang 16. Berlin: July 2, 1934, p. 99.
[20]Anzugordnung für das Reichsheer. H.Dv. 122, Abschnitt A. Berlin: November 14, 1934, p. 16 & 108.

Early Wehrmacht troops still wearing their Reichsheer uniforms. Note field caps with only the national cockade worn.

This enlisted man wears the pre-1936 national emblem and wreath on a "Tellerform" cap.

An excellent example of a transitional visored cap for a Reichsheer general. Note the thin piping, cap cords and the medium green-colored cap band. The first model insignia is worn.

## Wreath

The first model wreath was made of thin stamped metal with two pairs of clips on its reverse to be pressed through the cap band and flattened on the inside of the cap. This oakleaf wreath (Eichenlaubkranz) measured 6.4 x 4.1cm and consisted of eight oakleaves and six acorns, joined at the bottom center by a band. The detail of the oakleaves imitated the embroidered form, rather than actual leaves, as depicted on the second pattern wreath. The latter was roughly the same size as the first model wreath, but the second model wreath was slightly thicker and vaulted. The leaves and acorns were executed in a much more detailed fashion, showing the leaves to have veins, and the acorns to have a checkered pattern to their caps. The central band was also modified, having a beaded design.

Both the oakleaf wreath and national emblem were produced in varying qualities, depending on whether the cap was an issue piece or a private purchase (the latter usually having higher-quality insignia), and what materials were available at the time of purchase. Materials from zinc-based metal (used late in the war) to aluminum were used. The finish also varied, according to the desire of the purchaser, and the availability of the material, from natural-colored metal to a highly frosted finish, polished as well as unpolished.

NOTE:

"Sonderführung" (special workmanship) in the same metal was also manufactured, being silvered or gilded. (Assmann-Katalog, Ausgabe 1936/37, p. 2 and Katalog Dr. Franke & Co., p. 1.)

P. Pauwels

First model wreath in metal.

This enlisted man wears the first model national emblem and wreath in metal.

Len Champion

Jäger (grass-green piping) enlisted man's visored cap with fine quality metal insignia.

Second model wreath.

John Coy

Panzer (pink piping) officer's visored cap with a combination of metal and wire insignia.

Author's Collection

(Left) Officer's hand-embroidered wire wreath with metal rosette and (right) with hand-embroidered wire rosette.

21

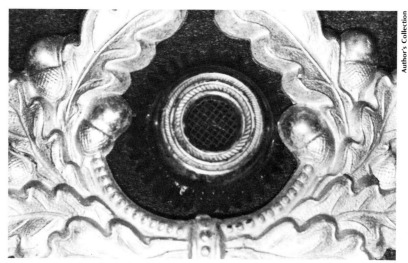

Metal national cockade having a wire mesh center commonly found on caps made by the Erel firm.

It was not uncommon for junior NCOs, such as the one above, to privately purchase their visored caps (called Eigentumsmütze). He wears officer-quality, embroidered insignia.

As stated previously, officers could wear the national emblem, wreath and cockade worked in hand-embroidered silver wire; they could also wear a combination of both metal and bullion insignia, e.g., metal national emblem with bullion-embroidered wreath and metal or bullion cockade. Again, the backing color for the hand-embroidered national emblem and wreath was initially field-grey; this was changed to dark blue-green in 1937.[21] Generals, likewise, often opted to wear wire insignia, first in silver, then, in 1943, in gilt wire. The cockade always remained in its black/white/red form, regardless of a person's rank. By July 1938 generals were permitted to wear uniform insignia embroidered in gold-colored "Celleon."[22] The insignia color for general ranks' cap insignia was officially changed to gold on January 1, 1943.[23]

P. Pauwels

Note the embroidered, grey thread first model wreath and metal first model national emblem on this enlisted man's visored cap.

---

[21]HVBl. "Hoheitszeichen, usw." Nr. 745, Jahrgang 1937, p. 293.
[22]Ibid., Nr. 258, 1938, pp. 191-192. Celleon was a substitute material (Austauschwerkstoff) which reduced costs considerably, while increasing length of wear and tenability.
[23]Davis, German Army Uniforms. p. 97.

James Boulton

Detailed photo of the Model 1943 general's visor cap showing the insignia in gold Celleon on a dark green material.

O. Spronk

General Schmidt wears his visored cap with the insignia in gilded metal.

24

By 1931, the visored cap was modified and became more "modern" in appearance, that is, modern in the sense of the form associated with the Third Reich. The field-grey cap top was now 11.8cm high with a loose wire inside. The visor was made slightly wider (25cm long, lacquered in light brown or tan on the underside). In 1934 the visored cap was once again modified. The cap band color was of field-grey cloth (Abzeichentuch), 4.5cm wide. It was piped in the aforementioned manner (.2cm wide), and the insignia described previously were retained.

The early "saucer" shape visored cap in wear.

In 1934, officers' caps issued from uniform depots were lined in light brown cotton (the color of the lining varied on caps that were privately purchased), with a sweatband made of calf or sheep leather, often perforated at the front of the band. During the war, the sweatband was also produced by the firm of Alkor-Werke (Karl Lissmann) from a material called "Alkor," a cheapter substitute for the more scarce and costly leather.[24] Between the interior side of the cap band and the sweatband was positioned a 15 x 3cm cork or red sponge rubber pad, to ease the weight of the cap on the wearer's forehead (hence the designation, "Stirndruckfrei" sometimes found stamped onto the sweatband itself). Issue caps worn by enlisted men and non-commissioned officers were initially lined in field-grey material, but around 1934, rust-colored waterproof material became the standard lining.[25] A cheesecloth lining was sewn between the cap top and the inner lining. Between the underside of the cap band and sweatband was a piece of cardboard, 5.3cm wide,[26] which constituted the support for the band and retained the shape of the cap body. A plain hair oil shield

[24]Uniformen-Markt (UM). September 15, 1939, p. 276.
[25]Anzugordnung fur das Reichsheer. Abschnitt A, November 14, 1934, p. 16.
[26]Ibid., pp. 14,15.

was sewn to the top of the lining. Sometimes the cap size was stamped in black ink onto the lining, with the wearer's unit number, etc., stamped in ink on the underside of the sweatband.

Officers' caps were generally lined in various colors of rayon. A celluloid sweat shield was sewn to the cap top lining as well. On the shields, in the caps of both officers and men, a small rectangular portion was sewn on three sides, to allow the owner to place a name tag into this slot. The cap size and maker's name, logo, etc., were stamped onto the lining under the shield or impressed directly into it. The year of manufacture (Lieferjahr) was sometimes stamped on the left underside of the sweatband on enlisted ranks' caps only.[27]

A narrow steel wire was sewn or fit into the crown seam of the cap to retain its shape. Though explicitly prohibited,[28] some elected to remove this loose spring to give their cap a more "salty" look.

Saris

In late 1935 the field-grey cap band was officially changed to dark blue-green.

This enlisted man wears his visored cap with steel wire removed from the inside crown seam.

### Cords and Chin Strap

Enlisted men and non-commissioned officers* [29] wore a 3-part black leather chin strap (1.5cm wide and 1-1.5mm in thickness), affixed to the cap at each side of the visor by two semi-domed buttons (1cm in diameter).

*The non-commissioned ranks of Oberfähnrich, Unterarzt, Unterveterinär and Oberfeuerwerker, who were aspirant officers, were permitted upon passing the Offiziersprüfung, to wear officers' silver cap cords on their enlisted visored caps (as well as Zahlmeisteranwärter in the Oberfeldwebel rank). In 1937 the wearing of cords was also permitted by active Unterapotheker, Unterarzt, Unterveterinär and Unterapotheker on leave, but they had to be privately purchased. In 1940 Fahnenjunker-Ingenieure (engineering officer candidates) and Feldingenieure (field engineers) were also permitted to wear the aluminum cap cords.

[27]Anzugordnung für das Reichsheer. Abschnitt A, November 14, 1934, p. 16.
[28]HVBl. "Verbesserung der Dienstmütze. Jahrgang 1931, Nr. 253, p. 112.
[29]Rundschau deutsches Schneiderfachblatt. "Bekleidung der aktiven Unterapotheker, sowie der Unterärzte, Unterveterinäre, und Unterapotheker des Beurlaubtenstandes," August 21, 1937, p. 1200.

Officers from the ranks of Leutnant through Oberstleutnant, and Musikmeister, wore a pair of woven silver cap cords, which were held together at each end by a heavy cardboard or metal frame, over which was woven silver wire in a plaited pattern. Directly behind each of these slides was a silver knot, followed by a silver bullion loop. The loop fitted over a silver pebbled button (1.3cm) attached at each side of the cap band, at the end of the visor sides. Generals wore the same pattern cords, but gold in color with pebbled gilt buttons. These side buttons were affixed with pins or were sewn in place.

NOTE:

Period publications often created confusion with uniform regulations. For example, in 1941, green/silver cap cords were offered for sale for Werkmeister and others, but this offering was an error as these cords were never authorized.

Saris

**Gefreiter Kurt Krüger wearing his visored cap according to regulations with the leather chin strap, 1937. He was a member of the 2./-Mar.Ers.Schützen-Batl.3.**

Gary Walker

Early General's visored cap with thicker piping and cap cords. The cap band color is darker than that shown on page 19.

Pre-1943 general's visored cap with gilt bullion piping and cords, and aluminum wire insignia.

Ron Kwan

Pre-1943 general's visored cap with gilt wire piping and cords, and silver-colored metal insignia.

Author's Collection

Post-1943 general's visored cap with gilt wire piping, cords, and wire insignia.

Ron Kwan

Generalleutnant Theodor Scherer wearing the 1943 general's visor cap with gold Celleon insignia.

Post-1943 general's visored cap with gilt metal insignia.

**Note:**

Generals and officials of general rank were to wear gilt metal insignia after January 1, 1943.

John Coy

Gen. d. Pz. Tr. Heinrich Freiherr von Lüttwitz, commander of the 2nd Panzer Division in 1944, wearing a general officer's visored cap with unique insignia of hand-embroidered gilt wire.

**General Lüttwitz's visored cap as worn at left.**　　31

Enlisted man's peaked cap with black leather chin strap (pink piped).

Freising
Adolf Hillerolz
Tel. 375
Frischluft
D.R.G.M. 1419757

An excellent example of a Sattelform (saddle-shaped) visored cap with a unique ventilation system. (Above) Notches are shown on the sides of the wreath which allow air to circulate through the cap. (Right) Interior view of the cap showing the ventilation grommets and the flap which folded over the holes to stop the air flow.

Officer's peaked cap with woven aluminum cap cords (grass-green piped).

Ron Kwan

Saris

O. Spronk

This officer wears his visored cap, contrary to regulations, with the spring removed to form a more jaunty-looking cap.

This enlisted man is shown still wearing his visored cap in 1941. Normally, the field cap was worn with the walking-out dress during the war.

## Uniform Cap for Armed Forces Wartime Officials
## (Schirmmütze für Wehrmachtbeamte auf Kriegsdauer)

Officers serving in a limited capacity for the duration of the war (auf Kriegsdauer) wore the standard army visored cap, with the exception of having a blue-grey cap band.[30] The cap crown piping and the band pipings were dark green (except general officer equivalents). This blue-grey material was standard Luftwaffe cloth. The Soutache for the field cap was dark green. The Corps of Wartime Officials was dissolved on August 11, 1943 and its officials were transferred to the General Administration Service (Allgemeiner Heeresverwaltungsdienst). The late war general's cap below would, therefore, technically be from the latter service.

Officer's visored cap with dark green piping and medium blue-grey cap band (Wehrmachtbeamte auf Kriegsdauer), with twisted aluminum cap cords.

Ron Kwan

An extremely rare example of a visored cap worn by Wehrmacht-Beamten im Generalsrang. The crown and bottom edge of the grey-blue cap band are piped in gold, while the top of the cap band is piped in dark green. The insignia is gilt, denoting post-1942 manufacture.

## Armed Forces Officials (Wehrmachtbeamte)

Wehrmachtbeamte wore the same visored cap as that for Wehrmachtbeamte a. Kr., but the cap band was of the basic dark blue-green material, piped in dark green.

---

[30]*Uniformen-Markt. 1940, p. 99.*

## Army Chaplains (Heeresgeistlichen)

However the National Socialists tried to destroy the influence of the church, clergy did serve within the ranks of Wehrmacht. Both the Protestant and Catholic churches in Germany are considered, in a limited capacity, to be institutions with very close ties to the state. Its clergy are, to a degree, considered to be civil servants, similar to the capacity of postal workers. For example, clergymen are provided with a pension, health insurance, and other benefits as state "officials."[31]

Between 1933 and 1935 no official uniform regulations were issued for army clergy.[32] By May 25, 1935, officials wore a field-grey uniform. This uniform was worn in addition to the normal black suit with collar and black felt hat or top hat (no national emblem was worn on these distinctively "civilian" hats, but a gold or silver breast eagle, embroidered on black cloth, was worn on the black coat).

O. Spronk

The two members of the army clergy at right of photo carry the black felt hat and top hat according to the initial regulations.

The visored cap designed for wear by army clergy in early 1935 consisted of the basic army cap with violet piping around the crown as well as a violet cap band (the band color was changed to dark blue-green with violet piping in late 1935);[33] a Gothic cross embroidered in silver wire was worn on the cap top between the national emblem and cockade.[34] The cross was changed to bright white aluminum in 1937.[35] Heerespfarrer and Heeresoberpfarrer wore silver

[31]*Private interview, May 17, 1989.*
[32]*Ibid.*
[33]*HVBl. "Dienstkleidung der planmässigen Heeresgeistlichen," Nr. 289, 1937, pp. 117, 118 (also HVBl. Jahrgang 1935, Nr. 183, p. 98).*
[34]*UM. July 1, 1935, p. 2.*
[35]*HVBl. "Dienstkleidung der planmässigen Heeresgeistlichen, Nr. 289, 1937, pp. 117, 118.*

**Gothic cross in hand-embroidered aluminum wire.**

O. Spronk

**This Heeresgeistliche wears the officers' field cap (Offiziersfeldmütze) with machine-woven national emblem and cross.**

cap cords. The rank of Feldbischof was accorded the status of an army general. Accordingly, a Feldbischof wore a visored cap piped around the crown and along the lower cap band in gold; the upper portion of the band was piped in violet. Gold cap cords with gilt pebbled buttons were worn on the visored caps of Feldbischofe.[36]

**Heerespfarrer/Heeresoberpfarrer visored cap with white metal cross below the national emblem.**

Ron Kwan

[36]Hettler, Eberhard, Uniformen der Deutschen Wehrmacht. Berlin, 1939, p. 50.

In 1939, the army clergy wore a violet Soutache on the front of their field caps. By March 1942 the mountain-style field cap ("Einheitsfeldmütze 42") was also issued to them.[37]

Machine-woven insigne for the field cap in "T" form.

### Specialist Officer Ranks (Sonderführer im Offizierrang)

Sonderführer (e.g., Kriegsärzte (wartime doctors), Dolmetscher (interpreters), etc.)[38] wore a field-grey visored cap with a blue-grey cap band and piping (introduced in Spring 1940).[39] Cords worn on the visored cap were of the standard officer pattern. However, they were changed in the summer of 1943 and segmented into two blue-grey sections to two aluminum sections.[40]

The Soutache color for the field cap was blue-grey.

### Headdress for Army Forestry Officials
### (Kopfbedeckungen für Wehrmachtbeamte im Forstdienst (Heer))

1. Schirmmütze

Army forestry officials were drawn from the state forestry and were considered Wehrmachtbeamte. These officials were first ordered to wear the new national emblem on their uniforms on February 28, 1935.[41] The army national emblem, instead of the Prussian eagle, was worn on the visored cap (for a time, a Landeskokarde was worn on the cap band until being replaced by the black/white/red cockade).

The Sattleform, grey-green visored cap was worn from 1935 until 1938. The cap band color and cap piping were dark green.[42] According to regulations (November 1935), army forestry officials were to wear gilt-colored insignia

[37]"Allgemeine Heeresmitteilungen (HM)." Jahrgang 1942, Nr. 642, July 7.
[38]UM. Nr. 9, May 1, 1940, p. 65.
[39]Uniformen-Markt. Nr. 9, May 1, 1940, p. 65.
[40]DUZ. August 15, 1943, p. 8.
[41]Dienstbekleidungsvorschrift für die Heeresforstbeamten (H. Dv. 120). Berlin: February 28, 1935.
[42]HVBl. Nr. 646, October 1935.

An army forestry officer's visored cap with top and cap band piped in dark green. The cap band is green velvet and the cap cords are aluminum officer's style instead of the specified gold/green.

(army-pattern). However, the army forestry visored cap is most often encountered having silver insignia. Forstanwärter wore a black patent leather chin strap, while officers (Forstbetriebsbeamte) wore green cords with gold flecking (main color is green). The higher ranks (Forstverwaltung) wore gold cords with green flecking (main color is gold). In 1939 the cords were simplified to either all silver or all gold in color.[43]

2. Visored Field Cap (Baschlikmütze)

Basically the same as an army mountain cap, the Baschlikmütze was of greygreen material, having functional flaps secured above the cloth-covered visor by two green pebbled metal buttons, 16mm in diameter. The national emblem and cockade were embroidered onto a grey-green or dark green backing, measuring 2.3 x 5.3cm, and was sewn to the cap front.[44]

3. Brimmed Hat (Hut)

Officials could wear a brimmed hat (Hut) made of grey-green felt, having a dark green hat band (5cm wide, enlarged to 6cm in 1939) and brim edging. The brim was 7cm wide. The national emblem (initially 2.9 x 5.0cm, then 2.5 x 6.7cm), was in white metal until November 1935, then in gold, and was worn in the center of the hat,[45] the lower portion of it extending over the top border of the hat band. In 1939 the national emblem was in aluminum for Forstbeamte through Oberlandforstmeister, but changed to gold in January 1943. A brush made of boar-, deer-, badger- or chamois-hair, was positioned on the left side of the hat,[46] secured by a large (3cm in diameter) metal national cockade.[47] A straw hat could be worn during the summer months.

[43]Nimmergut, Jörg. Mützen von Staat und Partei, 1933-1945. Munich: Verlag Jörg Nimmergut, 1978, pp. 114, 115.
[44]Dienstbekleidung für den Staatsforstdienst (DKV), Berlin. April 22, 1938, pp. 5-7.
[45]HVBl. Nr. 646, October 1935.
[46]E. Hettler, Uniformen der Deutschen Wehrmacht. p. 116.
[47]HVBl. Nr. 646, 1935.

John Coy

Hat worn briefly by Wehrmachtbeamten im Forstdienst (Heer) (army officials serving in the Forestry Service). Note the large metal national cockade and brush.

### 4. General Issue Field Cap (M43) (Einheitsfeldmütze)

The Einheitsfeldmütze (commonly referred to as the M43 cap) was piped around the cap seam and flaps in dark green with the army national emblem and national cockade worn in the center of the cap front. This brimmed field cap replaced the Baschlikmütze in 1944. The national emblem and cockade were machine embroidered onto a common trapezoid-shaped (2.5 x 5.5cm), grey-green backing. The thread color was silver-grey for forestry officials having the ranks of Forstbeamte through Landforstmeister. Higher officials (Oberlandforstmeister) wore golden-yellow insignia after January 1943.

### 5. Field Cap (Feldmütze)

This cap was in the form of the officers' "old-style" cap, having a pliable leather visor. Note that a cap of light-weight cloth was permitted for summer wear. It was piped in the same colors as the Schirmmütze. The oakleaf wreath was worn on the dark blue-green cap band (presumably in BeVo weave), but no national emblem was worn on the cap top until approximately 1939. It was replaced in 1944 by the Einheitsfeldmütze (cloth visor mountain cap).

Officials with NCO status wore the cap insignia machine woven in silver-grey thread upon a grey-green or dark green backing. Officials holding officer rank wore BeVo insignia in silver. From 1943-1945, Oberlandforstmeister wore their insignia machine woven in gold. The size of the insignia varied slightly from 4.0 x 6.7cm to 4.1 x 6.2cm. From 1943 on, the Schirmmütze and Feldmütze for these officials were no longer manufactured.

### Truppensonderdienst der Deutschen Wehrmacht

By a decree of January 24, 1944, the so-called rank of "Offiziere im Truppensonderdienst" was instituted in the army. The final decision regarding the uniform design was to be decided after the war. Some minor regulations were issued, however, mainly concerning shoulder boards.[48] In June 1944, members of the TSD were to turn in their visored caps to be refitted with light blue piping (a shade of blue that varied from that worn by medical and transportation troops). This new Waffenfarbe represented administrative officials (Verwaltungsdienst). The color of wine-red was also used by the TSD, representing army judicial officials (Wehrmachtsrichter).[49] The refitting order created problems among those firms authorized to manufacture army visored caps; they simply could not accommodate the additional workload. To remedy this situation, firms who were not officially allowed to make army caps were contracted for the job. The cloth for these pipings was readily available.[50]

Generals of the Special Services (Generale der Sonderlaufbahnen), which included doctors, veterinarians and TSD-Generals (Truppensonderdienst), were to change their color after April 1944 (base of collar patches, shoulder boards, and greatcoat lapels) from bright red to their appropriate branch color.

### Field Postal Officials (Feldpostbeamte)

Personnel serving in the Feldpost wore the basic army visored cap piped in dark green.[51] Those holding the rank equivalent of general wore gold cap cords.

O. Spronk

Heeresfeldpostmeister Ziegler (second from left) speaks with the Staffelkäpitan der Feldpoststaffel Joas, at Biala Podlaska on May 1, 1942.

---

[48]DUZ. Nr. 4, 1944, p. 2.
[49]HVBl. "Uniformänderungen," Nr. 225, June 17, 1944.
[50]Ibid., Nr. 436, September 6, 1944.
[51]UM. 1939, p. 297.

O. Spronk

**Unloading the mail plane at Biala Podlaska on May 1, 1942.**

## Civilian Army Drivers (Zivilkraftfahrer im Heer)

Civilian drivers wore a Klappmütze (visored cap with ventilation grommets on the underside of the cap top) of mottled-grey whipcord. The underlying band color was also mottled-grey, measuring 4cm wide. Overlaying the band was another, this one of black rayon, woven in an oakleaf pattern (it is assumed that this black band fitted over the grey band). Black twisted rayon cords with knots were secured to the cap by two black lacquered buttons.

The interior of the cap exhibited a brown waterproof lining. The cap was piped in black, with the usual cellophane sweat shield sewn onto the top of the lining.

A metal wreath and national cockade were secured to the center of the cap band, while a removable national emblem (with a safety pin attachment) was worn in the center of the cap top.[52]

The actual service life of this organization is not known, nor could photographs confirm if this cap was worn, but for the interest of the reader this information is enclosed. It was, however, specially mentioned in the An-zugordnung and, therefore, probably produced.

---

[52]*UM. Nr. 5, March 3, 1941, p. 44.*

## Umpires' Cap Band (Mützenband)

Army officials acting as umpires during field exercises wore a white ribbed cotton band with fastening clamp over the cap band of both the visored cap and the officers'"old-style" field cap. The white ribbed cotton band was 4cm wide, having a length of approximately 75cm. The buckle was matte-white-colored stainless steel, measuring 1 x 4.7cm.[53]

A very unusual example of an army infantry officer's visored cap with white capband. One may assume that it was used by an umpire, but regulations only call for the removable white cap band.

An army umpire (right) watches as pre-war maneuvers are conducted. He wears the white removable band on his visored cap.

## Carrying Case and Suitcase for Visored Caps
## (Mützenschachtel und Mützenkoffer für Schirmmützen)

To store or safely transport the visored cap, two forms of cases were available: 1) the Mützenschachtel, being oval-shaped and manufactured in black imitation leather and finished with a bright colored leather brim, was designed to carry two visored caps. The price of the Mützenschachtel in 1939 was RM 7,50. 2) A higher-quality, more sturdy Mützenkoffer was also available. It was made of black "Autoduck," and was lined in moire. The case was reinforced on the outside with nickeled metal strips and had a nickel lock. A carrying handle was attached to the top of the lid. The Mützenkoffer would also accommodate two visored caps. The price was, for the period, very expensive, being RM 14,50.[54]

---

[53]Anzugordnung für das Reichsheer, (H. Dv. 122). Abschnitt A. Berlin: November 14, 1934, p. 72.

[54]Preisliste der Heeres-Kleiderkass. Berlin: May 1, 1939, p. 10.

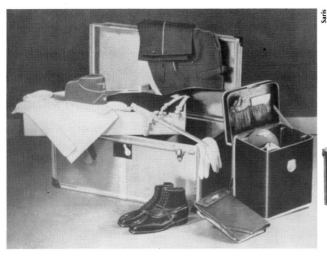

## Field Cap (Feldmütze or allgemeine Feldmütze)

Around 1920 a new cap was introduced. Its design was similar to the officers' "old-style" cap, but the visor was cloth covered. The top[55] measured 9cm. A cloth state cockade[56] was worn on the band until being replaced in 1933 by the black/white/red Reichskokarde (only one cockade was permitted to be worn on the cap,[57] i.e., no combination of state and national cockades was worn). A machine-woven wreath was being worn on the cap band by 1933. Though prohibited, some wore the metal version of the wreath and cockade. The national emblem was not introduced for wear on this cap until 1935.

The new-style field cap with cloth visor, adopted for the Reichsheer, is worn, but with a metal cockade.

---

[55]HVBl. "Bekleidung und Ausrüstung des Reichsheeres." Nr. 77, Jahrgang 2. Berlin: December 20, 1920, p. 1014.

[56]"Die Deutsche Reichswehr--Das Deutsche Reichsheer," May 9, 1930, p. 22.

[57]HVBl. "Verordnung über die Hoheitszeichen der deutschen Wehrmacht." Nr. 121, Jahrgang 15. Berlin: March 17, 1933, p. 39.

This field cap with its cloth-covered visor could be worn under the steel helmet to provide additional warmth.[58] The use of this cap was discontinued and replaced by the introduction of the field cap.

### Officers' Old Style Field Cap
### (Offiziersfeldmütze alter Art)

One of the most favored forms of headdress was the officers' "old-style" field cap. It was basically the same form and shape as the visored cap proper, but there were several differences. Regardless of rank, no cap cords were

Officer's "old style" field cap. Note the flat silver wire machine-woven insignia. The piping color is orange.

The officer's "old style" or Model 1933 field cap being worn.

[58]*Die Deutsche Reichswehr in neuen Uniformen. 1920, p. 12.*

worn on the cap. During the course of the war, officers sometimes added cords to their cap, in spite of regulations. The visor was made of black pliable leather, without the usual raised outer rim. Examples also exist with cardboard visors. The early model of this cap did not carry a national emblem and in the center of the cap band was positioned a national cockade, attached by prongs to the center of a punched-out oak-leaf wreath of white cloth (4.5cm high and 7cm wide). The national emblem (introduced in 1935) was worn in its silver machine-woven form (BeVo), as was a silver BeVo wreath and cockade (the first wreath worn on this cap featured a metal cockade; the completely machine-woven wreath/cockade combination came about later). The cap was piped (0.2cm) in the appropriate branch-of-service color around the crown seam and at each border of the field-grey (but darker than the top) cap band (4.5cm wide). General ranks' caps were initially piped in silver, then in gold. Wehrmachtbeamte with the rank of general wore gilt piping around the crown and lower band, but the upper piping around the cap band was dark green. This soft field-grey cap had a crown 11.8cm high.

Administrative official's "old style" field cap with white cotton thread insignia.

These caps were lined in various colored fabric, having a leather or composition sweatband, measuring 4.5cm wide, often perforated at the front. Like the Schirmmütze, this visored cap could feature a rubber sponge or cork pad.

Officers and Wehrmachtebeamte im Offizierrang wore insignia woven in silver wire; Wehrmachtbeamte without officer status wore the insignia in white cotton thread.[59]

Officially, the use of the "old-style" cap was to be discontinued by April 1, 1942.

---

[59]E. Hettler, Uniformen der Deutschen Wehrmacht. p. 14.     45

Machine-woven, silver wire national emblem and wreath for wear by officers and administrative officials of officer rank.

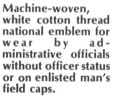

Machine-woven, white cotton thread national emblem for wear by administrative officials without officer status or on enlisted man's field caps.

Generaloberst Heinrici wears the general officers' field cap for 1934 regulations. Many officers preferred this style cap to the Model 1938 field cap.

Generalmajor Freiherr von Waldenfels wears a general officer's "old style" field cap.

(Below) General officer's "old style" field cap.

Roger Waterman

Bundesarchiv

This assault gun officer from the "Grossdeutschland" Division wears a red piped "old style" field cap, the Ukraine, January 1944.

47

Unissued, white-piped officer's "old style" field cap.

Red-piped officer's "old style" field cap with metal national emblem and wreath hand-embroidered directly onto the cap band.

48

## Field Cap (Feldmütze)

Most sources give the date of introduction of the Feldmütze as 1938. However, photographic evidence shows that this cap existed as early as 1934. Documentation proves this as well.[60]

The November 1934 (H.Dv 122) dress regulations for the army explained the difference between the field caps for enlisted men and officers. Officers were to wear the visored field cap (Officer's Old Style Field Cap). The cap for NCOs and enlisted men was in "Bootsform", in field-grey material, and somewhat heavier than the material used for officer's caps. It had flaps that sloped toward the front at a greater angle than the cap that was in the later "Schiffchenform". On each side an air hole was positioned in the form of a field-grey grommet with an inside diameter of 5mm. Another grommet was positioned 3cm below the top of the cap front to fasten the national cockade with prongs.

A wool piping (Soutache) in the branch-of-service color (4mm) thick was positioned on the upper front of the cap at an angle of 60 degrees. The corner of this "Soutache" was approximately 8cm below the top of the cap. The lining was field-grey twill and the weight was approximately 100 grams.[60a] The flaps were fastened by two pronged buttons with a 1.2cm diameter.

The style of this cap was modeled after that worn by the United States Army. For reasons undetermined, the Feldmütze was referred to in the early years as a "Krätzchen", although the Krätzchen worn mainly in the early 1920s and before, was more round in shape and had a small, stiffened cap band.

Enlisted men wearing the early Reichsheer field cap. Note the position of the cockade and the Soutache worn by the man on the right.

In October 1935 the Model 1934 field cap was slightly modified. The Soutache was now manufactured in cotton and at a 90 degree angle; the tip was positioned approximately 4mm from the upper edge of the flap. The grommet for the cockade was eliminated, as were the two flap buttons. The

[60]HVBl. "Feldmütze ohne Schirm", Nr. 149, 1934, p. 49.
[60a]Anzugordnung für das Reichsheer, H.Dv.122, Abschnitt A. Berlin, November 14, 1934, pp. 11-13.

Soutache was no longer positioned on the upper portion of the cap, but on the flap front. The cockade, in woven cotton on a field-grey backing, was now positioned within the Soutache. In the center of the cap front a small woven national emblem was positioned (white on a field-grey backing).[60b] The bottom edge of this field-cap was to be worn approximately 1cm above the right eyebrow with the cockade in the middle of the forehead.[60c]

**Oberfeldwebel Portsteffen wears the modified M1934 field cap complete with national emblem, cockade and Soutache.**

John Coy

**Machine-woven insignia for the field cap.**

**(Right) Modified M1934 field cap for enlisted men. The national emblem is machine-woven in mouse-grey thread.**

---

[60b]*Uniformen-Markt. Nr. 12, December 1, 1935, p. 2.*
[60c] *Unterrichtsbuch für Soldaten. Berlin, 1938, p. 45, and HVBl., "Sitz der Feldmütze", Nr. 153, Jahrgang 1936, p. 43.*

Feldmütze n/P (neuer Probe)

On December 6, 1938 a field cap in the style worn by NCOs and enlisted men (but slightly modified) was introduced for wear by officers and officials as a replacement for the visored field cap.[60d] The crown of this cap was piped in aluminum for officers and in gilt for generals, and the front scallop was also piped in aluminum or gilt. A Soutache in the branch-of-service color was also ordered to be worn on the lower front of the cap by officers.

Author's Collection

The man at left wears the M1942 Feldmutze with front buttons, while the man at right wears the modified M1934 pattern cap.

M1938 cavalry officer's field cap with golden-yellow Soutache.

Author's Collection

The national emblem was of machine-woven aluminum or hand-embroidered aluminum wire on a bluish-dark green cloth backing and was positioned 1cm above the edge of the flaps. The hand-embroidered national cockade (2.2cm), bordered by a small aluminum cord, was to be worn by officers in 1940, but this order was often ignored and a metal cockade was worn instead.

Lower ranking army officials wore the field cap as ordered for enlisted men. Generals officers could wear this cap, but they often preferred the old-style visored field cap. The wear of this "old-style" cap was officially allowed until April 1, 1942.[61]

---

[60d]HVBl. "Feldmütze für Offiziere usw.", Nr. 456, December 6, 1938, p. 294.
[61]Uniformen-Markt. Nr. 4, February 15, 1939, pp.56, 60.

Generalfeldmarschall von Reichenau wears the Model 1938 Feldmütze für Offiziere. Note the gold piping, Soutache, and the high-quality hand-embroidered cockade.

The front of this cap measured 10cm high, 9.5cm in the center, and 7.5cm at the back. The inside of the top was reinforced with padding to keep its shape. A field-grey ventilation hole was positioned 11cm from the front of the cap and 1cm below the top seam.

The flaps were 5cm high in front, raising to 8cm at the top portion of the flap scallop, and dropping to 6cm at the back of the cap. The 12cm scallop (on each side) was piped in aluminum cord, 2mm wide, or in gilt cord.

The lining for these caps was field-grey satin with a piece of leather (3cm wide) sewn in the inside front. Often, a leather sweatband was added, but regulations did not require it.

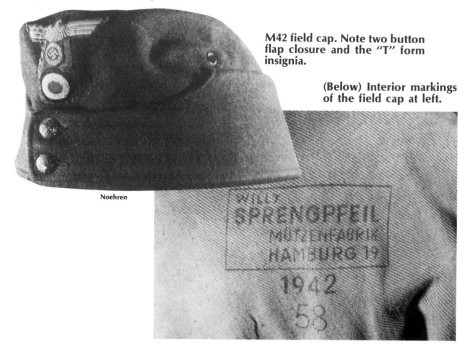

M42 field cap. Note two button flap closure and the "T" form insignia.

(Below) Interior markings of the field cap at left.

Noehren

WILLY
SPRENGPFEIL
MÜTZENFABRIK
HAMBURG 19
1942
53

The flap buttons for enlisted men's caps were normally manufactured in aluminum, however, a molded button of the "Spritzguss" style was experimented with but proved to be too expensive.[62]

Feldmütze 42

An order dated July 21,1942 introduced a new style field cap giving more ear and neck protection against the cold. In the Heeres-Verordnungsblatt, the description was as follows: Instead of the field cap introduced in 1934 for enlisted men, and based on experiences during the first winter on the eastern front, a new field cap in the shape of the mountain-cap, but without visor, will be introduced.[63] The flaps of these caps could be folded down and fastened by two small field-grey buttons (see section on Kopfhaube and Kopfschützer). A combined machine-woven, national emblem/cockade insigne on a trapezoid-shaped field-grey backing was positioned on the front upper center of the cap.[64]

The wear of this field cap was restricted to enlisted men and NCOs only, but it has been observed that officers also wore it, but with the crown piped with 2 or 3mm aluminum cord. The wearing of the Soutache was to be stopped during the summer of 1942, however, some personnel continued its wear.[65] The Feldmütze 42 was never authorized to carry the Soutache.

The above field caps were to be replaced in 1944 with the visored field cap (Einheitsfeldmütze).

General der Panzertruppe v. Senger-Etterlin is shown wearing a Model 1942 Feldmütze with gold piping around the crown and gold flap buttons.

Willy Schenk wears the Model 1942 Feldmütze with two metal front buttons and machine-woven, mouse-grey insignia. His cap is worn according to regulations, 1cm above the right eyebrow.

[62]Ibid., Nr. 21, November 1, 1940, p. 62.
[63]HVBl. Nr. 642 "Feldmütze 42", August 7, 1942, p. 327.
[64]Deutsche Uniformen-Zeitschrift Nr. 1/2. May 31, 1943, p. 15.
[65]Uniformen-Markt. Nr. 21, November 1, 1942, p. 165.

Ron Manion

Foreign uniform stocks were sometimes utilized. In the illustrated examples (left and above), a Slovak field cap was utilized with the addition of standard German Army, enlisted ranks' insignia.

The Feldmütze was produced in khaki for wear in arid climates. The national emblem was embroidered in light-blue upon a copper-brown backing and the cockade was machine-embroidered upon a copper-brown square backing. Officers wore their normal insignia and silver or gold piping around the crown and the front scallop. These caps were always lined in red.

J.R. Angolia

Tropical field cap of olive-colored meterial with light blue machine-woven on tan insignia. This particular specimen has copper-brown piping on the edge of the turn-up (reconnaissance), which was an uncommon practice.

Tan tropical field cap with pink Soutache.

The tropical field cap in wear.

Tank crews were also issued a Feldmütze in black (in either the "old" or "new" form). The national emblem for enlisted men was machine-embroidered on black material in white or grey thread. The Soutache was worn on the cap for a time. Although it was strictly prohibited, some crews elected to wear the field-grey, instead of the black Feldmütze.[66]

Saris

These four members of Pz.Abt. 65 are shown, during the invasion of Poland, wearing the field-grey field cap with their black uniform.

[66]HVBl., "Tragen der Feldmütze zur schwarzen Sonderbekleidung der Panzer-truppen," June 6, 1944, Nr. 246.

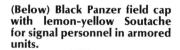

M1934 (modified) black Panzer field cap with pink Soutache.

J.R. Angolia

(Below) Black Panzer field cap with lemon-yellow Soutache for signal personnel in armored units.

J.R. Angolia

This Panzer man wears the black field cap with pink Soutache.

This young Panzer enlisted man wears a white metal SS-style skull on the left side of his field cap. The significance of this badge is unknown.

Author's Collection

Enlisted ranks' national emblems for the black field cap. The white machine-woven version at top is a Model 1936 (first pattern).

M1938 army Panzer officer's black field cap.

Bud Hasher

Author's Collection

Three young tank officers in conversation, 1942. The officers in center and right wear the standard officers' field caps while the officer at left wears and enlisted ranks' version which has been upgraded by the addition of aluminum piping around the front scallop of the turn-up.

### Mountain Cap (Bergmütze)

A special cap was introduced for mountain troops around 1930, its design being based on that worn by Austrian Army mountain troops (Hochgebirgstruppen).[67] It was made of field-grey material (Strichtuch, giving the impression of woven material having stripes, perhaps meaning whipcord). The top was unusually high, being 9cm, with a cloth-covered visor. The cap was lined in field-grey twill. Functional side panels sloped downward and were fastened together by the two buttons in the front-center of the flaps. Before December 1927 these buttons, approximately 12mm in diameter, were of matte-silver. This was later changed to bright silver; the buttons had either a pebbled or smooth finish. The button color was soon changed to field-grey for men and NCOs, silver for officers and gilt for generals.

Prior to the introduction of the Reichskokarde in 1933, a Landeskokarde was worn on the front of the cap top. Initially, a national emblem was not worn on this Bergmütze.[68]

A white camouflage cover is worn over the Bergmütze, March 25, 1943 on the Carolingian front.

The standard army Bergmütze in wear. Note the Heeres-Bergführer badge on left breast pocket.

---

[67]*Die Deutsche Reichswehr--Das Deutsche Reichsheer, May 9, 1930, p. 35.*
[68]*HVBl., "Verordnung über die Hoheitszeichen der Deutschen Wehrmacht," Nr. 121, Jahrgang 15, March 17, 1933, p. 39.*

O. Spronk

This NCO from Gebirgsjäger-Rgt. 54 is wearing a darker green mountain cap with two "Steinnuss" flap buttons.

By 1934 the buttons were 1.3cm in diameter and made of "Steinnuss," i.e., corozo nut. The lining existed in muslin, and a 4.5cm sweatband of leather was sewn to the inside.

A white cotton/tricot cover was available to wear over the Bergmütze for snow camouflage.

Around 1936 the national emblem (5.3cm wide) and cockade, combined on one piece of cloth backing, was sewn to the modified cap front. Enlisted men and non-commissioned officers wore the emblem embroidered in grey thread on a field-grey or dark green backing; officers wore a gilt or silver machine-woven national emblem.

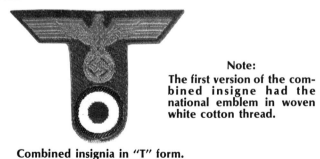

**Note:**
The first version of the combined insigne had the national emblem in woven white cotton thread.

Combined insignia in "T" form.

The mountain cap now had horsehair padding in the inside front for strengthening and support. It was slightly modified again in August 1938 with the additions of a field-grey air grommet, 0.5cm, positioned on each side 1cm below the top seam.

A metal Edelweiss was worn on the left side panel of the Bergmütze (see Tradition and Special Formation Badges).

## Tropical Headdress (Tropische Kopfbedeckungen)

### Tropical Field Cap (Tropeneinheitsfeldmütze)

In 1940, olive-colored clothing was introduced, on an experimental basis, to troops serving in the Afrikakorps and other tropical areas. The colors worn on these experimental uniforms varied from olive-green to various shades of brown. The Einheitsfeldmütze was officially introduced for units in Africa in 1941. It was based in design on the Bergmütze, but the cap top was much less pronounced, and the visor was longer. The tropical Einheitsfeldmütze was

Tropical, olive-colored visored field cap with tropical insignia and pink Soutache.

J.R. Angolia

Author's Collection

Author's Collection

The soldier above wears the skull and crossbones traditional badge of Infanterie-Regiment Nr. 17 on the front of his tropical visored field cap.

Oberst Hans Cramer wears the tropical version of the visored field cap. Note officer's piping and pink Soutache.

constructed of olive-brown cotton material. A seam gave the effect of a flap, but no flaps were provided for on this cap. It was piped along the front of the "flap" scallop and around the crown in aluminum wire for officers, gold for general officers. The Soutache was worn for a short time. The national emblem was machine-woven light-blue thread on a copper-brown cloth backing for NCOs and men. Officers could wear their silver or gold insignia.

This member of Sonderverband 288 wears an Einheitsfeldmütze which has been sun-bleached to a pure white.

**Notes:**
1. Because the sun bleached tropical headgear, various shades of color are encountered based on the amount of wear.
2. Tropical field caps were manufactured well into 1944 for troops in the Mediterranean area.

This Afrikakorps member is wearing the tropical visored field cap with the left-side shield from the tropical helmet.

### Tropical Helmet (Tropenhelm)

In 1941, forces stationed in North Africa were the first to receive the Tropenhelm (the style of these helmets was based on a navy model already in use). Prior to receiving the tropical helmet, troops often used captured ones (British, French, Dutch). The first issue Tropenhelm was cork covered in olive-green (later tan), canvas, having a medium-width band. The red lining of the helmet had several large ventilation slots, which allowed air to circulate up through the helmet and out the rounded, vented knob at the top of the crown. The liner was held in place by cotter pins and the leather chin strap was fastened to the aluminum inner rim. The first model helmet had a tan leather sweatband. The front brim of the helmet was shorter than the rear brim, and was edged around with olive-green or light brown leather trim.

**First model Tropenhelm.**

Two stamped brass, aluminum or zinc shields were worn on both models of Tropenhelmen. A shield bearing the national emblem (silver eagle and swastika on a matte black backing with silver border) was worn on the left side of the helmet: the national tri-color shield was worn on the right side. These shields were affixed to the helmets by two or three pins.

The second pattern tropical helmet was similar in design, but was made of one piece of pressed olive drab felt. The chin strap and brim edging were of olive drab leather. The interior of this cap was the same as its predecessor.

Tropical helmet stamped aluminum shields. The early productions were of stamped brass.

The metal parts (frame, cotter pins, ventilation system, and shields) were chiefly manufactured by the firm of F.W. Assmann & Söhne of Lüdensheid.

**Note:**
**Army issue tropical helmets were all lined in red.**

Second model Tropenhelm.

(Above) The first model tropical helmet is worn by the Afrikakorps member with his walking-out dress.

(Left) A "Heeresgeistliche" wears the tropical uniform according to regulations.

Captured Dutch tropical helmets were utilized early in the North African campaign, with the addition of the side plates.

A white tropical helmet was produced for wear with a white cotton version of the standard tropical uniform. This uniform was worn as a dress or parade uniform in Tripoli. No shields were worn on this helmet; rather a large, highly-detailed white metal national emblem was secured to the front of this white Tropenhelm. This form of national emblem was illustrated in the F.W. Assmann & Söhne catalogue. The wearing of any other insignia on this helmet was prohibited.[69]

Ron Manion

John Coy

O. Spronk

Army personnel wearing straw sunhats in a tropical area.

[69]*UM. Nr. 6, May 1, 1941, p. 81.*

## Visored Field Cap (Einheitsfeldmütze (M43))

The Model M43 cap produced for wear on the continent was made of field-grey material, having functional flaps that were secured in the middle above the cloth-covered brim by two pebbled buttons, field-grey in color for enlisted men, silver for officers, gilt for generals.[70] The regulation insignia was a combination of the national emblem and cockade embroidered upon a field-grey

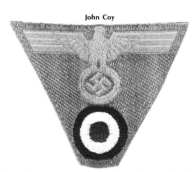

John Coy

**Machine-woven combined insignia for wear on the M43 cap.**

**Oberfeldwebel Josef Schreiber wears the standard field-grey M43 cap.**

John Coy

**A machine-embroidered version.**

**Generalmajor Kurt Freiherr von Mühlen, commander of the 559. Volksgrenadier Division, wears an M43 cap with gold piping around crown.**

[70]DUZ. Nr. 4, July 15, 1943.

**Knight's Cross holder Kurt Klein wearing an M43 cap with two-piece insignia.**

**Knight's Cross holder Otto Loose has a rosette (without backing) sewn directly onto his M43 cap.**

trapezoid, but other variations were worn as well. The cap was piped only around the crown for officers and generals. The cap was not piped in Waffen-farben, but officers below the rank of Generalmajor wore silver aluminum cord around the crown; generals wore gilt piping.[71] The cap was also produced in black wool for Panzertruppen, similarly piped.

The Einheitsfeldmütze was often worn with the newly-designed and authorized "Feldgrau-44" uniform.

General officers' M43 cap with gilt wire piping around crown, gilt buttons, and a metal edelweiss on the left side flap.

Officers' M43 cap with aluminum piping around crown and two-piece insignia. Note tailor's label in cap (below).

[71]HVBl. "Hoheitszeichen an der Bergmütze, usw." Nr. 190, February 11, 1936, p. 57.

This army officer wears the M43 cap with additional aluminum piping on the edge of the front turn-up.

(below) Enlisted ranks' M43 cap.

J.R. Angolia

Rare 1945 marked M43 cap of a late-war, grey-brown material. The grey national emblem and cockade are on a similarly colored backing. Note Jäger badge on left flap.

P. Stahl

69

Panzer combined insignia in "T" form (left) and on a triangular backing (right).

Black Panzer M43 cap (enlisted ranks) which has been upgraded to an officer model by having aluminum cord added around the crown.

Oberstleutnant Franz Bäke wears the officer's pattern M43 field cap in black for Panzer troops. Note the additional aluminum piping around the scallop in front.

Charita

## Panzer Beret (Schutzmütze)

A protective "helmet" was produced for wear by crews of motorized vehicles, specifically, Panzertruppen. The helmet consisted of a thick oval-shaped cap, lined with black oil cloth and ventilated on the sides by four hard rubber vents, over which fitted a loose black beret. Because motorized crews were liable to have their uniforms heavily soiled by grease and fuel, black was chosen as the uniform color, since such stains would not be readily visible. Panzertruppen were to receive a new Schutmütze every two and a half years.[72]

Army tank crew Schutmütze. The insignia is machine-woven white thread.

Initially, only a machine-woven wreath and cockade was worn on the beret. In 1935, a machine-woven national emblem was introduced to be worn 0.4cm above the wreath. The lowest line of the wreath was to be positioned approximately 1.2cm from the edge of the beret.[73]

The insigne on the first model beret consisted of an oakleaf wreath of white thread with a metal Reich cockade. Occasionally, the first pattern peaked cap wreath was also worn.

[72]Der Unteroffizier. Heft 4, "Der Bekleidungsoffizier," Berlin: 1939, pp. 104 and 121.

[73]HVBl. "Hoheitszeichen, usw." Nr. 646, Jahrgang 1935, p. 226.

The national emblem and wreath/cockade were machine-woven in white cotton thread on black cloth. By 1939 the national emblem was silver-grey cotton for men and NCOs; bright aluminum for officers (photographs indicate that the Schutmütze was also worn by general ranks).[74] The oakleaf wreath was silver-grey (excluding the cockade, which retained its original color scheme) for all ranks. Some units retained this protective headgear throughout the war.

Beret insignia in white.

In grey.

The Army Panzer beret in wear.

John Coy

**Note:**
The white insignia (above left) was introduced on October 30, 1935 and was replaced in 1939 by the silver-grey thread version.

One of the features of an original beret top is the circular weaving radiating out from the 2.5cm long lappet.

[74]*E. Hettler, Uniformen der Deutschen Wehrmacht. Berlin 1939, p. 49.*

Assault gun crews wore the Panzer-style uniform in field-grey;[75] and some units wore a Schutzmütze with a field-grey cloth-covered base. The field-grey top had BeVo insignia in mouse-grey on dark-green only. The Schutzmütze was officially withdrawn from issuance on January 15, 1941.

The field-grey beret was produced in limited numbers as assaultguns were introduced shortly before the use of the Schutzmütze was ordered to be discontinued. These berets were reissued and used, late in the war, by some crews of Panzerwerfer vehicles (rockets mounted on half-tracks). Many of the discontinued Schutzmützen had the cloth covers replaced with fur covers for use as winter headgear.

George Petersen

George Petersen

---

[75]*Introduced on May 29, 1940 for wear by gun crews of assault gun units of the artillery.*

A tanker's winter protective helmet was developed and issued. The padded headpiece was as that worn with the Panzer beret, but the cover was of field-grey cloth and fur. This winter model exists in two variations: one with removable fur cover, and the other permanently attached.

Tanker's winter protective helmet, front view.

Side view.

Experimental, protective headgear which was introduced for wear in 1940 with the dark green collared, field-grey uniform for self-propelled assault gun crews, but neither were adopted for use. Below is an interior view of the experimental protective helmet.

75

### Fur Caps (Pelzmützen)

During the winter of 1941-1942 Pelzmützen (fur caps) were instituted for wear in extremely cold zones. The Oberkommando der Wehrmacht sought to quickly provide its forces in the East with sufficient headdress. The current forms of head covering had proven to be practically useless against the harsh cold. A prototype Winterschützmütze was sent to the Fachuntergruppe Uniformenindustrie in Berlin for consideration. It was described as being made of field-grey material, lined in camouflage white material so that the cap color could be reversed.[76] The Winterschutzhaube consisted of an oval, heavily quilted cap, field-grey (colors varied) on the outside, though sometimes white was used. Two long fur flaps were sewn to the bottom edge of the cap, and when not in use, were tied across the crown of the cap. A fur flap was provided for the front and back of the cap as well.

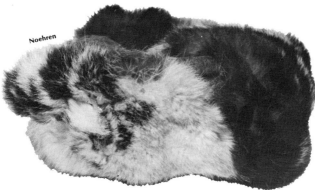

Noehren

An army-issue winter fur cap of field-grey wool and rabbit fur flaps.

O. Spronk

A black winter fur cap with white trim in wear.

The official German fur cap was identical to that worn by the Russian Army. Captured Russian caps were often worn, sometimes having a German national emblem of some form (metal, from the tunic, etc.) and, in some cases, a national cockade, attached to the cap front.

Almost every form of headdress was modified with a fur covering, including the field cap, M43 and Schutzmütze. Einheitsfeldmützen were produced with fur flaps, as were field caps. German troops in Lappland often wore white caps as used by the Finns, with the addition of German insignia.[77]

---

[76]Report to the Fachuntergruppe Uniformenindustrie, "Beschreibung der Winterschutzhaube für das Heer."

[77]UM. Nr. 6, March 15, 1943, p. 42.

Russian winter fur cap, often used by the Germans, who usually added a national emblem and roundel.

Obstlt. Graf Strachwitz wears a black field cap with black fur flaps for winter use.

**Illustrated are several of numerous versions of fur-covered caps utilized by German personnel.**

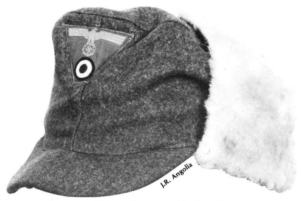

M43-style cap with fur flaps.

"Grossdeutschland"          "Grossdeutschland"

Gen. d. Inf. Heinrici is at far right, January 1943. Note the wear of wreath and rosette by man at left.

Note Finnish-style winter cap with metal national emblem from a white summer tunic.

Luftwaffe-style fur cap with army insignia.

"Grossdeutschland."

In September 1942 regulations were issued in anticipation of the coming winter. Special head protection (Kopfschützer) and a cowl (Kopfhaube) were manufactured. These forms of protective headdress covered the back of the head, neck (this portion could be fastened snugly by a lace) and chin, as well as the mouth and nose. The Kopfschützer was of field-grey material. Material for the Kopfhaube was field-grey or green wool. Those who did not receive the Kopfhaube received two Kopfschützer. A protective shawl or wrap was also available.[78]

J. de Jonge

The Kopfschützer for protecting the back of the head, ears, neck, and chin. It could be raised to also protect the mouth and nose.

J. de Jonge

The Kopfhaube was worn over the Kopfschützer as illustrated at right.

[78]*Anleitung zum Verpassen und Gebrauch von Bekleidungsstücke im Winter. Berlin: September 1, 1942, reprint 1943, pp. 12, 13, and 19.*

The Kopfhaube is fastened with a fabric tape around the neck.

The soldier at left wears the Kopfschützer while the one at right wears regulation earwarmers.

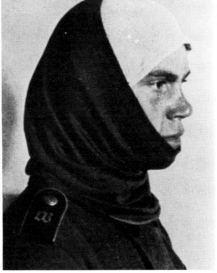

The use of two different Kopfschützer, as illustrated above, was by troops who were not issued the Kopfhaube or fur cap. The field-grey Kopfschützer was pulled over the head and around the neck, while the white or grey one was pulled over the back of the head covering the ears and forehead. The first Kopfschützer was then pulled up over the back of the head totally covering the neck and chin.

As worn with the field cap, mountain cap, or steel helmet.

In extreme cold, the field-grey Kopfschützer was pulled up over the mouth and nose, and the flaps of the field cap or mountain cap were pulled down and fastened by the two front buttons.

A side view of the above right manner of wear.

These German prisoners on the eastern front are wearing the Kopfschützer as intended, and not rags or cloth remnants as one would think.

The Kopfhaube was also produced in a reversible form (camouflage on one
side and white on the other), to be worn with the camouflage winter suit. This
could be worn with a face mask which was fastened by tapes at the back of the
head (see below). It appears that neither the camouflage Kopfhaube or face
mask were produced in large numbers, and not normally worn with the winter
suits.

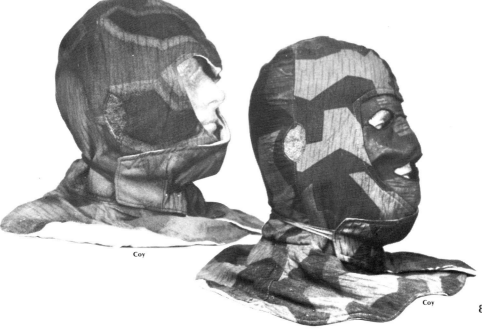

Coy

Coy

## Army Female Communications/Signal Auxiliaries
## (Nachrichtenhelferinnen des Heeres)

Also referred to as "Blitzmädel," (taken from the lightning bolt insigne worn on their caps), army female auxiliaries wore by 1940 a striking uniform which was highly praised by the German public. The first Helferinnen were incorporated into the army from the Deutsches Rotes Kreuz (German Red Cross); the new uniforms were partially delivered from DKR depots.[79] This new uniform was officially sanctioned in November 1942. Helferinnen wore a stone-grey cap with yellow piping (the same color worn by men of army signal units) around the crown seam and on the front flap scallop.[80] A national emblem (white machine-woven thread on black) was sewn to the center of the cap flap; no cockade was worn. A black oval with an embroidered yellow "Blitz" (lightning bolt), striking downward, was sewn to the forward portion of the left flap. Lower ranking Helferinnen did not wear piping around the oval.

George Petersen

J.R. Angolia

Female signal helper's field cap with yellow piping and "Blitz," as worn by enlisted grades. The national emblem is machine-woven white thread on black. The "Blitz" is machine-embroidered rather than the often encountered machine-woven version.

The piping for the field-grey cap in 1940 was as follows:[81]

| | | |
|---|---|---|
| 1. Führerin | Yellow cord on flap and around oval; |
| 2. Oberführerin | Yellow/silver cord on flap and around oval; |
| 3. Hauptführerin | Gold cord on flap and around oval. |

In 1943 the Schiffchen was piped as follows for these ranks:

---

[79]UM. Nr. 21, November 1, 1940, p. 162.
[80]Ibid., 1940, p. 175.
[81]Ibid., 1940, p. 175.

| | |
|---|---|
| 1. Unterführerin | Silver or white machine-woven eagle, yellow/black cord on flap, crown and around oval; |
| 2. Führerin | As above, with yellow/black cord on flap, crown and around oval; |
| 3. Oberführerin | As above, with yellow/silver/black cord on flap, crown and around oval; |
| 4. Hauptführerin | As above, with silver cord on flap, crown, and around oval; |
| 5. Stabsführerin | As above, with gold cord on flap, crown and around oval; |
| 6. Oberstabsführerin | As above.[82] |

Helferinnen were also provided with an M43-style cap.

J.R. Angolia

**Female signal helper's garrison cap for the rank of Unterführerin (yellow/black piping). The national emblem has been removed from this particular specimen.**

Author's Collection

**These three Nachrichtenhelferinnen have just been awarded the War Merit Cross with Swords, 2nd Class, for performance of duty during an air raid, July 10, 1944.**

---

[82]DUZ. June 1943, pp. 9-10.

### Female Army Staff Aides (Stabshelferinnen des Heeres)

A uniform was authorized for wear by those women serving on army command staffs in the east and northern countries, probably from the fall of 1942. A garrison cap, like that worn by Nachrichtenhelferinnen, was worn by these Stabshelferinnen, however, the woven national emblem in white on black was sewn to the front of the cap, above the flap. This field cap was piped along the crown seams and around the flaps in silver wire.[83]

### Army Female Horse Trainers (Wehrmachtbereiterinnen)

In the summer of 1943 the OKW began experimenting with using female auxiliaries, instead of male personnel, in riding and driving schools, as well as in training horses.[84] While working with horses, a stone-grey Einheitsfeldmütze with national emblem was worn. The Schiffchen, also in stone-grey, and piped in yellow, was worn. These caps were delivered with the stocks for the Nachrichtenhelferinnen.[85]

O. Spronk

(Above) Wehrmachtbereiterinnen lined up for a briefing. Note that their caps have only one fastening button and the national emblem only. The rider, 3rd from right, is wearing either a "German Horseman's Badge" or a "Badge for the Care of Horses."

(Right) A Schiffchen being worn by a Wehrmachtbereiterinnen during the training of a horse.

O. Spronk

---

[83]*Ibid., Nr. 1/2, May 31, 1943, p. 11.*
[84]*Front und Heimat. Horisonten. Nr. 19, September 1944.*
[85]*DUZ. Nr. 6, September 15, 1943, p. 8.*

## Tradition and Special Unit Badges

Some units were permitted to wear "tradition badges" to commemorate former units of the old Imperial German Army.

1. A matte-white metal Totenkopf with crossed bones, to be worn only on the visored cap, by the following:

- 1. and 4. Kompanie of the Infanterie-Regiment Nr. 17, to commemorate the former Braunschweiger Infanterie-Regiment Nr. 92; and

- 4. Eskadron of the 13. Reiter-Regiment (4th squadron of cavalry troop Nr. 13) to commemorate the former Braunschweiger Husaren-Regiment Nr. 17 (later this Totenkopf was also manufactured in gold-washed metal).[86]

O. Spronk

The Totenkopf to commemorate Braunschweiger Infanterie-Regiment Nr. 17 and Infanterie-Regiment Nr. 92 is worn by the above soldier of Infanterie Truppenteil 20 (circa 1919). This style of skull was worn until 1940 when it was replaced with the chinless version.

[86]Katalogue F.W. Assmann & Söhne. Lüdenscheid: Ausgabe 1937, pp. 4-5.

Infantry officer's visored cap bearing the traditional badge of Infanterie-Regiment Nr. 17.

Knight's Cross holder, Gerhard Boldt.

In this pre-1935 photo, the above officer wears the skull and crossbones traditional badge between the state and national cockades on his visored cap.

These two enlisted men wear the Braunschweig
Infanterie-regiment Nr. 17 tradition badge on their field
caps, which was against regulations.

2. A matte-white (silver) metal chinless Totenkopf (Leib-Husar), having
crossed bones resting under the teeth (the style used by Panzertruppen) was
only to be worn on the visored cap by:

- 1. and 2. Eskadron of the 5. Reiter-Regiment to commemorate the former
  Leib-Husaren-Regimenter Nr. 1 and 2.

The Leib-Husaren-Regimenter Nr. 1 and 2 tradition badge is worn by this NCO from
Truppenteil 8 (cavalry), approximately 1919. It
was worn until 1945 on the visored cap only.

Bill Rentz

Visored cap with the traditional badge worn by the 5. Kavallerie-Regiment.

(Left) The tradition badge for Reiter-Regiment Nr. 5 is worn on the visored cap according to regulations.

O. Spronk

(Right) The un-authorized wear of the "Dragoner or Schwedter Adler" on the Einheitsfeld-mütze.

3. A small matte gold Imperial eagle (without crown and device in 1930) was worn on the visored cap by:

- 2. and 4. Eskadron of the 6. Reiter-Regiment, to commemorate the former Brandenburger Dragoner-Regiment Nr. 2.[87] This eagle varied in material and style. Brass was also used with an eagle having no sword and scepter. Before 1930 the same style might have been worn as the 1934 model, with the addition of the crown. In 1934 this eagle was renamed the "Dragoner-Adler" (dragoon eagle), and then had the ribbon with "Mit Gott für König und Vaterland (with God for King and Nation). It was also manufactured in gold-anodized aluminum.[88]

[87]Die Deutsche Reichswehr--Das Deutsche Reichsheer. May 9, 1930, p. 33.
[88]Anzugordnung für das Reichsheer (H. Dv. 122). Abschnitt A, Berlin: November 14, 1934, p. 109.

Model 1930 Prussian eagle traditional badge. Note the absence of the sword and scepter.

James Boulton

Dragoon eagle with sword and scepter.

As above but mounted on a field-grey backing.

A. Breuker

Walter Gorn.

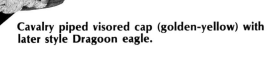

Cavalry piped visored cap (golden-yellow) with later style Dragoon eagle.

91

By order in 1938, the text of the regulations concerning the wearing of tradition badges was changed:

1. An aluminum Totenkopf with crossed bones, to be worn only on the visored cap by the following:

- Regimentsstab I. and II. Bataillon; the 13. and 14. Kompanie of Infanterie-Regiment 17, to commemorate the former Braunschweig Infanterie-Regiment Nr. 92; and

- II./Kavallerie-Regiment Nr. 13 to commemorate the former Husaren-Regiment Nr. 17 from Braunschweig.

Note:

> This skull, worn by those with Braunschweig tradition, was abolished in the Spring of 1940 and replaced by the chinless version worn by the I./Kavallerie-Regiment Nr. 5.

2. An aluminum chinless Totenkopf (style as for Panzertruppen) to be worn by:

- Regimentsstab und I./Kavallerie-Regiment Nr. 5 (including trumpet corps) to commemorate the former Preussische 1. und 2. Leib-Husaren-Regiment.

3. A small form of the Dragoner-Adler with device, crown, sword and scepter for wear on the visored cap by:

- Regimentsstab 2. and the 4. Schwadron of Kavallerie-Regiment Nr. 6; and

- Kradschützen-Bataillon Nr. 3, commemorating Dragoner-Regiment Nr. 2.[89] This Dragoon Eagle was manufactured in matte-yellow aluminum or brass, the latter being prohibited at that time, but its prohibition was often ignored.[90]

### Jäger Badge

Jäger divisions were authorized in October 1942 to wear a special white or bronze stamped metal badge, the "Eichenlaubbruch der Jägerdivisionen." It was of aluminum or silver-grey colored metal, 55mm high and 37mm wide, and consisted of a sprig of three oakleaves and one acorn. The badge was worn

Ron Kwan

[89]HVBl. "Erinnerungsabzeichen," Nr. 71. Jahrgang 1938, pp. 49-50 and Uniformen der deutschen Wehrmacht, Berlin: 1939, pp. 12-13.
[90]Unterrichtsbuch für Soldaten (mit Anlage). Berlin: 1938.

Knight's Cross holder Max Sachenheimer wears the Jäger badge on his field cap.

on the left side of the field cap and Bergmütze. It was granted for wear only by members of Gebirgsdivisionen, Gebirgsgeneralkommandos and Gebirgsarmeeoberkommandos.[91]

## Skijäger Badge

In fall 1944, the Chef des Generalstabs granted Skijäger-Brigade 1. permission to wear a special badge.[92] The badge was of stamped metal, consisting of a sprig of three oak leaves and a single acorn, in the style of that worn by Jäger, but with the addition of a ski, positioned across the leaves at approximately a 45-degree angle. The lower edge of the badge was to be positioned horizontally

The Skijäger cap badge.

---

on the left cap flap.[93] Field-made pieces exist with metal hand-made skis soldered over the standard Jäger leaves.

The Skijäger Badge is shown being worn in Russia in 1944.

## Edelweiss

In May 1939, German mountain troops were authorized to wear a metal Edelweiss, the flower commonly found growing in the mountains, and the traditional emblem of mountain climbers, on the Berg- and Schirmmütze.[94]

A metal Edelweiss with stem and two leaves was worn on the left side of the mountain cap (40mm wide, 57mm high). The badge was white metal, excluding the stamen, which were gilt colored. Specimens also exist in hand-

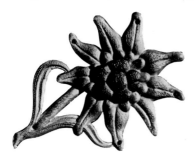

Metal Edelweiss as worn on the left flap of the mountain cap.

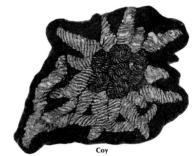

A hand-embroidered wire version of the Edelweiss.

[93]HVBl. "Abzeichen für Skijäger-Brigade 1," Nr. 400, Aug. 21, 1944.
[94]Uniformen-Markt. Nr. 24, December 15, 1939, p. 326.

**Members of Austrian-originated units as well as by members of the non-Austrian 1st Mountain Division wore the metal Edelweiss on a green cloth backing.**

O. Spronk

George Petersen

Stemless Edelweiss for the visored cap.

embroidered aluminum wire. A stemless metal Edelweiss (28mm wide, 30mm high) was worn on the cap top of the visored cap between the national emblem and wreath/cockade.

Steve Trompeter, photo: N. Malcolm

**Bright green piped, officer's visored cap with stemless metal Edelweiss. (Right) Interior photo.**

Enlisted ranks' visored cap
with stemless Edelweiss attached.

Black piped (Pionier) officer's visored cap with
Edelweiss metal insignia, belonging to an officer of a mountain engineer unit.

## Windhund

Members of the 116. Panzer-Division wore one of several semi-official cap
badges.[95] It was an oval with the figure of a running whippet in silver with a
wavy line and three sprigs of grass beneath the hound. The dog and lines/grass
were silver against a dark grey or black background.

John Coy

France, August/
September 1944.

96

## Sardinia Shield

Troops of the 90. Panzer-Grenadier Division wore a stamped metal badge in the shape of the island of Sardinia superimposed with a sword,[96] after July 1943.

This badge was manufactured locally and measured 16mm wide by 26mm high.

---

### Note:

Many unofficial unit badges were utilized. Those listed below are but a sampling.

---

## 2. Gebirgs-Division

A deer head was probably worn, but available photographs of this badge being worn were too unclear to give specific details.

## 4. Gebirgs-Division

The tactical emblem for this division, the "Enzian" (a flower), has been observed being worn in photographs. The badge was made of lightweight metal, measuring approximately 12mm x 23mm. The colors are thought to have been blue upon a greyish background. A stick pin was attached on the reverse of the badge.

(Above) A close-up view of the "Enzian" badge. (Right) The "Enzian" being worn next to the Edelweiss badge.

---

[95]Davis, p. 92.
[96]Angolia and Schlicht. Uniforms and Traditions of the German Army, Vol. I, p.

### 5. Gebirgs-Divison

This badge was observed being worn on the cap of the divisional commander, General Ringel, in Crete in 1941. Also unauthorized, the emblem was a chamois, the tactical symbol of the division. The approximate size was 25mm x 10mm. The cover of an issue of the "Neue Illustrierten Zeitung" dated February 29, 1944, shows a Jäger of this division in Italy wearing the chamois behind the regulation Edelweiss badge.

It is possible that this badge existed in two versions, stamped of brass or aluminum.

(Above) The "chamois" badge. (Right) General Ringel, the division commander, wearing the "chamois" next to his Edelweiss (Crete, 1941).

### Hochgebirgs-Bataillon 3 and 4

In January 1945 the commander of these battalions was known to have worn an eagle's head badge on the left side of his Bergmütze.

### Hochgebirgs-Kompanie 1

On at least one occasion eagle feathers (the sign of this unit) were presented to the men of this company by their commander, Hauptmann Groth, while in the Caucasian mountains in 1942.

## "Brandenburger"

This badge was in the form of the heraldic lion of the state of Thüringia (without the Swastika), and has been observed in only one photograph, taken in Greece, being worn on the tropical Einheitsfeldmütze.

## "Sonderverband 288"

It is possible that members of this mountain company wore a small brass version of the mountain troop Edelweiss patch worn on the right tunic sleeve.

It is also probable that members of "Sonderverband 288" wore this badge on the left side of their cap.

## Unknown Unit

A photograph of a machine-gunner in Italy in the Spring of 1944 shows him wearing two versions of the Edelweiss, in addition to an unidentified, but possibly Italian badge, in the style of the "Stellete" (collar badge).

### 20. Infanterie-Division

The commander of this division, General Gräser, was observed in a photograph wearing the tactical symbol, an anchor, on the left side of the cap band on his "old-style" visored cap.

Klaus Patzwall

General
Gräser

### 34. Infanterie-Division

The "Mosel-Dreieck," or "Mosel Triangle" was the tactical symbol of the 34. Infanterie-Division. A badge in this shape, measuring approximately 16mm x 21mm, was manufactured in brass and consisted of a shield bisected by a double-edged wave. The colors of this emblem are not known.

### 290. Infanterie-Division

Members of this division wore a sword, estimated to have been 10mm x 30mm. On some occasions, the badge was made from grenade fragments. A photograph shows the commander of Gren. Regt. 502, Oberst Warrelmann, wearing a small version of the sword.

(Left) A variant sword. (Right) Illustration of an actual sword observed being worn.

## Hoch- und Deutschmeister

The "Hoch- und Deutschmeister" cross (also known as the "Stalingrad Cross) normally worn on the shoulder straps and boards by members of grenadier regiments, was sometimes used as an unofficial cap badge.

## 1. Panzer-Division

The oakleaf was the tactical symbol of the 1. Panzer-Division from 1935-1940, and from 1943-1945. This symbol was worn on the sides of divisional members' caps, however, only during the later years of the war.

This Oberleutnant from Pz. Rgt. 204 carries the tactical symbol of the 22nd Pz. Div. on the left side of his black field cap.

Klaus Patzwall

An officer of Pz. Rgt. 23 wears an un-authorized badge on the left side of this officer's field cap, probably the tactical symbol of the regiment.

A. Breuker

Tactical symbol of the 1. Kavallerie-Division until November 1941 when it was reorganized as the 24. Panzer-Division. The unauthorized cap badge is illustrated above.

## "Sonderverband Bergmann"

Members of this unit, formed in 1941, wore an emblem in the shape of a "Kindjal," a Caucasian dagger, on the left side of the Bergmütze. Like most badges of this type, it was never formally authorized for wear.

The sabre measured approximately 10mm x 70mm and was manufactured of lightweight metal, probably aluminum. The colors of the badge are undetermined. A safety pin was affixed to the reverse of the sabre for attaching to the mountain cap flap.

Saris

A line illustration of the "Kind-jal."

Klaus Patzwall

A Georgian member of the "Sonderverband Bergmann" wears only the "Kindjal" on his field cap.

Germans wore this badge behind the authorized Edelweiss; Georgian volunteers wore only the "Kindjal." It is estimated that more than 1,000 of these badges were produced.

An officer's field cap with a variant "Kindjal" on the left flap.

George Petersen

## Other Badges

George Petersen

**Gen. d. Pz. Tr. Fritz-Hubert Graser.**

## Army Foreign Volunteers (Freiwillige im Heer)

Many foreign volunteers served in the German Army during the war. For the most part, German uniforms were worn, combined with the insignia peculiar to the wearer's nationality. The regular army-style national emblem was usually worn on the headdress, but the cockades varied greatly.

In publications dated 1942, articles illustrated various styles of headdress being worn by these volunteers, especially the fur caps worn by the Cossacks from the Don, Kuban, Wolga or Terek. Don Cossack black fur caps were tall with a red top; Kuban Cossack black fur caps were low-cut with a red top; Terek Cossack black fur caps were also low-cut with a cornflower blue top; and the Siberian Cossack white fur caps were tall with a yellow top. The colored cap tops were decorated with a cross pattern of white braid for enlisted and NCO ranks, and silver braid for officers. These Cossack fur caps were Russian-made with officers' models having a higher quality fur covering.

---

Cockades

1. Russische Befreiungsarmee

   Officers: white or bright aluminum fluted cockade, 45mm in diameter, a dark blue oval with a red center (the old Russian colors).

   Men and NCOs: Oval, 34mm in diameter, dark blue with red center.

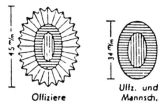

Offiziere — Uffz. und Mannsch.

Sometimes members wore the insignia that was meant for caps worn by SS-Helfer or SS-Luftwaffenhelfer. In this case they wore a silver diamond with a silver shield in the center, bordered twice in blue. This badge was superimposed with the Andreas cross.

---

(All further cockades, with the exception of those for Estland, Lettland and Lituania, were in the aforementioned sizes).

## 2. Ukrainisches Befreiungsheer

Officers: Corn-yellow fluted cockade with a light-blue center.

Men and NCOs: as above.

Offiziere

Uffz. und
Mannsch.

A silver diamond with a blue border, superimposed with a gilt Ukrainian trident was sometimes worn as well.

## 3. Estland:

Instead of an oval cockade, as worn by most units, a round cockade having a diameter of 23mm, was worn by all ranks. The colors were dark-blue/black/white.

A white diamond with a yellow border was also worn. It consisted of a green shaft of wheat bordered in yellow, over which was positioned a golden sword pointing upward. A gold and green ribbon rested horizontally over both the sword and the wheat shaft.

### 4. Lettland

All ranks: Round red/white/red cockade, 23mm in diameter.

The diamond consisted of a white diamond surrounding a red diamond; in the center, a white diamond having a red-canted swastika. The color of red was replaced by purple, probably in 1943.

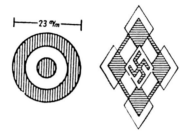

### 5. Litauen

All ranks: Round corn-yellow/green/red cockade, 23mm in diameter.

A red diamond, bordered in white with the form of a silver knight mounted on horseback in the center, was worn.

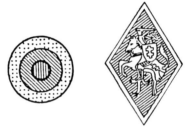

### 6. Don-Kosaken

Officers: A dark blue fluted cockade with red center.

NCOs and men wore a dark blue/red oval cockade.

Offiziere

Uffz. und
Mannsch.

## 7. Terek-Kosaken

Officers: A black/white/dark blue fluted oval cockade.

Men and NCOs wore an oval cockade in the colors of black/dark blue.

Offiziere

Uffz. und
Mannsch.

## 8. Kuban-Kosaken

As above, but with a red, instead of the dark blue center.

Offiziere

Uffz. und
Mannsch.

## 9. Sibir-Kosaken

Officers: A dark blue fluted oval cockade with a golden-yellow center.

Men and NCOs wore a dark blue/golden yellow oval.

Offiziere

Uffz. und
Mannsch.

## 10. Turkistaner

Officers: Fluted oval dark blue/red cockade. Men and NCOs wore the same colors.

Olliziere

Ullz und
Mannsch

**Note:**

Nos. 10-15 show oval cockades based on original German records. A number of these also existed in a round format as evidenced by existing examples.

## 11. Wolga-Tataren (probably Krim-Tataren also)

Officers: Fluted oval green/dark blue cockade.

Men and NCOs wore the same colored oval cockade. The diamond was silver, superimposed with a heraldic shield, partitioned per pale and green sinister (left) with a silver half moon and silver star, blue dexter (right) imposed with a silver "T."

Olliziere

Ullz und
Mannsch.

## 12. Nordkaukasier

Officers: Fluted white/orange oval cockade with white center.
Men and NCOs wore a white/orange/white oval cockade.

Offiziere

Uffz. und
Mannsch.

## 13. Aserbeidschaner

Officers: Fluted light blue/red/green oval cockade.
Men and NCOs wore a light blue/red/green oval cockade.

Offiziere

Uffz. und
Mannsch.

## 14. Armenier

Officers: Fluted red/dark blue/orange oval cockade.
Men and NCOs wore a red/dark blue/orange oval.

Offiziere          Uffz. und
                   Mannsch.

15. Georgier

Officers: Fluted red/white/black oval cockade.

Men and NCOs wore an oval cockade in the same colors.[97]

Offiziere

Uffz. und
Mannsch.

For the field cap, cossacks wore a bluish dark-green oval, in the center of which were two white crossed spears surmounted by a vertical red stripe. The same bluish dark-green oval without the crossed spears, having only the vertical red stripe was worn by other volunteers, with the exception of the Turkistaner battalions and Cossacks.[98]

16. Weissruthenien

The state colors for Weissruthenien are white/red/white, however, it is not known whether a cockade was worn. The diamond consisted of a white field bordered in yellow. In the center was a red vertical bar, imposed with a vertical golden double cross, the ends being scalloped, covered by a downward-pointing gold sword, which was crossed by an upward-pointing gold spade (the ends of both the sword and spade extended into the white back field). The letter "c" was positioned sinister (left) in the white field; the "m" dexter (right) in the white field, while a larger "b" was centered over the crossed sword and spade ("CMB" referred to the "Sajus bjelarusskaje Moladesi," the youth organization).

## 17. Galizien

Blue diamond, bordered in silver, having the gold lion of Galicia in the center.[99]

Other nations served in the German Army as well, often wearing regular caps. Variations did exist, however (see following photographs).

(Left) A "Freies Indien" volunteer wearing his traditional headgear . . . the turban.

(Below) Volunteers wearing the black fur cap with national emblem, oakleaf wreath and a cockade.

[97]*HVBl./B, Nr. 289, July 17, 1944.*
[98]*Ibid.*
[99]*DUZ. Heft 8, 1944, p. 4,*
*Ibid., Heft 6, 1943, p. 6,*
*Ibid., Heft 10, 1944, p. 5.*

# WAFFENFARBEN

**1919-1921**

| | |
|---|---|
| Kriegsministerium, Generalstab; | carmine |
| Infanterie; | white |
| Schützen-, Jäger-, Maschinengewehr-Abteilungen, Maschinengewehr-Scharfschützen-Abt., Gebirgs-Maschinengewehr-Abteilungen; | light green |
| Kavallerie; | golden yellow |
| Leichte Artillerie, Schwere Artillerie, Flak-formationen, Gebirgs-Artillerie, Minenwerfer, Artillerie-Messtrupps, Artillerie-Parks; | bright red |
| Train (army trains), Traindepots | light blue |
| Pioniere, Ingenieurkorps; | black |
| Fliegertruppen, Luftschiffertruppen; | brown |
| Eisenbahntruppen; | light grey |
| Kampfwagentruppen, Kraftfahrtruppen; | pink |
| Nachrichtentruppen, Vermessungsabteilungen; | carmine |
| Sanitätsformationen, Sanitätsoffiziere, Unterärzte; | cornflower blue |
| Veterinäroffiziere, Unterveterinäre; | golden yellow |
| Tierblutuntersuchungsstellen; | golden yellow |
| Bekleidungsämter, Versorgungsämter; | white |
| Landwehrinspektionen, Bezirkskommandos; | white |
| Zeugoffiziere, Zeugfeldwebel, Feuerwerksoffiziere, Feuerwerker; | bright red |
| Festungsbauoffiziere, Festungsbaufeldwebel, Oberwallmeister, Wallmeister; | black |
| Oberschirrmeister, Schirrmeister; | according to branch of service |
| Militärbeamten. | dark green[100] |

---

[100]*Die Deutsche Reichswehr in neuen Uniformen. 1920, pp. 17-18.*

**1921-1934**

| | |
|---|---|
| Generale; | branch-of-service color (this changed in 1927 to gold) |
| Reichswehrministerium; | carmine |
| Inspektion für Waffen und Geräte; | carmine |
| Truppengeneralstab; | carmine |
| Infanterie; | white |
| Jäger; | light green |
| Kavallerie; | golden yellow |
| Artillerie; | bright red |
| Pioniere; | black |
| Fahrtruppen; | light blue |
| Kraftfahrtruppen; | pink |
| Nachrichtentruppen; | light brown |
| Sanitätsabteilungen, Sanitätsoffizieren; | cornflower blue |
| Veterinäroffiziere; | carmine |
| Waffenschulen; | branch-of-service color |
| Zeugämter; | bright red |
| Militärbeamten; | dark green |
| Führerstäbe. | carmine[101] |

---

[101]*Bekleidung und Ausrüstung des Reichsheeres. Nr. 1368, Jahrgang 1920, p. 1027.*

**1934-1937**

| | |
|---|---|
| Generale | metallic gold |
| Reichswehrministerium; | carmine |
| Offiziere der Führerstäbe; | carmine |
| Truppenführerstab; | carmine |
| Gruppen- und Wehrkreiskommandos; | carmine |
| Infanterie; | white |
| Jäger; | light green |
| Kavallerie; | golden yellow |
| Artillerie; | bright red |
| Pioniere; | black |
| Fahrtruppen; | light blue |
| Kraftfahrtruppen; | pink |
| Nachrichtentruppen; | light brown, then changed to lemon yellow, fall 1936 |
| Sanitätsabteilungen und Offiziere; | cornflower blue |
| Veterinäroffiziere und Unterveterinäre; | carmine |
| Wachtruppe Berlin; | white |
| Dienststellen der Nachschubverwaltung und sämtliche Feuerwerker; | bright red |
| Waffenschulen; | branch-of-service color |
| Militärbeamten; | dark green[102] |
| Inspektion für Waffen und Geräte; | carmine |
| Zeugämter, Munitionsanstalten. | carmine[103] |

In January 1936, the color of orange-red was introduced for members of the Wehrersatzdienststellen.[104] At this time the Reichswehrministerium was renamed Reichskriegsministerium.

[102]*Anzugordnung für das Reichsheer (H.Dv. 122). Abschnitt A. Berlin: November 14, 1934, pp. 129-130.*
[103]*Der Dienstunterricht im Heere, Ausgabe für den Reiter. Berlin: March 1935, p. 135.*
[104]*HVBl. "Uniform der Unteroffiziere und Mannschaften der Wehrersatzabteilungen," Nr. 78, Jahrgang 1936, p. 24.*

**1937-1940**

| | |
|---|---|
| Reichskriegsministerium; | carmine |
| Generale; | metallic gold |
| Generalstab und Oberkommando der Wehrmacht; | carmine |
| Ergänzungs-Offiziere im OKW und Wehrkreisen; | orange-red |
| Infanterie, Maschinengewehrbattailonen; | white |
| Jäger; | light green |
| Wachtrupp Berlin; | white |
| Radfahrabteilung; | golden yellow |
| Kavallerie; | golden yellow |
| Artillerie, Beobachtungsabteilung; | bright red |
| Pioniere; | black |
| Nachrichtentruppen; | lemon yellow |
| Fahrtruppen, Kraftfahrtruppen; | light blue |
| Nebeltruppen; | bordeaux red |
| Panzertruppen, Panzerabwehrtruppen; | pink |
| Aufklärungsabteilungen, Schützenregimenter, Kraftradschützenbattailonen; | pink |
| Sanitätsabteilungen (including Sanitätsoffiziere und Unterärzte); | cornflower blue |
| Veterinär, as well as Unterveterinäre; | carmine |
| Reserve- und Landwehroffiziere, Sanitäts- und Veterinäroffiziere der Reserve- und Landwehr; | branch-of-service color |
| Wehrmachtbeamten; | dark green |
| Planmässigen Heeresgeistlichen; | violet[105] |
| Sonderabteilungen; | light grey |
| Zeugämter, Munitionsanstalten. | bright red |

[105]*Uniformen, Abzeichen, Dienstgrade, usw., der Deutschen Wehrmacht. Stand February 1938, pp. 8-9.*

**1940-1945**

| | |
|---|---|
| Generale; | metallic gold or yellow Celleon |
| OKW und OKH, Stabsabteilungen des OKH, Offiziere des Generalstabes, Reichskriegsministerium; | carmine |
| Gruppen-und Generalkommandos; | white |
| Unterstab des Wehrmachtbevollmägtichten beim Reichsprotektor (Unteroffiziere und Mannschaften); | white |
| Militärbefehlshaber im Generalgouvernement; | white |
| Stäbe der leichten Division und Gebirgsdivision; | bright green |
| Andere Kommandobehörden und höhere Stäbe; | branch-of-service |
| Schützenbrigadestäbe; | pink or grass-green, according to unit detachment. |
| Infanterie-Regimenter; | white |
| Jäger-Bataillone und Gebirgs-Jäger-Regimenter; | bright green |
| Infanterie-Regiment "Grossdeutschland," Wachbataillon Berlin, Wachbataillon Wien; | white |
| Maschinengewehr-Bataillone; | white |
| Radfahrabteilungen; | golden yellow (also Begleitbatterie in 1941) |
| Kavallerie- und Reiter-Regimenter; | golden yellow |
| Artillerie-Regimenter; | bright red |
| Reiter-Artillerie-Abteilungen; | bright red |
| Heeres-Flakartillerie; | bright red (1941) |
| Beobachtungs-Abteilungen; | bright red |
| Nebel-Einheiten; | bordeaux red |
| Panzer-Einheiten, Panzer-Jäger-Einheiten der Pz.-Jäger. Abt.; | pink |
| Eisenbahn-Panzerzüge; | pink |
| Aufklärungs-Abteilungen; | golden yellow (decided from case to case) |
| Motorisierte Aufklärungsabteilungen; | copper-brown |
| Motorisierte Schützen-Regimenter; | pink, golden yellow or grass-green, according to unit detachment. |

| | |
|---|---|
| Kraftradschützen-Bataillone; | as above, or also white and copper brown |
| Festungspioniere; | black |
| Desgleichen in Planstellen für Nachrichtendienst; | lemon yellow |
| Pioniere-Bataillone; | black |
| Eisenbahn-Pioniere; | black |
| Nachrichtenabteilungen; | lemon yellow |
| Fahr- und Kraftfahr-Abt.; | bright blue |
| Sanitäts-Abt.; | cornflower blue |
| Feldnachrichtenkommandanturen; | lemon yellow (1941)* |
| Werkstattkompanien; | bright red (1941)* |
| Veterinäreinheiten, bewegliche Veterinäruntersuchungsstellen; | carmine |
| Pferdetransportkolonnen; | carmine |
| Schulen; | branch-of-service |
| Feuerwerker; Waffenmeister; | bright red |
| Kriegsschule; | white |
| Kriegsakademie; | carmine |
| Ingenieur-Offiziere-Akademie; | orange-red |
| Heeres-Unteroffizierschulen--und Vorschulen, Musikschulen; | white |
| Heeresschule für Hunde und Brieftaubendienst; | lemon yellow |
| Heeresgasschutzschulen; | bordeaux red (officers: branch-of-service color) |
| Heeresluftschutzschule; | as above |
| Lehr- und Versuchstruppen; | branch-of-service color |
| Heeresfeldzeugmeisterei; | bright red (orange in 1944) |
| Bautruppen; | light brown (1940) |
| Propagandatruppen; | bright grey (1943) |
| Truppensonderdienst | light blue (1944) (this is a color in shading between the blue for Fahrtruppen und Sanitätseinheiten) |

---

*These colors and dates could not be positively determine.*

| | |
|---|---|
| Geheime Feldpolizei; | dark green (light blue--secondary color on shoulder straps/boards) |
| Feldpost; | dark green (lemon yellow--secondary color on shoulder straps/boards) |
| Wehrmachtbeamten; | dark green |
| Heeresgeistlichen; | violet |
| Reserve-und Landwehroffiziere, usw.; | branch-of-service |
| Reserve-Offiziere (W); | bright red |
| Landwehr-Offiziere (W); | bright red |
| Festungswerkmeister; | black[106] |
| Offiziere des OKW und OKH; | in 1943 changed to branch-of-service color[107] |
| Offiziere (W), Feuerwerker. | changed to orange in 1944.[108] |

Due to material shortages, the old branch-of-service color for Offiziere(W) and Feuerwerker was retained until the end of the war. However, newly-commissioned officers did wear this color.[109]

---

[106]*Heeresverwaltungs-Taschenbuch. Berlin: 1942-1943, pp. 915-924. Also several publications in Uniformen-Markt, HVBl, and Heeresmitteilungen.*
[107]*UM. Nr. 4, February 15, 1943, p. 26.*
[108]*Allgemeine Heeres-Mitteilungen. 1944, pp. 252-253.*
[109]*Ibid., 1944, p. 362.*

## ━━━━━━━━━ Dress Regulations (Anzugsbestimmungen) ━━━━━━━━━

These regulations were standard for all soldiers, including army officials, when ordered in 1930 to wear a uniform.

a. Feldanzug (field dress: with field cap (Feldmütze). Mountain troops wore their Bergmütze;

b. Dienstanzug (service dress) with visored cap (Dienstmütze or Schirmmütze);

c. Paradeanzug (parade uniform); with steel helmet, with the exception of mountain troops, who wore the Bergmütze.

d. Meldanzug (reporting dress); with the visored cap.

e. Kleiner Gesellschaftsanzug für Offiziere (evening dress for officers); with the visored cap (the Schirmmütze was also worn with the more formal evening dress (Grosser Gesellschaftsanzug) (full decorations, not just ribbon bars));

f. Ausgehanzug (walking-out dress) with visored cap;[110]

g. Kleiner Dienstanzug für Offiziere und dienstleitende Unteroffiziere (small service dress for officers and NCOs in service); with visored cap and later the field cap.

Special regulations were in preparation for members of Kraftfahrab-teilungen (motorized vehicles) in 1935.[111]

For b: The uniform visored cap was worn by officers and Unteroffiziere mit Portepee. Other NCOs and men wore the field cap.[112]

━━━━━━━━━━━━━━━━━━━━━━━━━━━━━━━━━━━━━━━━━━━━

[110]*Die Deutsche Reichswehr--Das Deutsche Reichsheer. May 9, 1930, pp. 34-35.*
[111]*Der Dienstunterricht im Heere, Ausgabe für den Reiter. Berlin: March 1935, pp. 122-127.*
[112]*Anzugordnung für das Reichsheer, (H.Dv.). Abschnitt B, Berlin: 1935, p. 7.*

# CHAPTER

# 2

## GERMAN MOTORIZED COMPANY
## (COMPAGNIA AUTOCARRATA TEDESCA)

On June 2, 1940 the governor of Eritea (Italian East Africa), General Frusci, ordered the institution of a motorized company made up of German volunteers living there. These men were largely refugees from British colonies in Africa and sailors who had been stranded in the harbor of Massaua when hostilities broke out in September 1939. The company was designated "Compagnia Autocarrata Tedesca," or in German, "Deutsche Motorisierte Kompanie."

The total strength of this unit was approximately 138 men. Their commander was Kompaniechef Oberleutnant Gustav Hamel (his CAT rank was Tenente). On July 10, 1940 the Compagnia Autocarrata Tedesca paraded before Governor Frusci. This was the first occasion that the CAT appeared in their uniforms. Less than a year later, on May 20, 1941, the entire company was annihilated in action.

The uniforms, as well as arms and equipment, came from Italian Army stocks, the only difference being the insignia worn. The visorless field cap and tropical helmet were supplied with a round white cloth badge, bordered in red, called a "Kokarde." The black canted swastika worn in the center diverged slightly from the well-known design. A black "Helvetic" cross (one in the shape of that worn by the International Red Cross) was sometimes worn instead. The size of the cockade varied. A bigger one was worn when the uniform tunic had the swastika positioned in the upper portion of the collar tabs (open version blouse). A small cockade was worn when the swastika was positioned at the front of the tab (closed version blouse).[1] The German press indicated that this variation was to distinguish between two different groups within the company, but this has not been confirmed.

Other forms of headdress were worn as well. The Italian field cap was like that worn by members of the SA-Wehrmannschaften, having a flap which folded over the top and a front brim, which was usually worn turned up, but could be worn down, serving as a short visor. When folded up, this visor was

---

[1]*UM. Nr. 22, November 15, 1940, pp. 155, 164.*

(Below) Three members of the German Motorized Company. (Left) Helvetic cross cockade on an Italian field cap, as worn by man at far left of photo. (Below right) Reconstruction of the CAT uniform worn in Eritrea and taken from Italian stocks.

Grey-green and khaki colored field caps.

secured to the front of the cap by a snap. The Italian field cap was made of grey-green gabardine. Khaki-colored caps were used as well.

The khaki tropical helmet had a squarish crown and brim. A cloth band was positioned at the base of the crown. The cockade is known to have been worn on the right side of this tropical helmet; whether this was according to regulation is not known.[2]

---

[2]Unknown newspaper article about the "Deutsche Freiwillige in Italienisch-Ostafrika."

# 3

# PEOPLE'S ARMY
# (DEUTSCHE VOLKSSTURM)

By a decree of the Führer dated September 25, 1944, it was ordered that a home guard be created to defend German soil from any hostile force which might set foot on it.[1] Two days later, further orders arranged its organization, training and equipment.[2] The "Volkssturm" consisted of men between the ages of sixteen and sixty years old who were able to bear arms. The Peoples' Army was segmented into battalions and was meant to be a reinforcement for the German armed forces fighting within the country. This new "army" was divided into four summons to take up arms, called "Aufgebote."

On October 12, 1944 the first orders regarding uniforms appeared. Without deference to rank, it was the duty of the individual to procure some sort of military-looking clothing. Sports and work clothes were suitable for wear as well.[3]

Upon "Das erste Aufgebot" (the first summon), Volkssturm members had to be uniformed. Clothing often came from NSDAP stocks, and had to be dyed "Einsatzbraun," a dark shade of brown similar to the color of the SA mountain tunic (Gebirgsrock).

Upon other Aufgebote, members were to wear grey uniforms. They were to strive for a unity in headdress; caps in the style of those worn by the army and political visorless garrison caps (Einsatzmütze der NSDAP) were most often used. A national emblem was worn on the front of the headdress.[4] The shortages of war deemed that an enormous variety of headdress was worn by the Volkssturm. It can be literally said that anything was possible regarding what sort of uniform was worn.

---

[1]"Erlass des Führers." September 25, 1944.
[2]Anordnung 277/44. "Ausführungbestimmungen über die Bildung des deutschen Volkssturmes," September 27, 1944.
[3]Anordnung 318/44. "2: Ausführungbestimmungen," October 12, 1944.
[4]DUZ. Nr. 12, December 1944, p. 1.

A wide variety of civilian headwear is shown in this photo of marching Volkssturm members.

This businessman wears his civilian hat and leather overcoat with "Deutscher Volkssturm/Wehrmacht" armband, December 1944.

The commander of a Volkssturm battalion instructs two of his men on how to build a defensive position. Note the Hitler Youth style cap and the leather motorcyclist helmet in wear.

Two styles of cap often worn by the "Deutsche Volkssturm".

Otto Spronk

Two older members of the "Deutsche Volkssturm" from the second summons (Das zweite Aufgebot) wearing a hodgepodge of clothing. The mountain-style caps were supplied with proper insignia.

Paul Geers

This youngster from the third summons (Das dritte Aufgebot) wears a single-button Luftwaffe cap and is well armed.

# CHAPTER

# 4

## REICHSMARINE/KRIEGSMARINE

As previously stated, the Reichsmarine (German Navy) was formed simultaneously with the Reichsheer (German Army) on March 23, 1921. On April 5, clothing and equipment regulations were issued for the Reichsmarine.[1] Old regulations and traditions were either partially altered or entirely superseded.

### Visored Cap (Schirmmütze)

The visored cap worn by officers of the Reichsmarine in 1919 was still in the old style, circa 1890. The top was of either dark blue doeskin or white material, and was smaller in size than that worn later by Kriegsmarine officers. Like its successor, this visored cap featured a black mohair cap band, 4cm in width, and a black lacquered visor and chin strap (the chin strap was worn by all officer ranks, including Admirale and Kommodore). The latter was secured to the cap sides by two gilt buttons embossed with an anchor motif. Regulations often refer to anchors as "klarer" or "unklarer." "Klarer" indicates an anchor without a rope or "unfouled," and "unklarer" indicates an anchor with an interlaced rope or "fouled."[2]

### Insignia

### Wreath and Cockade

Prior to 1919, officers wore a hand-embroidered, gilt wire wreath surmounted by an Imperial crown (with a portion of the crown extending above the top band seam. The wire national cockade was in black and silver (representing white), with a red felt center.[2]

James Boulton

---

[1]*Marineverordnungsblatt (MVBl). Jahrgang 1921, Nr. 142, p. 203*
[2]*Halcomb, Jill. The SA: A Historical Perspective. Overland Park, KS: Crown/ Agincourt Publishers, 1985, p. 216.*

## Form I

### Reichs- (Adler-) Kokarde

In accordance with Article 3 of the constitution of the Weimar Republic, dated August 11, 1919, and the new uniform regulations, it was ordered that the black/white/red cockade was to be replaced by the new metal Reichs- (Adler-) Kokarde, a black Weimar eagle on a gold oval background (in the same style as that worn by the Reichsheer) for wear on the visored cap (enlisted ranks were to wear a cloth Landeskokarde on their field-grey Feldmützen (field caps)). See Reichsheer chapter.

The new cockade was worn within the oakleaf wreath, in the position formerly occupied by the black/white/red national tri-color by all naval officers, as well as by officers of navy-brigades (Marinebrigaden) and coastal-protection units (Küstenwehr). It was to be in use by January 1, 1920.[3] The Reichs- (Adler-) Kokarde was available in hand-embroidered bullion for wear by the ranks of Admiral and Kommodore.

A round version of this eagle cockade was worn by enlisted men on the Matrosenmütze.

Frailey

This Reichsmarine officer wears the cap wreath with the Reichs- (Adler-) Kokarde. (Above right) Kokarde in hand-embroidered wire. (Right) Metal Kokarde.

A. Breuker

---

[3]*MVBl. "Reichskokarde." Nr. 354, Jahrgang 1919, p. 464.*

*Marineschule Muerwick*

(Above) White top visored cap with hand-embroidered oakleaf wreath and Reichsadlerkokarde.

(Right) Early blue top visored cap for officers worn with the frock coat.

*Marineschule Muerwick*

Marineschule Muerwick

Enlisted man's Matrosenmütze with metal Reichsadlerkokarde and "Torpedobootsflottille" tally.

**Early Matrosenmütze with metal Reichsadlerkokarde and "Marineschule Muerwick" tally being worn.**

**Marine-Küstenartillerie, field-grey visored cap with Reichsadlerkokarde being worn.**

Marineschule Muerwick

129

Metal wreath for wear with the metal Reichs-
(Adler-) Kokarde.

## Form II

In 1933 the Reichs- (Adler-) Kokarde was replaced by the newly-reinstated black/white/red national tri-color, constructed in the following manner:

a. Base: 1.0mm fluted and black lacquered, pressed metal, being 23mm in diameter. The use of Vulkanfiber parts in manufacturing was replaced by aluminum in 1935.

b. Roundel: Prior to 1935, in matte "Neusilber," later in matte aluminum, 0.5mm thick, covered in clear lacquer, 4mm high, having a diameter of 1.75cm. The first type had four retaining clips on the reverse; the later type had only two pins to attach the roundel to the base. A red piece of cloth (Abzeichentuch) was glued to a piece of cardboard, giving the roundel its red center.[4]

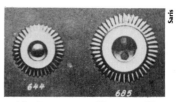

Several types of cockades in use with the navy, as illustrated in the Ad. Baumeister catalogue (Ludenscheid (W)). Numbers 12028 and 5369½ were regular styles and numbers 644 and 685 had a white enameled middle section surrounding a red glass "Bull's eye."

Naval officers on extended furlough (Offiziere des Beurlaubtenstandes) wore a silver cross, 6mm in diameter, in the center of the red field of the cockade.[5] This practice was discontinued in 1936 (see "Offiziere des Beurlaubtenstandes" further in this chapter).

---

[4]*Bekleidungsvorschrift für die Kriegsmarine. "Die Beschreibung der sonstige Abzeichen." Berlin. Ausgabe 1935 and 1938.*

[5]*Uniformen-Markt. Nr. 8, August 1, 1935, p. 4.*

Cockade for naval officers on extended furlough.

## Wreath

### Wreath (for the field-grey visored cap)

The first pattern oakleaf wreath was made of gilt-colored (Tombak) metal or galvanized brass (matte as well as polished). It was identical in design to the first pattern wreath worn by the army. In 1935 this wreath was replaced by the new style (same as the army)[6] and yet another version was introduced. The last type was the most commonly used wreath until the end of the war.

The wreath extended in the same manner as for the blue-visored cap and the cloth backing was in the same color as the cap-band for the field-grey visored cap. A special pattern, army style, was manufactured which featured polished

This member of the VIth Coastal Artillery Battalion wears the early style cockade and gilt wreath in metal as shown above.

sides and was fabricated in lightweight metal or aluminum, and was gilt anodized.[7]

The standard army pattern wreath, but in gilt, was also worn on the field-grey visored cap.

### Wreath (for the blue and white visored cap for officers, officials, NCOs and Fähnriche)

The wreath as introduced in 1933 was normally manufactured in hand-embroidery on a black or very dark blue background, but due to manufacturers' procedures, variations in appearance are to be found.

The wreath surrounded the cockade and was in gold wire or yellow thread for naval officers, in silver for officials, and was padded to give a vaulted appearance. The wreath bottom extended to the lower piping (or brim) of the cap band.[8] On the left and right were four leaves with the inside leaves pointing above the cockade and the stems touching the horizontal leaves. The short leaves, as well as the horizontal leaves were fastened by a simple ribbon. The four acorns were positioned as such: two on the horizontal angle of the outer leaves; and the other two in the top vertical space, between the two middle leaves.

The size of the wreath is 5cm high and 4.5cm wide between the horizontal leaves. The width between the two lowest acorns is 5.8cm; between the short outside leaves, 6cm; and between the upper acorns, 3.8cm. The cloth backing was to extend approximately 2mm from the wreath proper.[9]

Before 1938 the wreath was embroidered in "echt Gold" or "echt Silber" and after that date in aluminum as well as Celleon, a substitute material. The woven thread insignia was introduced to save material as well as cut costs.

During the first year of the war a metal version was also introduced, which had larger dimensions. The wreath extended upward so that the top portion of it continued above the cap band and onto the cap top (dimensions approximately 6.4cm x 5.4cm). The cockade was also produced in metal and the wreath was stamped to resemble embroidery. Originally the wreath was of gilt aluminum or in white metal and was available in either a matte or polished

[7]*Uniformen-Markt Nr. 12, December 1, 1935, p. 2.*

[8]*Bekleidungsvorschrift für die Kriegsmarine (M.Dv.-260). Berlin, 1935 and 1938, "Beschreibung fertige Stücke für U-Offiziere mit Portepee u. Fähnriche," p. 119.*

[9]*Ibid. Pp. 156-169.*

Gilt wire version of the naval cap wreath worn by officers and NCOs.

Yellow Celleon thread national emblem and cap wreath.

A variation yellow Celleon thread wreath.

Konteradmiral Werner Scheer wearing the appropriate gilt wire insignia on his peaked cap.

finish, and was mounted on a cloth backing. These metal wreaths were also sold by the Assmann Firm without the backing. (This pertains to the national emblem also.)[10]

Author's Collection

Visored cap worn by an officer candidate (Fähnrich). Note the absence of any decoration on the visor.

John Coy

A metal wreath and cockade were also worn on senior NCO and junior officers' visored caps.

George Petersen

The senior NCOs above wear the metal wreath on their caps.

[10]F.W. Assmann Katalog, Supplement 1940, p. 8a.

## National Emblem (Hoheitszeichen)

A national emblem, consisting of the eagle and swastika, was worn on the cap top in conjunction with the wreath. The first pattern was in the same form as that worn by the army, but was gilt in color. It was officially instituted for wear in August 1934.[11] The periodical "Die Deutsche Uniform" (Nr. 1, dated August 1934) stated, however:

> ". . . The national symbol as a sign of recognition for the new state; in the course of the first months of this year (1934) this symbol was also introduced for the navy, police and other organizations."[12]

Saris

The first pattern national emblem for the navy was sold in two versions (for example by Ad. Baumeister in Lüdenscheid): regular version at left, and version with black painted swastika at right. The latter was usually worn with the walking-out uniform.

O. Spronk

Bernard Rogge, commander of the raider "Atlantis" wears a hand-embroidered first pattern national emblem on his visored cap.

[11]MVBl. Nr. 273, Jahrgang 1934, p. 191.
[12]Die Deutsche Uniform. Nr. 1, August 1934, p. 2.

The national emblem initially was made of gilded Neusilber, but was changed in 1935 to gilt lightweight metal, as well as gilt aluminum.

The second pattern national emblem was introduced in April 1935, and could be found in either metal or embroidery, in various designs and styles.

a. Enlisted men and non-commissioned officers (without Portepee): Stamped eagle having a thickness of 0.4cm. The wingspan was 5cm (the first model span was 3.7cm). The height of the national emblem was 2cm (compared to the former eagle, 2.1cm).

For a short period, the national emblem and cockade worn on the Matrosenmütze were separately attached to the cap, before being combined into one piece (around 1936). A long pin was soldered on the reverse for attaching the national emblem/cockade to the cap top. This combined insigne measured 5.1cm (wingspan) x 4cm (height).[13] (Assmann Nr. 23541 DRGM).

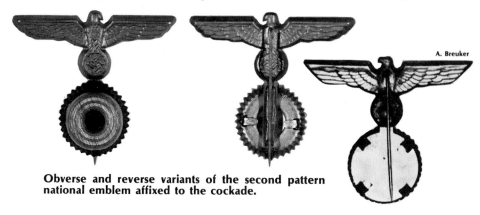

A. Breuker

Obverse and reverse variants of the second pattern national emblem affixed to the cockade.

b. Officers: Wingspan approximately 6.3cm (formerly 4.8cm). The height was 2.3cm, compared to the earlier height of 2.8cm.

Second pattern national emblem in hand-embroidered gilt wire, and in gilt metal.

[13]F.W. Assmann Katalog. Jahrgang 1936, p. 8.

In the 1938 regulations, the dimensions of the national emblem remained unchanged, but another version was discussed:

a. Sergeants I. Class and Cornets: For the blue cap, an embroidered national emblem having a wingspan of 6.6cm, the width of each wing was 0.9cm. The height of the eagle was approximately 3cm. The dark blue cloth backing was to extend 3mm around the edge of the national emblem.

b. For wear on the white top, a gold-stamped national emblem, measuring 6.6cm x 2.6cm, having a thickness of 0.4cm, with a stickpin for attaching to the cap top soldered to the reverse.[14]

### Blue Visored Cap (For Unteroffizier with Portepee and Fähnrich)

In 1935 the naval visored cap was modified in several ways, the most notable being that the top was larger, 12cm high. For example, the diameter for the top of a size 57 cap was 28.5cm.

The visored cap worn by the ranks of Unteroffizier mit Portepee and Fähnrich consisted of a dark navy-blue top, made of "Feldwebeltuch," a material of lesser quality than doeskin, having a black mohair cap band, 4cm in width. The crown of the cap and the edges of the band were piped in dark blue "Grundtuch," a cloth almost identical to the "Feldwebeltuch."

P. Roelse

**A naval officer's visored cap being worn in 1934. Note the first pattern national emblem and lack of visor decoration, which was introduced in early 1936.**

[14]*Bekleidungsvorschrift für die Kriegsmarine, (M.Dv.-260). "Beschreibung der sonstige Abzeichen." Berlin, 1938.*

Konteradmiral Carls wearing the early style visored cap in late 1936. Note crown wire is still in place keeping the basic cap form.

The smooth visor was of black Vulkanfiber, the leading edge having a narrow black lacquered leather border. Above the visor rested a black leather chin strap with two leather slides and metal buckles. The width of this strap was 1.4cm. Originally, a black lacquered snap was always affixed to the strap so as to fasten on the wearer's left side. The chin strap was secured to the cap band at each end by a matte-gilt metal button embossed with an anchor.

The visored cap was lined in light blue satin. A brown leather sweatband was sewn along the inner bottom edge of the cap band.

The front of the cap top was padded to support its weight. A rust-proof wire was installed in the crown seam to keep the basic cap form, and another loose wire was positioned inside, but this was often removed to give the cap a more jaunty look. A white netting was installed between the lining and the cloth of the top. The cap front was firmed with a 5.3cm piece of cloth.

### Visored Cap with Removable Top

A visored cap could be purchased which had provision for interchanging the tops. According to regulations, the blue top was to be removed and replaced by a white top during the summer months.

The cap body, 5.4cm high (without the top) was constructed in such a manner as to accomodate the two covers. Above the top piping on the mohair cap band was a very strong cloth-covered wire, and the lower edge piping formed a raised edge to slip the cap top over and secure it. A 5.4cm-wide piece of cloth, covering a metal stiffener (0.4cm), was sewn to the inner portion of the cap

**NCO and officer candidate's visored cap with removable white top. Note metal and gilt wire insignia combination.**

band to support the cap top. The cap body was lined in its usual light blue satin, having a celluloid sweat shield sewn in the center. This shield could have the maker's name and logo stamped on it, or be void of markings. A white cheesecloth lining was sewn above the satin lining (between the lining and the cap top).

The blue top could be made of the aforementioned Feldwebeltuch, coarse cotton canvas or drill, or the more expensive and higher quality doeskin. The white top was made of picque, or bleached material, waffle-pattern cotton, or doeskin. The inside border of the blue top was edged by a 1-cm wide double-wrapped piece of black cloth. The inside rim of the white cover had a band of white,[15] instead black edging. The underside of the front of the blue top was padded with horsehair.

In 1935,[16] the white top was to be worn in Germany from May 1 until September 30, but later the season was moved back to April 20th.[17]

The white cover could also be worn out of the country while on duty overseas and in warmer climates. Generally, only the U-Boot commander wore the white top year round, as a form of distinction.

Usually the gilt metal national emblem was worn on the cap top, but an eagle embroidered on white or dark blue backing could also be used. The white-backed embroidered national emblem was affixed to the top, in most cases, by snaps sewn to its reverse. Oftentimes, two round machine-finished holes were made into the front of the cap top to accomodate various styles of metal national emblems.

[15]*Bekleidungsvorschrift für die Kriegsmarine (M.Dv.-260)-B.2. "Beschreibung fertige Stücke für U-Offiziere mit Portepee und Fähnriche." Berlin, 1938, p. 120.*
  [16]*MVBl. Nr. 186. Ostseestationstagesbefehl Nr. 77, Ziffr. II, Jahrgang 1937, April 10, 1937.*
  [17]*Bekleidungs- und Ausrüstungsbestimmungen für die Kriegsmarine (M.Dv.-260). Berlin 1935, p. 44.*

Note the pronounced cap wreath on this young officer's visored cap. He wears the French badge "Bretagne" on his cap band.

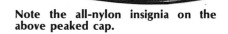

Note the all-nylon insignia on the above peaked cap.

Konteradmiral Schniewind wear a white-topped visored cap with a gilt wire national emblem on a white backing.

U-Boat commander, Kapitänleutnant Heilmann, wears the visored cap with removable white top and boat insignia (sea horse) on the cap band.

O. Spronk

A "Sonderführer" of the navy wearing his uniform according to the 1941 regulations. Note the anchors on the collar of his tunic.

141

## Model 1938 Visored Cap for Officers

In 1938, the cap was slightly modified, the basic design of the visored cap was retained; however, the top had a more definite saddle-shape. Instead of a smooth black lacquered visor in Vulkanfiber, officers wore a leather visor. It was 5.4cm wide for the rank of Leutnant and above; 5.6cm wide for Stabsoffiziere and Admirale. The obverse of the visor was often covered in fine dark navy blue felt-like material. Rank distinction was shown on the visor through the use of a gilt scalloped border or decoration. The leading edge of the visor was finished with a narrow strip of black leather.

The gold bullion decoration on the visor was added in 1936, emulating the insignia worn by naval officers of other countries,[18] and served to more readily distinguish officers. The system was as follows:

a. Leutnant to Kapitänleutnant: A 7mm-wide scalloped border.

b. Stabsoffiziere and, by 1938,[19] Musikinspizienten and Obermusikinspizienten (Musikmeister, Marineobermusikmeister and Stabsmusikmeister),[20] wore an 18mm-wide row of oakleaves (Eichenlaubranke) along the edge of the visor, just behind the leather border;

c. Admirale and Kommodore: A double row of oakleaves.[21]

**Visored cap worn by non-commissioned officers. The insignia is gilt wire while the cockade is metal. Note the non-standard chinstrap.**

O. Spronk

O. Spronk

A promotion at sea of a Kriegsmarine Leutnant. Top photo: cutting the scalloped border from a single piece of copper sheet metal.     Left photo: placing the scalloped border on the blue visored cap. Right photo: the newly-promoted Leutnant puts on his blue visored cap with unofficial, scalloped border.

[18]MVBl. "Uniformen, Abzeichen, usw., der Deutschen Wehrmacht." Leipzig, 1938, p. 25.
[19]Uniformen-Markt. Nr. 11, June 1, 1938, p. 163.
[20]Ibid.
[21]MVBl. Nr. 527, Jahrgang 1936, p. 27

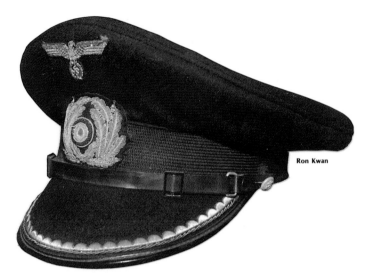

Ron Kwan

Visored cap for wear by ranks of Leutnant zur See through Kapitänleutnant. Gilt wire insignia and scalloped border.

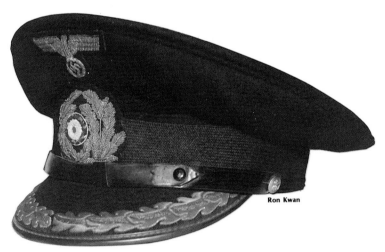

Ron Kwan

Visored cap for wear by Stabsoffiziere and Musikinspizienten, Korvettenkäpitan through Kommodore.

Note:
Many firms made naval caps but only those marked O.K.K. on the sweat shield were purchased directly from the Kriegsmarine Offiziere Kleider-Kasse (Officers' Clothing Sales).

Interior view, showing the owner's name, Dr. Moebs, perforated into the sweatband.

Visored cap for wear by ranks of Kommodore to Admiral.

**Generaladmiral Rolf Carls. He wears the double row of oakleaves on the visor of his cap.**

James Boulton

Yellow-gold nylon thread was often used instead of the corrosion-prone bullion.

The firms of F.W. Assmann & Söhne and Friedrich Linden manufactured the scalloped border and oakleaves in gilt metal, with fine detail resembling hand-embroidery (Stickereiimitationen). The lightweight gilt-anodized metal was available in four qualities, with either a polished or unpolished finish.[22] It has not been determined whether these metal rank distinctions were ever worn on the blue or white top visored caps. It is known, however, that they were used on the tan tropical visored cap.

Note:
The cap cords were not introduced for the naval officers' blue visored cap since the chinstrap was practical for use, especially on duty aboard ships.

---

[22]*F.W. Assmann & Söhne Katalog. Ausgabe 1936-1938, p. 9a and Katalog F. Linden. May 15, 1939, p. 2c.*

## Administrative Officials (Wehrmachtbeamte der Marine)

Navy administrative officials were uniformed and wore the same style caps as those worn by officers but with the following differences:

a. Naval officials, from 1921 on, wore the golden oakleaf wreath with the Reichsadlerkokarde and the leather chinstrap which was secured by golden anchor buttons. The white visor cap was also allowed. (MVBl. April 15, 1921, Nr. 142, p. 203.)

b. Civil naval officials wore the same headdress (since 1924), but the buttons and wreath were in silver. (Ibid., Nr. 4, January 26, 1924, Nr. 24, p. 21.)

c. Naval officials wearing field-grey did wear the golden or silvered metal insignia; embroidered pieces were allowed when privately purchased. (Ibid., 1921, p. 548.)

d. From June 21, 1933 the silver cords instead of the leather chinstrap were ordered for the field-grey visored cap. The eagle and wreath in gold was worn by Marine Zahlmeister. (Ibid., Nr. 16, July 1, 1933, Nr. 153, p. 108.)

e. On May 13, 1936, naval officials in the rank of officer up to the rank of Sea Captain (Kapitän zur See) wore the silver cords on the blue as well as the white visored cap. Admirals wore the gold cords. The other insignia was silver but the exact date of institution has not been determined. (Ibid., Nr. 27, October 1, 1936, Nr. 527, p. 372.)

**The white top visored cap as worn by administrative officials.**

Note:
Officials did not wear any visor decoration at all, no matter what their rank was.

**Silver wire national emblem and cap wreath for administrative officials.**

John Coy

Four groups of officials existed:

a. Those required to appear daily in uniform (for example, officials of the Marinegerichte, Marinejustizwachtmeister, Marinebauverwaltungen, Marinesanitätswesen, Marinewaffenbauwesen, etc.);

b. Those officials who were permitted, but not required, to wear the uniform;

c. Officials who were not permitted to appear in uniform;

d. Those officials with unique duties, e.g., Marineseelsorge (chaplains), Marineförster,* Leiter der Werftfeuerwehr (shipyard fire protection), Arrestanstaltaufseher (detention center supervisors,[23] etc.)

---

[23]*Bekleidungs- und Anzugsbestimmungen (M. Dv.-260). Berlin: 1935 and Nachdruck 1938, p. 70.*

    \*Although the designation of Marineförster was dis-
cussed in official uniform regulations, no evidence was
found which suggested that these officials wore anything
other than the standard navy administrative officers'
visored cap with silver insignia.

Lower ranking officials wore the black chinstrap in lieu of silver cords. Field
caps and other forms of headdress were worn by administrative officials, but
with the characteristic silver insignia.[24]

From January 1, 1943 the administrative rank of Admiral was to wear gold,
instead of the former silver, insignia. Metal insignia was also permitted.[25]
Wehrmachtbeamte der Marine wore silver Agraffe on their fore-and-aft hat
(see "Zweispitzhut für Offiziere" further in this chapter).

Officers and officials of the navy.

## Marine Clergy (Marineseelsorge)

    The first regulations concerning the uniforming of marine clergy (Marine-
pfarrer) were issued in October 1934. The visored cap was like that worn by officers, with either a blue or white top, but the cockade was replaced by a Latin
cross worn in the center of the oakleaf wreath.[26]

---

[24]*Ibid, p.* 69.
[25]*Uniformen-Markt. Nr. 4, February 15, 1943, p. 26, repeated Nr. 6, March 15,
1943, p. 44.*
[26]*Nachricht der Marineleitung. B. Nr. 4635AVc, October 19, 1934, &
"Bekleidungsvorschrift für die Kriegsmarine," Berlin, 1935. (M.Dv.-260).*

A Marinepfarrer wearing the white visor cap with the cross within the wreath, according to 1934 regulations.

Prior to 1938 marine clergy were not required to be uniformed, but on March 24, 1938, the commander-in-chief of the navy, Generaladmiral Dr. H.C. Raeder, ordered that the clerical ranks of Marinepfarrer and Marineoberpfarrer were specifically to appear in uniform.

The visored cap worn was the same as that for administrative officials, having silver insignia and cords. The senior dean on duty (Dienstälteste Dekan) wore gilt cap cords on his visored cap. A cross (Christus Kreuz) was embroidered directly above the black/white (silver)/red cockade, within the top portion of the wreath.[27] Whether two styles of crosses existed to distinguish between the protestant and catholic clergy has not been determined. In 1939 a new version of the wreath and cross was issued, this one having the cross above the wreath.

Navy chaplain's visored cap with leather chinstrap and cross positioned directly above the national cockade.

[27]*MVBl.* Nr. 293, Jahrgang 1938, p. 190 (OBd. M25738/37CLA, March 24, 1938); "Ostseestationstagesbefehl," Nr. 93, April 15, 1938, p. 3; "Die besondere Verwaltungsanordnungen," Nr. 31; MBVL, "Bekleidungs- und Anzugsbestimmungen für die Kriegsmarine," B. Nr. 3601, M. Wehr. II, April 23, 1938.

Ron Kwan

Navy chaplain's visored cap with aluminum cap cords. Note positioning of cross on the wreath.

J. Zienert

Marineschule Muerwick

(Left) A Marinepfarrer wearing the service dress. The cross is above the wreath on his visored cap, according to the 1939 regulations. (Right) An excellent example of a variation metal cross positioned on the upper portion of the wreath and extending into the swastika of the national emblem.

While these uniform orders were issued, marine clergy were slow to accommodate these changes; so slow that the commander-in-chief repeatedly had to summon them about this matter.

Other forms of headdress were issued to clergy during the war.

A Marinepfarrer wearing the white top visored cap.

A white top visored cap for navy chaplains, with the cross positioned within the wreath.

### Marine Post (Feldpostdienst der Kriegsmarine)

Postal (Feldpost) officials were recruited from the Deutsche Reichspost and were activated in September 1939. All officials wore the army uniform and visored cap, piped in lemon yellow.

### Truppensonderdienst (TSD)

The Truppensonderdienst was confirmed by an order of Hitler on January 24, 1944. On May 3, 1944 the OKM (Oberkommando der Kriegsmarine) authorized special uniform regulations for their officers serving in the TSD. They wore the standard navy officers' visored cap with gilt insignia (quite often, the stamped metal insignia was preferred to the hand-embroidered type), although their status was equated with the administrative and judicial ranks of Marinezahlmeister through Admiralsoberstabsintendant and Marineoberstabsrichter through Admiraloberstabsrichter.[28]

The field cap worn by marine officials of the TSD was fashioned after that worn by the army, with navy insignia according to rank.

### Dismissed Officers (Verabschiedete)

Those Imperial naval officers who were not incorporated into the new Reichsmarine or were otherwise dismissed from duty were permitted to wear their uniforms on special occasions. The style and insignia was that of the Imperial navy, and was not to be upgraded. For these officers, the regulations of 1909 were still in effect.[29] The cap wreath was hand-embroidered gilt wire and

In 1926, retired naval officers wear the Imperial crown insigne on their blue visored caps during the Honor Day ceremonies of the old army and navy. Admiral von Schroeder stands between Franz Seldte and Theodor Duesterberg of the Stahlhelm organization.

The Imperial, hand-embroidered, gilt wire insigne was permitted for wear by "dismissed" naval officers on special occasions.

surmounted by a gilt hand-embroidered Imperial crown. It was positioned in the center of the cap band with a portion of the crown extending above the top band seam. A wire national cockade in black and silver (representing white), with a red felt center, was positioned within the frame of the oak leaf wreath.

### Officers on Extended Furlough (Offiziere des Beurlaubtenstandes)

These officers wore the standard visored cap, but with the addition of a silver Maltese cross in the center of the cockade, 6mm in diameter. Navy artillery officers wore this cross in the cockade on their field-grey visored caps.[30] The use of the cross was discontinued in June 1936.

---

[28]*Deutsche Uniformen Zeitschrift. Nr. 4, 1944, & Ibid., Nr. 6, June 20, 1944, p. 1.*
[29]*Bekleidungs- und Anzugsbestimmungen für die Kriegsmarine (M.Dv.-260).* Berlin, 1935, p. 53.
[30]*Uniformen-Markt. Nr. 8, August 1, 1935, p. 4.*

### Military and Civilian Drivers
### (Militärkraftfahrer/Zivilkraftfahrer)

Military drivers in service of the Kriegsmarine wore a standard field-grey field cap. A blue visored cap was worn with the walking-out or parade dress.

Civilian drivers wore a black field cap with a national emblem (the color of which has not been determined, but is thought to have been silver) and cockade.[31]

### Naval Pilots (Marinelotsen)

Personnel serving as naval pilots were permitted to wear a dark blue visored cap with a black mohair band after 1921. The band insigne was worked upon an oval piece of cloth, piped in gold, having two gilt embroidered crossed anchors. On the shaft the "Lotsenflagge" was worn. The black Reichsadler upon a golden field was worn on the cap top.[32]

According to regulations dated December 22, 1934, these Marinelotsen were now to be classified as officials (MVBL. Nr. 13, May 1, 1938, Nr. 293, p. 190).

### Naval Coastal Police (Marineküstenpolizei)

Consisting mainly of personnel from the Wasserschutzpolizei, the naval coastal police wore the uniform of the Wasserschutzpolizei until 1941. Afterward, they were supplied from navy stocks. The gilt metal (or yellow

O. Spronk

---

[31]*Bekleidungsvorschrift für die Kriegsmarine, (M.Dv.-260). Berlin: 1938, Anhang K.*

[32]*MVBl. Nr. 40, March 1, 1926, p. 37.*

machine-woven) for enlisted ranks, or gilt wire hand-embroidered national emblem for officers was in the pattern as for police formations.[33]

The visored cap featured a dark navy-blue tricot top (police or navy style), black mohair cap band, black visor, having a green underside, and either a black leather chin strap or matte yellow cords (according to rank). A white top could be worn instead of the blue cover, until its use was discontinued in 1943.[34] Officers from the rank of Obermeister and above were allowed to wear a dark blue "Hausmütze" (field cap), having the yellow police national emblem embroidered upon a black backing.[35] A metal police national emblem was also allowed. (Also see "Die Deutsche Polizei" chapter.)

### Sailing Cap (Segelmütze)

A special cap was introduced in 1934 for wear by yacht crews in service of the navy. It consisted of a knitted tube-shaped cap, having three white and three navy blue alternating stripes. At the closed end of the cap was a navy blue "pompom" (thus the designation, "Pudelmütze," or "poodle cap"). The total unrolled length of the cap was 40cm.[36]

O. Spronk

The so-called "Segelmütze" in wear. In this case, however, in black or dark blue.

[33]*Bestimmungen für die Marine-Küstenpolizei, IV., 16, 1941.*

[34]*MVBl. Nr. 204, April 3, 1943, p. 287.*

[35]*Reichsministerialblatt für die Innere Verwaltung. Jahrgang 1938, p. 1297, & Jahrgang 1939, p. 2348.*

[36]*Bekleidungsvorschrift für die Kriegsmarine (M.Dv.-260). Berlin: 1935, also Nachdruck 1938, p. 99.*

## Fore-and-Aft Hat for Officers
## (Zweispitzhut für Offiziere)

This hat was introduced for wear by officers no earlier than July 1925,[37] and was officially referred to as a "Zweitspitzhut" until 1934; afterward it was simply called a "Hut." It was constructed of black felt with a 4.5cm Moiré band. A golden Agraffe (claps of twisted cords) was attached at the back of the hat, near the bottom edge. In the end of this loop was positioned a large gilt button (2.5cm in diameter) embossed with an upright anchor. The Agraffe extended from the lower back of the hat to the top forward portion of the brim upturn. Another button, this one being an embroidered version of the Reichsadlerkokarde, was secured at this end of the cords.

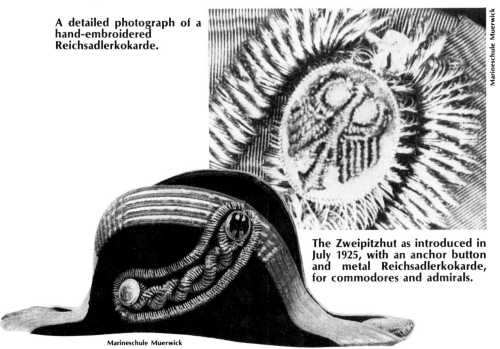

A detailed photograph of a hand-embroidered Reichsadlerkokarde.

Marineschule Muerwick

The Zweipitzhut as introduced in July 1925, with an anchor button and metal Reichsadlerkokarde, for commodores and admirals.

Marineschule Muerwick

Officers having the rank of Admiral wore the aforementioned hat, but the Moiré band was replaced by gold lace (5 sections), 3.5cm wide.

Administrative officials wore the basic Hut for officers, but the button and Agraffe were silver. Wehrmachtbeamte holding the rank equivalent of an Admiral wore the Hut with silver Tresse, Agraffe,[38] and button.

In 1933 the Reichsadlerkokarde was replaced by a silk-like rosette, in the colors of black/white/red, sewn under the upper forward Agraffe. The design of the hat was modified slightly in 1934, with only a slight visual difference. The 3cm anchor button was replaced in 1935 with one embossed with the

[37]*MVBl. Nr. 40, August 1, 1925, p. 117.*
[38]*Bestimmungen über die Uniformen der Wehrmachtbeamten der Marine. Berlin: 1935, p. 15.*

"Wehrmachtadler" (armed forces national emblem). The button had a simulated twisted rope border.

The fore-and-aft hat to be worn was the Galarock, frock coat or the "Grosse Uniform," or at any high social or official occasion.

Naval officers from the "Königsberg" and "Leipzig" during a visit to England in 1936.

P. Roelse

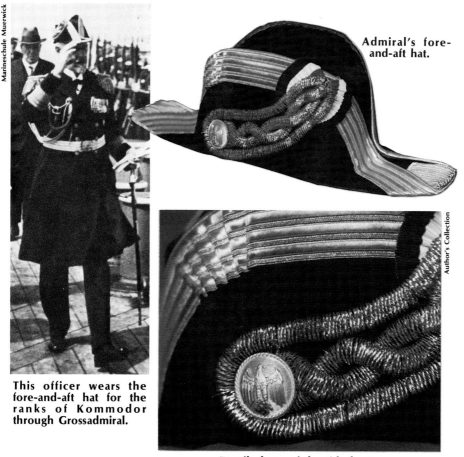

Marineschule Muerwick

Admiral's fore-and-aft hat.

Author's Collection

This officer wears the fore-and-aft hat for the ranks of Kommodor through Grossadmiral.

Detail photo of the side button.

Bud Hasher

**Reverse view of the fore-and-aft hat worn by Kriegsmarine officers. Note the detail of the national emblem on the button.**

Marineschule Muerwick

Author's Collection

**Detail of the cockade.**

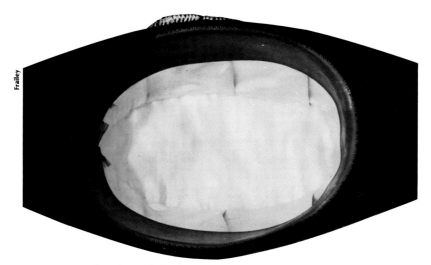

Interior view of the fore-and-aft hat. Lining is white silk.

Storage box for the fore-and-aft hat, dress belt and epaulets.

## Enlisted Ranks' Cap (Mannschaftsmütze)

The Matrosenmütze is quite a traditional form of headdress in the German Navy, dating back to its initial conception in 1848. In 1853 a new model, designed like that worn by French sailors, was introduced, and was worn until 1863. Many forms were tried in the following years, including one based on that worn by British sailors, before another form was introduced in 1878. This form was the basis for the cap that became known as the Model 1921.

The cap worn in 1878 was dark blue, being 11cm high, with a black wool cap band, 5.2cm wide. The diameter of the top was 27cm. This "Matrosenmütze," with the exception of the lower edge, was made of cotton. A brown sheepskin sweatband, 4.1cm wide, was sewn to the inside bottom edge of the cap. The inside of the band was supported by a stiff linen wall. The interior of the cap top was quilted. Around the top and the lowest edge of the cap band was sewn piping in the color of the cap top. The piping was supported by a thin, round whalebone. The cap band tally was 47cm in length and 8mm wide. A white cover was available for wear.[39]

A new model appeared in 1886, having a white cotton drill top. Improvements, such as a supporting wire in the cap top and loops for the cap band tally, were incorporated for the blue cap in 1885.

In 1887, crews of torpedo divisions were permitted to wear red piping around the cap top.[40] Use of this piping was discontinued by orders in 1920.[41]

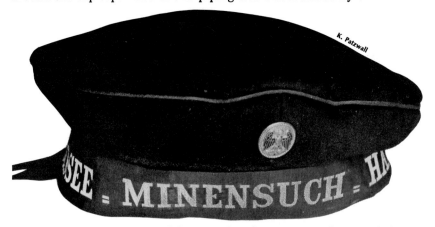

The blue Matrosenmütze, Model 1901, with red crown piping for torpedo boat crews. This style was abolished after 1921. The "Nordsee-Minensuch-Halbflottille" tally was originally worn during the Imperial period. Note the Reichsadlerkokarde.

In 1892 the cap was again modified. The top was reduced to 8.5cm from the former 11cm, and an iron (changed to brass in 1901) wire was installed into the cap top.[42]

---

[39]*Admiralitätsverfügung B. Nr. 3 4877 XI, December 7, 1878.*
[40]*Ibid., 2385 XI, April 14, 1887.*
[41]*Verfügung des Reichswehrministeriums, Chef der Admiralität, B. Nr. Cd. 11011 Vm, August 17, 1920.*
[42]*RMA, B. Nr. C1, 7975, November 27, 1901.*

The blue Matrosenmütze, Model 1921, with Reichsadlerkokarde, no colored piping, and the "Linienschiffe Hannover" tally in Latin lettering. This style lettering was used until the autumn of 1929 when Gothic lettering was introduced.

Regulations dated April 5, 1921 were issued concerning clothing and equipment for the Reichsmarine.[43] The Matrosenmütze reached its basic form in 1901. Only dark blue material was used for piping. The Reichsadlerkokarde[44] was worn on the cap top, and the tally lettering was embroidered in gold.[45] The white top was not to be worn in Germany; it was only to be worn in tropical regions. A new visorless cap with a removable white cover was introduced in April 1926.[46]

The blue Matrosenmütze with Reichsadlerkokarde and short cap band tally, all according to 1921 regulations.

[43]MVBl. Nr. 142, Jahrgang 1921, p. 203.
[44]Ibid. Nr. 354, Jahrgang 1919, p. 464.
[45]Ibid. Nr. 142, Jahrgang 1921. p. 204.
[46]Ibid. Nr. 96, Jahrgang 1926, p. 91.

The visorless "Tellermütze" was developed in December 1931 (this cap was also referred to in the Marineverordnungsblatt as "Schlöffelmütze," describing a cap with a removable white or blue cover).

The basic construction of the Matrosenmütze consisted of a navy blue band, 5.1cm wide, the lowest edge having a dark blue piping (Vorstoss) to prevent the tally from slipping. Since the top was interchangeable, the top of the band had a piping reinforced with a wire; 1cm below this was another piping, in dark blue (this piping was visible when the top was in place). The inside of the upper cap band was strengthened by a cloth-covered, rustproof iron wire. In the front was positioned a flat metal wire sewn in an approximately 4.5cm white piece of cloth. This extended vertically 5cm above the edge of the cap band base. A type of chin strap, 45cm in length x 0.8cm wide, was secured to the left interior of the cap. Four vertical and two sloping black loops were attached to the outside of the cap band for securing the tally. The inside of the cap band was finished with a brown leather sweatband.

The name of the manufacturer was stamped on the inside of the sweatband on the left. The cap size was stamped on the inside of the support.

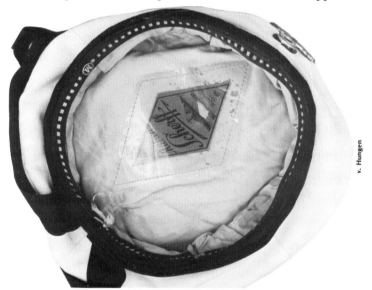

A privately-purchased "Schlöffelmütze" with white removeable cover. Note tailor's label.

## Blue Cover

The top and piping was in blue cloth, lined in black, with the exception of the side panels, which had no lining. The top had a diameter of 28.5cm (for a size 57). A doubled 1cm-piece of black cloth was sewn along the inner edge of the top. Between the usual lining was a cheesecloth lining. The size and manufacturer's name (abbreviated) were stamped in washable ink on the back portion of the lining. An extra wire, 1.85mm wide was fitted into the top for additional support.

The cap tally, "1. Schiffsstammab-teilung der Ostsee 1" is shown being worn.

In 1933 the eagle cockade was replaced by the black/white/red national tri-color.[47] The national emblem was introduced to the top of the cap in 1934.

## White Cover

The white cover was basically made like the blue cover, however, the piping at the bottom of the cover was white, instead of dark blue. The 1cm edging was white instead of black. Two small finished holes were incorporated onto the front of the cover, to accommodate the insignia.

The abbreviated name of the manufacturer was stamped in washable ink on the edge of the 1cm edging. The size was written on the back of the lining.[48]

"Panzerschiff Admiral Graf Spee" tally is shown being worn on the white visorless cap.

---

[47]*MVBl. Nr. 65, Jahrgang 1933, p. 47.*
[48]*Bekleidungsvorschrift für die Kriegsmarine, (M.Dv.-260). "A. Fertige Stücke für Mannschaften," Berlin: 1938, pp. 98-99.*

## White Visorless Cap for Duty on Board

The cap was in the form of the Matrosenmütze, having a white top lined in "Bramtuch," a coarse, strong canvas-like material.[49] The same cap, without the tally, was worn by stokers while on duty stoking the engines.[50]

Only the blue top was authorized for wear on the Matrosenmütze during the war, but the white cover could be worn in tropical climates. In fact, it was ordered in the Spring of 1940 that no white top headgear (with the exception of the Bordmütze) was to be worn. This order, issued to regulate raw materials and washing products, was generally ignored. No regulations have been discovered to reintroduce the use of the white visorless cap.

The tally designation, "Kriegsmarine," was instituted in 1939.

Model 1934 enlisted ranks' blue-topped visorless cap.

Roger Waterman

**Model 1931 enlisted ranks' white-topped visorless cap with "Kriegsmarine" tally.**

George Petersen

George Petersen

**The "Kriegsmarine" tally in wear on the white-topped visorless cap.**

---

[49]*Bekleidungsvorschrift für die Kriegsmarine (M.Dv.-260). Berlin: 1938, p. 99.*
[50]*Bekleidungs- und Anzugsbestimmungen für die Kriegsmarine, (M.Dv.-260),*
*1935, p. 44.*

## Cap Band Tallies (Mützenbänder)

The cap band tally designations were changed in August 1919 to reflect the new government. For example:

| Old Style | New Style |
|---|---|
| KAISERLICHE MARINE | REICHSMARINE |
| SMS DEUTSCHLAND | DEUTSCHLAND |
| M.B. KAISERLICHE MARINE | M.B. MARINEBEKLEIDUNGSAMT |

"II. Marineartillerieabteilung II." cap tally being worn in 1926.

The lettering for these tallies was in Latin. The length was 47cm, the width being 8mm. In April 1921 the tally length was changed to 116cm x 3.2cm.[51] The Latin lettering was changed to Gothic in October 1929.[52] The first ship to receive this new style tally was the cruiser "Karlsruhe." The remainder of the Reichsmarine soon followed with the appropriate tally designations.

The embroidery on the tallies was in golden thread on black silk. In 1925 a yellow cotton embroidery was introduced, then abolished, then reintroduced in 1936. Woven tallies were commonly used, as well as embroidered ones, and tallies embroidered in artificial silk thread (rayon). The tally crossed over the back of the cap, the right ribbon over the left.

During this research some color variations were observed:

a. A black silk tally with "MARINE VORSCHULE BERLIN" woven in silver;

## MARINE VORSCHULE BERLIN

---

[51]*MVBl. Jahrgang 1921, Anlage 4, p. 12.*
[52]*Ibid Nr. 246, Jahrgang 1929, p. 156.*

b. A white silk tally (for wear on the white duty cap) with "ZERSTÖRER LEBRECHT MAASS" embroidered in cornflower blue lettering;

c. A black silk tally embroidered in light blue lettering:

1. MARINEUNTEROFFIZIERSCHULE 1. This tally was worn by students, called "Jungmatrosen" and worn on the Matrosenmütze only with the walking-out dress.[53] If other types of color variations for schools were issued is not known. The above mentioned tally for Jungmatrosen was published by the German press in 1942;

d. The propaganda type tally for the Horst Wessel ship (see tally list);

Note:
A blue tally with "Segelschulschiff Horst Wessel" in light grey, machine-woven letters also exists, but was worn by the Marine-HJ.

e. ADMIRAL SCHEER, a specialty tally that was not worn officially, and was worn on children's caps. Special editions that were manufactured, though not worn officially, were:

1887 50 JAHRE TORPEDOWAFFE 1937

RESERVE HAT RUH

For obvious security reasons all tallies with varying designations were to be replaced on September 5, 1939 by all crews of ships, boats and vessels, as well as land-based units and authorities. The well-known KRIEGSMARINE tally became standard issue for the entire navy, and was worn until the end of the war.

John Coy

---

The "KRIEGSMARINE"
tally in wear.

O. Spronk

Prior to the generalization of the tally inscription, it was possible that tallies existed with different designations for the same ship, for example, when a ship received another command:

FLOTTTENTENDER SAAR      U-BOOTSBEGLEITSCHIFF SAAR
VERSUCHSBOOT GRILLE      AVISO GRILLE
TENDER HELA              AVISO HELA

Saris

Flottentender Saar

U=Bootsbegleitſchiff Saar

### Reichsmarine Cap Band Tallies

The following tally designations were found to have been used by the Reichsmarine at least until 1930:

ARTILLERIESCHULBOOT DELPHIN
ARTILLERIESCHULBOOT DRACHE
ARTILLERIESCHULBOOT FUCHS
ARTILLERIESCHULBOOT MARS
ARTILLERIESCHULBOOT LUDWIG PREUSSER
ARTILLERIESCHULBOOT ULAN

ARTILLERIESCHULBOOT CARL ZEISS
AVISO GRILLE
AVISO HELA
FISCHEREIBOOT ZIETEN
FLOTTENTENDER GAZELLE
FLOTTENTENDER HAY
FLOTTENTENDER HECHT
FLOTTENTENDER HELA
FLOTTENTENDER JAGD
FLOTTENTENDER SAAR
FLOTTENTENDER TSINGTAU
FLOTTENTENDER ZIETEN
I. FLOTTILLE I.
II. FLOTTILLE II.
1. HALBFLOTTILLE 1 (1 through 6).

The above tallies for the Halbflottille were carried over from the Imperial Marine and used until finally being discontinued (date unknown). The lettering was in yellow cotton, but examples existed in gold thread embroidery.

Additional tallies:

KREUZER AMAZONE
KREUZER ARCONA
KREUZER BERLIN
KREUZER HAMBURG
KREUZER KOELN
KREUZER KOENIGSBERG
KREUZER MEDUSA
KREUZER NIOBE
KREUZER NUERNBERG
KREUZER NYMPHE
I. KUESTENWEHRABTEILUNG I (I through VI).

LINIENSCHIFF BRAUNSCHWEIG
LINIENSCHIFF ELSASS
LINIENSCHIFF HANNOVER
LINIENSCHIFF HESSEN
LINIENSCHIFF LOTHRINGEN
LINIENSCHIFF PREUSSEN
LINIENSCHIFF SCHLESIEN
LINEINSCHIFF SCHLESWIG-HOLSTEIN
LINIENSCHIFF ZAEHRINGEN

I. MARINEARTILLERIEABTEILUNG I (I through VI).

MARINEDIENSTSTELLE BREMEN
MARINEDIENSTSTELLE HAMBURG
MARINEDIENSTSTELLE KOENIGSBERG

MARINEDIENSTSTELLE LUEBECK
MARINEDIENSTSTELLE STETTIN

1. MARINE-DIVISION 1.
MARINESTATION DER NORDSEE
MARINESTATION DER OSTSEE

MARINESTATION DER OSTSEE

MARINESCHULE KIEL

MARINE VORSCHULE BERLIN

MARINESCHULE KIEL
MARINE VORSCHULE BERLIN (this tally existed in the old form with
  silver or gold lettering)
PEILBOOT HOOGE
PEILBOOG NORDEROOG
PEILBOOT SUEDEROOG
I. PEILBOOT I (I through VI).

REICHSWEHR
REICHSWEHRMINISTERIUM M.L. (land department)
REICHSWEHRMINISTERIUM M.S. (sea department)

SCHIFFSSTAMMDIVISION DER NORDSEE
SCHIFFSSTAMMDIVISION DER OSTSEE

SCHIFFSSTAMMDIVISION DER NORDS

I.A. SCHIFFSSTAMMDIVISION DER NORDSEE I.A.
II.A. SCHIFFSSTAMMDIVISION DER NORDSEE II.A.
A.I. SCHIFFSSTAMMDIVISION DER NORDSEE A.I.
A.II. SCHIFFSSTAMMDIVISION DER NORDSEE A.II.

I.A. SCHIFFSSTAMMDIVISION DER OSTSEE I.A.
II.A. SCHIFFSSTAMMDIVISION DER OSTSEE II.A.
A.I. SCHIFFSSTAMMDIVISION DER OSTSEE A.I.
A.II. SCHIFFSSTAMMDIVISION DER OSTSEE A.II.

SCHULBOOT FREYR
SCHULBOOT SPREE

SEGELSCHULBOOT GUD-WIN
SEGELSCHULSCHIFF NIOBE

STATIONSTENDER FRAUENLOB
STATIONSTENDER NIXE
STATIONSTENDER NORDSEE

STATIONSYACHT NIXE
TAUCHERSCHULBOOT TAUCHER
TENDER BLITZ
TENDER BROMMY
TENDER DAHME
TENDER DELPHIN
TENDER DRACHE
TENDER FUCHS
TENDER HELA

# TENDER HELA

TENDER KOMET
TENDER NORDSEE
TENDER PFEIL
TENDER SPREE
TORPEDOBOOT ALBATROS
TORPEDOBOOT FALKE
TORPEDOBOOT GREIF
TORPEDOBOOT ILTIS
TORPEDOBOOT JAGUAR
TORPEDOBOOT KONDOR
TORPEDOBOOT LEOPARD
TORPEDOBOOT LUCHS
TORPEDOBOOT MOEWE
TORPEDOBOOT SEEADLER
TORPEDOBOOT TIGER
TORPEDOBOOT WOLF

1. TORPEDOBOOTS-HALBFLOTTILLE 1.
2. TORPEDOBOOTS-HALBFLOTTILLE 2.
3. TORPEDOBOOTS-HALBFLOTTILLE 3.
4. TORPEDOBOOTS-HALBFLOTTILLE 4.

These four above existed with a varying designation, with the corresponding
numbers: TORPEDOBOOTSHALBFLOTTILLE

# 1. TORPEDOBOOTSHALBFLOTTILLE. 1.

# 4. TORPEDOBOOTS = HALBFLOTTILLE.

The tallies for TORPEDOBOOTSHALBFLOTTILLE in the cut and uncut version existed in either Latin or Gothic embroidery.

I. TORPEDOBOOTS-FLOTTILLE I.
II. TORPEDOBOOTS-FLOTTILLE II.
UZ-HALBFLOTTILLE
VERMESSUNGSSCHIFF METEOR
VERMESSUNGSSCHIFF PANTHER

# U Z = HALBFLOTTILLE

**Cap Band Tally Designations, 1930-1939**

a. Tally for those serving in the Reichskriegsministerium (Oberkommando der Kriegsmarine): OBERKOMMANDO DER KRIEGSMARINE

b. Personnel of marine communication centers with the name of the city in which it served (Marinenachrichtenstelle mit Ortbezeichnung):

MARINENACHRICHTENSTELLE BORKUM
MARINENACHRICHTENSTELLE BÜLK
MARINENACHRICHTENSTELLE CUXHAVEN
MARINENACHRICHTENSTELLE DÜSTERNBROOK
MARINENACHRICHTENSTELLE FLENSBURG
MARINENACHRICHTENSTELLE FRIEDRICHSORT
MARINENACHRICHTENSTELLE KIEL
MARINENACHRICHTENSTELLE LIST
MARINENACHRICHTENSTELLE MARIENLEUCHTE
MARINENACHRICHTENSTELLE MITTE
MARINENACHRICHTENSTELLE NEUMÜNSTER
MARINENACHRICHTENSTELLE PILLAU
MARINENACHRICHTENSTELLE STOLPMÜNDE
MARINENACHRICHTENSTELLE STRALSUND
MARINENACHRICHTENSTELLE SÜD
MARINENACHRICHTENSTELLE SWINEMÜNDE
MARINENACHRICHTENSTELLE WILHELMSHAVEN

The tally could also read only "MARINENACHRICHTENABTEILUNG."

# Marinenachrichtenstelle Süd

c. For personnel serving in commands of a marine station (Kommando der Marinestation) in Ost- or Nordsee, including telecommunications (Stations-,

Fernsprech-, and Fernschreibnetzes), inspections of training facilities (Inspektion des Bildungswesen), torpedo and mine inspections (Torpedo- und Sperrwaffeninspektionen), commands of communications testing units (Nachrichtenmittelerprobungskommandos), the marine health resort Holsteinische Schweiz (Marinegenesungsheim), the entire personnel of the "Schiffsstammabteilungen" in the Ost- and Nordsee, including the inspections for personnel (Personalinspektionen), the offices for liquidation (Abwicklungsamt), and the teaching and repair stations (Lehr- und Reperaturwerkstätten), all assigned to the I., II., or III. Abteilung.:

MARINEGENESUNGSHEIM HOLST.SCHWEIZ
MARINELEHRWERKSTATT KIEL
MARINELEHRWERKSTATT WILHELMSHAVEN
MARINENACHRICHTENMITTELERPROBUNGSKOMMANDO KIEL
1. SCHIFFSSTAMMABTEILUNG 1. (these were numbered 1 through 24);

## 6. Schiffsstammabteilung 6.

1. SCHIFFSTAMMABTEILUNG DER NORDSEE 1. (1 through 4);
1. SCHIFFSTAMMABETILUNG DER OSTSEE 1. (1 through 4);
1.A. SCHIFFSSTAMMDIVISION DER NORDSEE 1.A.
2.A. SCHIFFSSTAMMDIVISION DER NORDSEE 2.A.

1.A. SCHIFFSSTAMMDIVISION DER OSTSEE 1.A.
2.A. SCHIFFSSTAMMDIVISION DER OSTSEE 2.A.

STATIONSTENDER NIXE
STATIONSTENDER NORDSEE

d. For the regular personnel and all those who spend six or more weeks as instructing pupils in schools, as well as personnel attached to the inspections of marine artillery (Inspektion der Marineartillerie), after being incorporated into such a unit:

KÜSTENARTILLERIESCHULE or KÜSTENARTILLERIE-SCHULE
MARINEFLUGABWEHRSCHULE
MARINEGASSCHUTZSCHULE
MARINENACHRICHTENSCHULE

## Küstenartillerie-Schule

## Küstenartillerieschule

## Marinenachrichtenschule

MARINENACHRICHTENSCHULE AURICH
MARINENACHRICHTENSCHULE MÜRWICK

## Marinefanitätsfchule

MARINENSANITÄTSSCHULE
MARINENSCHULE FRIEDRICHSORT
MARINESCHULE KIEL
MARINESCHULE MÜRWICK
MARINESCHULE WESERMÜNDE
MARINESPORTSCHULE
1. MARINEUNTEROFFIZIERSLEHRABTEILUNG 1. (1 through 3)

## 3. Marineunteroffizierlehr

1. MARINE UNTEROFFIZIERSSCHULE 1. (1, 2, and 4: the number 3 was not observed during the research).
SCHIFFSARTILLERIESCHULE or SCHIFFSARTILLERIE-SCHULE

## Schiffsartillerie=Schule

## Schiffsartillerieschule

SPERRSCHULE
STEUERMANNSCHULE
TORPEDOSCHULE
UNTERSEEBOOTSSCHULE
MARINE VORSCHULE BERLIN

e. For personnel serving on commissions for testing submarines (Erprobungsausschusses für Unterseeboote), as well as for crews of the crafts of the test units (E.A.U: -Erprobungsausschuss für U-Boote):

ERPROBUNGSKOMMANDO FÜR UNTERSEEBOOTE (worn until mid-1936, then changed to, for example):

UNTERSEEBOOTSTENDER ARCHERON

f. For personnel of the blockade test commands (Sperrversuchskommandos), as well as for crews of vessels without a name used by these test units

SPERRVERSUCHSKOMMANDO

## SPERRVERSUCHSKOMMANDO

The cap tally inscription worn by this sailor indicates that he was a pupil at a communications school, the tally reads, "Marinenachrichtenschule." Such inscriptions were discontinued in 1939 and replaced with the "Kriegsmarine" tally.

This young sailor wears the two-piece cap insignia (the national emblem attached to the cap top separately from the cockade). Note the cap tally inscription, "Reichsartillerieschule."

g. For personnel of hospitals, as Marinelazarette:

MARINELAZARETT CUXHAVEN
MARINELAZARETT KIEL-WIK
MARINELAZARETT MÜRWICK
MARINELAZARETT PILLAU
MARINELAZARETT SWINEMÜNDE
MARINELAZARETT WILHELMSHAVEN

h. For the crews of armoured ships:

PANZERSCHIFF ADMIRAL GRAF SPEE
PANZERSCHIFF DEUTSCHLAND
PANZERSCHIFF ADMIRAL SCHEER
SCHLACHTSCHIFF BISMARCK (doubtful if produced)
SCHLACHTSCHIFF GNEISENAU
SCHLACHTSCHIFF SCHARNHORST
SCHLACHTSCHIFF TIRPITZ (doubtful if produced)

i. For the crews aboard liners:
LINIENSCHIFF SCHLESIEN
LINIENSCHIFF SCHLESWIG-HOLSTEIN
LINIENSCHIFF ZÄHRINGEN

(The tallies of these liners existed in both types of letter versions).

j. For crews on cruisers:
KREUZER EMDEN
KREUZER KÖLN
KREUZER KÖNIGSBERG
KREUZER KARLSRUHE
KREUZER LEIPZIG
KREUZER NÜRNBERG

All members of light cruisers serving in the Reichsmarine wore first the designation in Latin letters, but this was changed to Gothic letters in 1930.

The following designations were also worn:
KREUZER ADMIRAL HIPPER
KREUZER BLÜCHER (doubtful if produced)
KREUZER PRINZ EUGEN (doubtful if produced)

k. For the crews of survey ships (Vermessungsschiffen):
VERMESSUNGSSCHIFF METEOR

l. For crews serving aboard marking ships (Peilbooten):
1. PEILBOOT 1. (1 through 5).

m. For crews of school sailing ships (Segelschulschiffe):
SEGELSCHULSCHIFF GORCH FOCK
SEGELSCHULSCHIFF HORST WESSEL
SEGELSCHULSCHIFF LEO SCHLAGETER (possibly "Segelschulschiff ALBERT LEO SCHLAGETER" as listed in the book "Nauticus," dated 1939).

It is possible that another version existed, this being:
SEGELSCHULBOOT GUD-WIN

The crew of the "HORST WESSEL" flanked at each end by a swastika flag, for certain occasions, such as on trips to foreign countries. This was not an official, but rather a propaganda tally.

This seaman from "KREUZER EMDEN" pins his ship's tally on the sweater of an American female participant in the 1936 olympic games in Berlin.

Segelschulschiff Gorch Fock.

n. For crews of ships protecting civil fisheries:
FISCHEREISCHUTZBOOT ELBE
FISCHEREISCHUTZBOOT WESER

**FISCHEREISCHUTZBOOT ZIETEN**

Old-style lettering for the "Zieten," later renamed the "R-Bootsbegleitschiff Zieten."

**Fischereischutzboot Elbe**

o. For crews of destroyers (Zerstörerdivisionen):
1. ZERSTÖRERDIVISION 1. (1 through 6)

At no time did a tally bearing the designation ZERSTÖRERFLOTTILLE exist. Destroyers numbering from 1 to 22 wore names that were not classified with the aforementioned tallies. See explanation further in this chapter.

**5. Zerstörerdivision. 5.**

p. For members aboard torpedo flotillas:
1. TORPEDOBOOTSHALBFLOTILLE 1. (1 through 4).
1. TORPEDOBOOTSFLOTILLE 1. (1 through 6).

**2. Torpedobootshalbflottille . 2**

**2. Torpedobootsflottille 2.**

q. For members of submarine flotillas:
U-BOOTSBEGLEITSCHIFF SAAR
U-BOOTSBEGLEITSCHIFF WILHELM BAUER
U-BOOTSBEGLEITSCHIFF WALDMAR KOPHAMEL
U-BOOTSBEGLEITSCHIFF ERWIN WASSNER
U-BOOTSBEGLEITSCHIFF OTTO WÜNSCHE

According to the new regulations issued in 1939, the tally for Otto Wünsche was never manufactured. Further designations were:
UNTERSEEBOOTSFLOTTILLE EMSMANN
UNTERSEEBOOTSFLOTTILLE HUNDIUS
UNTERSEEBOOTSFLOTTILLE LOHS
UNTERSEEBOOTSFLOTTILLE SALZWEDEL (introduced no earlier than September 1, 1936)
UNTERSEEBOOTSFLOTTILLE WEGENER

O. Spronk

# erſeebootsflottille Weddigen

UNTERSEEBOOTSFLOTTILLE WEDDINGEN

UNTERSEEBOOTSTENDER DONAU
UNTERSEEBOOTSTENDER HAVEL
UNTERSEEBOOTSTENDER ISAR
UNTERSEEBOOTSTENDER D. HERTHA
UNTERSEEBOOTSTENDER LECH
UNTERSEEBOOTSTENDER MEMEL
UNTERSEEBOOTSTENDER MOSEL
UNTERSEEBOOTSTENDER D. ODIN
UNTERSEEBOOTSTENDER WARRNOW
UNTERSEEBOOTSTENDER WEICHSEL

# Unterſeebootstender Donau

The following tallies may have existed as well:

1. U-JAGD FLOTTILLE 1.
12. U-JAGD FLOTTILLE 12.
17. U-JAGD FLOTTILLE 17.

No others have been discovered. In 1938, examples, such as listed below, were abolished and absorbed in other units:

2. UNTERSEEBOOTSFLOTTILLE

Note:

On January 1, 1939 the tally "UNTERSEEBOOTS-SCHULFLOTTILLE" was introduced for NCOs and enlisted ranks.

r. For crews of Führerboote des F.d.M. and lower ranking persons serving on the staff (Unterpersonal des Stabes F.d.M.):

FÜHRERBOOT DES F.d.M.

This tally was also worn by other personnel of this department who were not attached to a ship or staff.

s. For crews of minesweepers or convoy flotillas (Minensuch- oder Geleit-flottille):

1. GELEITHALBFLOTTILLE 1.
2. GELEITHALBFLOTTILLE 2.
1. GELEITFLOTTILLE 1.
2. GELEITFLOTTILLE 2.

1. 𝕲𝖊𝖑𝖊𝖎𝖙𝖋𝖑𝖔𝖙𝖙𝖎𝖑𝖑𝖊. 1.

1. MINENSUCHHALBFLOTTILLE 1.
2. MINENSUCHHALBFLOTTILLE 2.
1. MINENSUCHFLOTTILLE 1.
2. MINENSUCHFLOTTILLE 2.
16. MINENSUCHFLOTTILLE 16.

(others may exist, but have not been observed during this research)

16. 𝕸𝖎𝖓𝖊𝖓𝖘𝖚𝖈𝖍𝖋𝖑𝖔𝖙𝖙𝖎𝖑𝖑𝖊 16.

t. For crews of torpedo boots with names:

TORPEDOBOOT ALBATROS
TORPEDOBOOT FALKE
TORPEDOBOOT GREIF
TORPEDOBOOT ILTIS
TORPEDOBOOT JAGUAR
TORPEDOBOOT KONDOR
TORPEDOBOOT LEOPARD
TORPEDOBOOT LUCHS
TORPEDOBOOT MÖWE
TORPEDOBOOT SEEADLER
TORPEDOBOOT TIGER

The walking-out dress as worn after 1930, with the new style "Torpedoboot Tiger" tally and Reichsadlerkokarde.

A seaman from the "Torpedoboot Jaguar."

Below: two versions of the "Möwe" tally. The pre-1930 tally has "OE" instead of "Ö."

## TORPEDOBOOT MOEWE

## Torpedoboot Möwe

TORPEDOBOOT WOLF

In 1938, the destroyers with names were incorporated into this group.

Z.1 ZERSTÖRER LEBRECHT MAASS

Z.2 ZERSTÖRER  GEORG THIELE

A.3 ZERSTÖRER MAX SCHULTZ

Z.4 ZERSTÖRER RICHARD BEITZEN
Z.5 ZERSTÖRER PAUL JACOBI
Z.6 ZERSTÖRER THEODOR RIEDEL
Z.7 ZERSTÖRER HERMANN SCHOEMANN
Z.8 ZERSTÖRER BRUNO HEINEMANN
Z.9 ZERSTÖRER WOLFGANG ZENKER
Z.10 ZERSTÖRER BERND VON ARNIM
Z.11 ZERSTÖRER HANS LODY
Z.12 ZERSTÖRER ERICH GIESE
Z.13 ZERSTÖRER ERICH KOELLNER
Z.14 ZERSTÖRER FRIEDRICH IHN
Z.15 ZERSTÖRER ERICH STEINBRINCK
Z.16 ZERSTÖRER FRIEDRICH ECKHOLD
Z.17 ZERSTÖRER DIETHER VON ROEDER
Z.18 ZERSTÖRER HANS LÜDEMANN
Z.19 ZERSTÖRER HERMANN KÜNNE
Z.20 ZERSTÖRER KARL GALSTER
Z.21 ZERSTÖRER WILHELM HEIDKAMP
Z.22 ZERSTÖRER ANTON SCHMITT

u. For members of Kleinbootflottille:

1. RÄUMBOOTSHALBFLOTTILLE 1.
2. RÄUMBOOTSHALBFLOTTILLE 2.
1. RÄUMBOOTSFLOTTILE 1. (1 through 7, 9, and 17).

The missing numbers may have existed, but could not be confirmed. The following were connected to the previously mentioned flotillas:

R-BOOTSBEGLEITSCHIFF ZIETEN (later, NETTELBECK)
R-BOOTSBEGLEITSCHIFF BROMMY
R-BOOTSBEGLEITSCHIFF VON DER GRÖBEN
R-BOOTSBEGLEITSCHIFF RAULE

Ships with the following names have been observed. Whether tallies existed for them is not certain. Tallies were planned for the Wissmann and Nachtigal, but due to new regulations, were never produced.

SCHNELLBOOTBEGLEITSCHIFF HERMANN VON WISSMANN
SCHNELLBOOTBEGLEITSCHIFF NACHTIGAL
SCHNELLBOOTBEGLEITSCHIFF ADOLF LÜDERITZ
SCHNELLBOOTBEGLEITSCHIFF CARL PETERS
SCHNELLBOOTBEGLEITSCHIFF TANGA

(It is not certain that a tally existed for ''CARL PETERS'' and ''TANGA'' as the names were observed only in documentation.)

The following may have existed in two versions:
S-BOOTBEGLEITSCHIFF TSINGTAU or
S-BEGLEITSCHIFF TSINGTAU

v. Members of artillery school ships (Artillerieschulschiffe) and boats, test or experimental ships (Versuchsboote), stationed tenders (Stationstender) and flottille tenders having a name:

AVISO GRILLE (this ship also had a Versuchsboot tally).
ARTILLERIESCHULBOOT DELPHIN
ARTILLERIESCHULBOOT DRACHE
ARTILLERIESCHULBOOT FUCHS
ARTILLERIESCHULBOOT HAY
ARTILLERIESCHULBOOT JAGUAR
ARTILLERIESCHULBOOT JUNGMANN
ARTILLERIESCHULBOOT ULAN

**Artillerieschulboot Hay**

The following artillery school ships with a name may also have had tallies:
ARTILLERIESCHULBOOT MARS
ARTILLERIESCHULBOOT LUDWIG PREUSSER
ARTILLERIESCHULBOOT CARL ZEISS
ARTILLERIESCHULBOOT BREMSE
ARTILLERIESCHULBOOT BRUMMER

Some of the above boats were carried over from the old Reichsmarine, therefore, two versions of lettering (Latin or Gothic) existed.
FLOTTENTENDER HAY
FLOTTENTENDER HECHT
FLOTTENTENDER HELA
FLOTTENTENDER JAGD
FLOTTENTENDER SAAR
FLOTTENTENDER TSINGTAU
FLOTTENTENDER ZIETEN
FLOTTENTENDER GAZELLE
STAIONSJACHT NIXE
STATIONSTENDER FRAUENLOB

**Stationstender Frauenlob**

TAUCHERSCHULBOOT TAUCHER
VERSUCHSBOOT ACHERON*
VERSUCHSBOOT ARKONA

*This tally was changed to "UNTERSEEBOOTSTENDER ACHERON" in November 1936, but the old tally was still per-

183

*mitted for wear. It is, therefore, possible that both tallies were worn at the same time on board the Acheron. (UM. Nr. 11, June 1, 1937, p. 164.)*

VERSUCHSBOOT CLAUS VON BEVERN
VERSUCHSBOOT OTTO BRAUN
VERSUCHSBOOT GRILLE
VERSUCHSBOOT NAUTILUS
VERSUCHSBOOT NIBELUNG
VERSUCHSBOOT PELIKAN
VERSUCHSBOOT SCHILBUNG
VERSUCHSBOOT STÖRTEBECKER
VERSUCHSBOOT STRAHL
VERSUCHSBOOT SUNDEWALL
VERSUCHSSCHIFF ALBERICH

w. For crews of sailing boats with names that had been given approval by the Oberbefehlshaber der Kriegsmarine to wear a tally:

SEGELJACHT ASTA
SEGELJACHT ORION
SEGELSCHONER DUHNEN

x. Members of marine artillery units (Marineartillerieabteilungen):
1. MARINEARTILLERIEABTEILUNG 1. (1 through 6).

y. For members of mine replacement units (Marineergänzungsabteilungen):

1. MARINEERGÄNZUNGSABTEILUNG 1.
2. MARINEERGÄNZUNGSABTEILUNG 2.

z. For all personnel connected with offices of commanders (Kommandturen):

KOMMANDANTUR BORKUM
KOMMANDANTUR CUXHAVEN
KOMMANDANTUR KIEL
KOMMANDANTUR NORDERNEY
KOMMANDANTUR PILLAU
KOMMANDANTUR SCHILLING

KOMMANDANTUR STRALSUND
KOMMANDANTUR SWINEMÜNDE
KOMMANDANTUR WANGEROOG
KOMMANDANTUR WESERMÜNDE
(probably existed)

KOMMANDANTUR WILHELMSHAVEN*

z1. Personnel serving organically in the Kriegsmarine (Dienststellen), as well as for personnel connected and stationed in the Baubelehrungskommandos (construction institutions), the latter until the formation of a separate marine unit. It is not known whether these were actually manufactured.

KRIEGSMARINEDIENSTSTELLE BREMEM
KRIEGSMARINEDIENSTSTELLE HAMBURG
KRIEGSMARINEDIENSTSTELLE KÖNIGSBERG
KRIEGSMARINEDIENSTSTELLE STETTIN

egsmarinedienststelle Hamburg

The following provisions were made for the wearing of other tallies:

1. The crews of ships without names and not classified wore the tally of the ship or marine unit to which the ship was connected.

2. Tallies were to be purchased from the sailor's uniform allowance.

3. On land, composed "Schiffstämme," as an independent marine unit, wore the tally bearing the name of the future ship.

4. Personnel of training schools in the Marine-Sonderabteilungen (specialty branches) wore the cap band tally of their former command with the walking-out dress.

5. Lower-ranking personnel of destroyer divisions and torpedo boat flottillas wore the tally of their division or flottilla, even though they may have been serving on the crew of a destroyer or torpedo boat with a name. For example: 5. ZERSTÖRERDIVISION 5.

During this research, the following tallies could not be classified to their exact commands. Therefore, they are listed in alphabetical order:

DONAUFLOTTILLE
FÜHRERBOOT DES B.d.M. (Befehlshaber der Marine)
FÜHRERBOOT DES B.d.U. (Befehlshaber der U-Boote)
FÜHRERBOOT DES B.d.T. (Befehlshaber der Torpedoboote)
FÜHRERBOOT DES B.d.Z. (Befehlshaber der Zerstörer)

GELEITFLOTTILLE
KRAFTFAHRKOMPANIE KIEL
KRAFTFAHRKOMPANIE WILHELMSHAVEN
KÜSTENSCHUTZ DANZIG
LEHRKOMMANDO

MARINEAKADEMIE (KIEL) (It has not been determined if the city name was included on the tally designation)
MARINEARCHIV BERLIN
MARINEARSENAL KIEL
MARINEARTILLERIEDEPOT CUXHAVEN
MARINEARTILLERIEDEPOT PILLAU
MARINEARTILLERIEDEPOT SWINEMÜNDE
MARINEARTILLERIEDEPOT WILHELMSHAVEN
MARINEBEKLEIDUNGSMAGAZIN KIEL
MARINEBEKLEIDUNGSMAGAZIN WILHELMSHAVEN
MARINEHAFENKAPITÄN KIEL
MARINEHAFENKAPITÄN WILHELMSHAVEN
MARINEINTENDANTUR KIEL
MARINEINTENDANTUR WILHELMSHAVEN
MARINEMUNITIONSDEPOT DIETRICHSDORF
MARINESCHIESSPLATZ ALTENWALDE
MARINEWASCHANSTALT KIEL
MARINEWASCHANSTALT WILHELMSHAVEN
MARINEWERFT DANZIG
MARINEWERFT KIEL
MARINEWERFT WILHELMSHAVEN
MINENDEPOT CUXHAVEN
MINENDEPOT FRIEDRICHSORT
MINENDEPOT WILHELMSHAVEN
NACHRICHTENINSPEKTION KIEL
NACHRICHTENMITTELVERSUCHSKOMMANDO KIEL, or possibly,
MARINENACHRICHTENMITTELVERSUCHSKOMMANDO KIEL
SALUTSTATION FRIEDRICHSORT
SONDERABTEILUNG DER KRIEGSMARINE
SPERRABTEILUNG
SPERRKOMMANDO
SPERRSCHULFLOTTILLE
STATIONSKASSE KIEL
STATIONSKASSE WILHELMSHAVEN
VERSUCHSKOMMANDO
VORPOSTENFLOTTILLE
TORPEDOLABORATORIUM
TORPEDO- UND NACHRICHTENSCHULE

## Torpedo=und Nachrichte

TORPEDOVERSUCHSANSTALT
W.E. INSPEKTION MÜNCHEN
W.E. INSPEKTION HAMBURG
W.E. INSPEKTION SCHLESWIG-HOLSTEIN
W.E. INSPEKTION KOBLENZ

These last tallies were worn for a short period (beginning in 1938) by members of the Wehrkreiskommandos.

In August 1938 members of the navy who were ordered into the L.w.K. (See) were to wear their regular uniform with the addition of a "LUFTWAF-FENKOMMANDO SEE" cap band tally. (UM. Nr. 18, September 15, 1938, p. 276.)

WACHBOOT BIRAGO

MOTORBOOT ENNS

MOTORBOOT MUR

MOTORBOOT KREMS

MOTORBOOT DRAU

MOTORBOOT TRAUM

MOTORBOOT SALZACH

SCHULBOOT GAZELLE

All of the above boats and ships were incorporated into the Kriegsmarine on March 23, 1938 and were the basis for the "Donauflottille," ordered to be formed on March 17, 1938. The Gazelle and Birago served continuously in this unit but the motor-boats were returned to their old duties with the Pionier-Bataillone in 1939.

Information on cap band tallies was acquired through the following:

Uniformen der deutschen Wehrmacht. E. Hettler. Berlin: 1939, also Nachtrag 1939-1940.

Uniformen-Markt, 1934 through 1939, several issues.

Bekleidungs- und Anzugsbestimmungen für die Kriegsmarine (M.Dv.-260). Berlin: 1935, also Nachdruck 1938, pp. 27-30.

Bekleidungsvorschirft für die Kriegsmarine. Berlin: 1935, also Nachdruck 1938.

Die Wehrfront. Several years and issues (1935-1936).

Oertzenscher Taschenkalender. Berlin: several issues 1938-1940.

Marineverordnungsblatt, Jahrgänge 1926-1939.

Nauticus, Jahrbuch für Deutschlands Seeinteressen. Berlin, 1939, pp.10-18, plus other issues.

Zeitschrift Die Kriegsmarine, several issues.

Schwert und Spaten, Fachzeitschrift der gesamten Ausrüstungsindustrie.

Various newspapers and periodicals during the years 1934-1939.

Notes:

1. Cap band tally illustrations by W. Saris.

2. The manner of writing or abbreviating cap band tally designations listed may vary from the actual tally text as reference books/magazines often used inaccurate designations.

A crewmember of the auxiliary cruiser "Atlantis," a raider, while the ship was disguised as the Russian ship "Kim." Note he wears the "Kriegsmarine" tally inside out making the letters look like Cyrillic script, and also a red star on his blue visorless cap.

This Kriegsmarine guard from the 2. Marine-Unteroffizier-Lehrabteilung Wesermünde is stationed in front of the new Reich Chancellery in May 1939.

Two crewmembers of the "Aviso Grille" wearing the special arm insignia for Adolf Hitler's ship.

The "Küstenschutz Danzig" tally being worn. Shortly before the outbreak of war in 1939, sailors were illegally brought to Danzig from Germany. Together with the members of the Marine-SA and the SS-Heimwehr from Danzig an approximately 100-man unit was raised and fought from inside Danzig during the battle of Westerplatte, starting on September 2, 1939. The unit's name was taken from the Küstenschutz of the Landespolizei Danzig. The death's head worn was the former tradition badge of the Danzig Leibhusaren. "Küstenschutz Danzig" was only in existence until September 10, 1939, when it was disbanded.

## Stamp Markings

Caps worn by enlisted ranks were stamped as follows (see drawings): The cover was stamped on the inside back portion. Markings were also stamped on the leather sweatband.

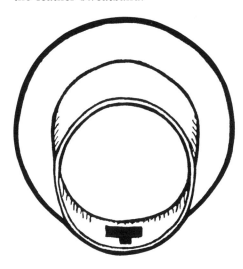

**Note:**
Only issued caps were so marked, whereas, private purchase caps were not.

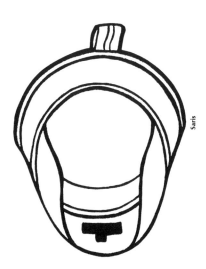

189

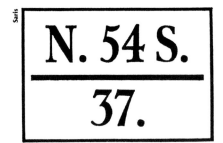

Explanation of numbers and figures:

B.A.K.    Bekleidungsamt Kiel
B.A.W.    Bekleidungsamt Wilhelmshaven

The date found on the cap is the date of sale, the Roman numeral indicates the size of the cap.

White caps for service aboard a ship and the white cover were stamped with smaller numerals and letters:

W.    10.1.30

The first letter indicates the name of the city of the Bekleidungsamt, followed by the date (day, month, year).

Other markings for the navy:

N    Nordsee
O    Ostsee
54    Stammrollnummer
S    seemännischer Laufbahn (seamanship career)
T    technischer Laufbahn (technical career)
37    Einstellungsjahr (year of call-up).

The size for this stamp was 3.5cm x 5cm in red ink, stamped at the right side of the sale stamp. It was permitted to sew over the red stamp with red thread.[54]

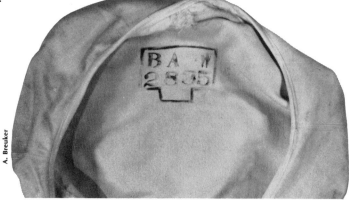

**BAW marking inside the white top for the Matrosenmütze.**

---

[54]*Bekleidungsvorschrift für die Kriegsmarine (M.Dv.-260), Berlin, 1935; also Nachdruck 1938, par. 41.*

## Garrison Cap (Bordmütze)

Introduced in November 1938, the blue cap (Gefechtsmütze, or "battle cap") was to be worn by all personnel wearing the blue battle dress and was meant mainly for crews working with headphones, optics and measuring instruments.

This cap similar in shape to that worn by members of the army, having gently-sloping side panels. The front of the cap was 7.5cm, in the center 9.5cm, and at the rear portion, 5.5cm. The flaps measured 4cm in the front, graduating to 7.5cm in the middle, then down to 4.5cm in the rear. To prevent the cap from becoming misformed, it was reinforced.

The national black/white/red cockade, in machine-woven or bullion form, was worn in the front center of the flap. The machine-woven version was worked upon a dark blue square backing, which was sewn standing on one point to the cap. The national emblem in golden-yellow thread, Celleon or gilt bullion, was sewn in the center of the cap top. The cap was lined in black Moiré. This cap was slightly modified in 1939, the shape being improved. The former support in the front was done away with. In the spring of 1939 this cap was also permitted for crews of sailing training ships while at sea (UM. Nr. 18, April 15, 1939, p. 118).

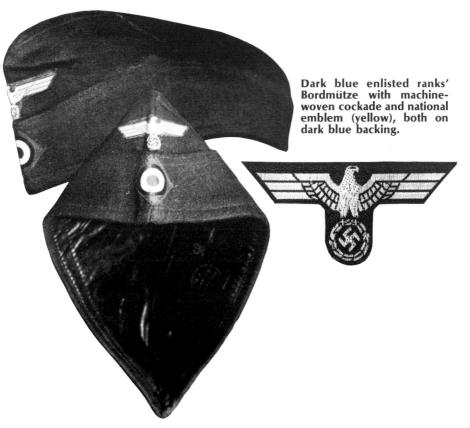

Dark blue enlisted ranks' Bordmütze with machine-woven cockade and national emblem (yellow), both on dark blue backing.

Officers wore the dark blue garrison cap with the addition of gold cord piping around the upper edge of the flap. Administrative officials wore this cap as well, but with silver cord piping. The Bordmütze was highly-favored and was widely issued. The rank of Admiral was not required to wear this cap, and no provision was made for this rank to wear a Bordmütze (Grand Admiral Carl Dönitz has been observed, however, wearing the blue Bordmütze)

Officer's Bordmütze with gold wire insignia and gold piping.

Note the 23. U-Bootsflottile insigne worn on the side of the officer's Bordmütze at right.

The white Bordmütze, introduced sometime before November 1939, was created to be worn in tropical climates, and was not to be worn in Germany or the occupied northern countries.[55] The national emblem was worked upon a white backing in light-blue thread. The cockade in its normal colors was embroidered upon a white square.

A special distinguishing mark for active, reserve and navy officers "budding" hands (Aktive, Reserve- und Kriegsoffiziere Nachwuchs) in the rank of Oberfähnrich was authorized for the Bordmütze by a 3mm golden lace around the upper edge of the cap flap.[56] This lace could be worn on the blue, field-grey as well as the khaki Bordmütze.

---

[55]*MVBl. Nr. 204, April 3, 1943, pp. 276-277.*
[56]*Deutsche Uniformen Zeitschrift. July, 1944, p. 1.*

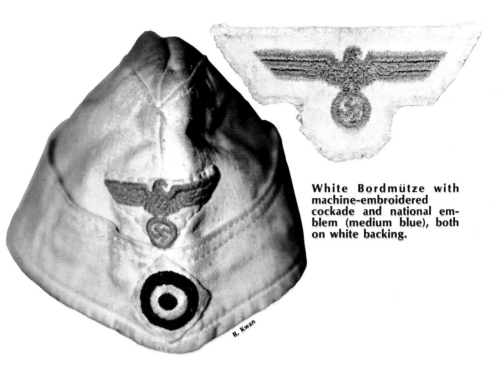

White Bordmütze with machine-embroidered cockade and national emblem (medium blue), both on white backing.

### Tradition Badges (Erinnerungsabzeichen)

Though officially forbidden by Kriegsmarine regulations, many crews of ships and submarines wore tradition badges on their headdress. These orders were especially overlooked during the war by U-Boot crews. Official orders and publications repeatedly stated that such insignia were not to be worn, as reflected in this 1941 article in Uniformen-Markt:

> "Specialty badges have often been offered for wear to navy artillery units, coast guards (Küstenschutz)[57] and other navy units. However, navy regulations forbid these, not only for the Edelweiss, but also for any other badge. This is not expected to change in the future."

The Marineverordnungsblatt stated in August 1944 that:

> "The wearing of the symbol for mountain units, the Edelweiss, as instituted for the army, as well as symbols for (army) Jägerdivisionen, are forbidden on authority of the Kriegsmarine."[58]

It is quite possible that literally hundreds of these unauthorized badges were worn. To include them all would be too great an undertaking. Therefore, the text is restricted to the most interesting, or the most-often-worn badges. Variations of the badges illustrated do exist. Actual pieces of jewelry were sometimes used as badges, as well as fantasy badges and knick-knacks. Con-

---

[57]*Uniformen-Markt. Nr. 16, August 15, 1941, p. 158.*
[58]*MVBl. Nr. 459, Jahrgang 1944.*

trary to orders, the following badges were known to have been worn by members of the Kriegsmarine:

Note:
The related U-boat number is given whenever possible and some were used on more than one boat. Also, on some occasions, more than one badge was worn at the same time.

---

### U-Boat Flotillas

For the 2.U-Flottille, detached at Wilhelmshaven, from June 1940 also Lorient. The last boats were in August 1944 detached in Norway. Also in use with the U-107, U-128, U-129, U-156, U-163, U-505, U-802, U-518 and U-3040.

For the 3.U-Flottille, at first detached in Kiel, but from October 1941 also in France: La Pallice and La Rochelle. Also used by the U-553, U-615 and U-739.

ECPA

This newly decorated KC recipient wears the "turtle" badge of the 3. U-Flottille.

For the 6.U-Flottille, detached at first in Danzig, later at St. Nazaire. Abolished in August 1944. The insignia for Danzig varied slightly, having another style of U-boat, with the lower edge sloping. Also in use with the U-228, U-260, U-264, U-766.

This U-boat crewman wears a varient of the above badge without the submarine. He is wearing two badges, one for the U-404 and the other is unidentified.

For the 7.U-Flottille detached in Kiel and since October 1940 also at St. Nazaire. In the last part of the war the remainder of the flotilla was detached in Norway. Also in use for U-46, U-47, U-48, U-69, U-71, U-74, U-75, U-94, U-96, U-103, U-135, U-207, U-213, U-221, U-224, U-227, U-267, U-382, U-406, U-434, U-436, U-442, U-454, U-455, U-551, U-552, U-553, U-567, U-575, U-576, U-578, U-593, U-594, U-607, U-617, U-618, U-662 and U-751. This badge might be the most often used one.

For the 9.U-Flottille, detached in Brest since November 1941, abolished in August 1944. Also in use with the U-91, U-92, U-211, U-214, U-217, U-218, U-230, U-409, U-450, U-591, U-595, U-604, U-659, U-664, U-744, U-755, U-764 and U-954.

For the 10.U-Flottille, detached in Lorient (France) since January 1942, abolished in October 1944. Also in use with the U-155, U-170, U-172, U-174, U-175, U-176, U-506, U-509, U-510, U-513, U-514, U-515, U-516, U-525, U-539, U-546, U-772.

For the 11.U-Flottille, detached at Bergen since May 1942. Also in use with the U-209, U-251, U-255, U-269, U-302, U-334, U-376, U-378, U-457, U-657 and U-703. The bear on this badge is looking to the left. There existed a similar badge, with the bear looking to the right (see further in this chapter).

For the 13.U-Flottille, detached at Drontheim since June 1943. Also in use with the U-293, U-302, U-307, U-312, U-354, U-362, U-739, U-965, U-968 and U-995.

For the 21.U-Boots-Schulflottille, detached at Pillau.

For the 23.U-Flottille.

For the 24.U-Flottille, training unit: was originally detached at Danzig, later in Memel, In between, at Drontheim. Also in use with the U-28, U-29, U-30, U-34, U-151, U-152, U-163, U-554, U-560 and U-561.

For the 29. U-Flottille, detached in La Spezia. Later also in Toulon, Pola, Marseille and Salamis. Also in use with the U-77, U-338, U-371 and U-617.

In use with the U-2 and U-121.

In use with the U-3, U-14, U-20, U-23, U-24, U-59, U-105, U-128, U-152, U-169, U-192, U-203, U-227, U-228, U-306, U-311, U-344, U-351, U-407, U-415, U-440, U-467, U-534, U-546, U-630, U-643, U-733, U-763, U-802, U-877, U-880, U-995, U-1007, U-1230.

In use with the members of the U-9 under the command of Oberleutnant Lüth.

In use with the U-17: a giraffe might have also been worn.

In use with the U-19 and U-569.

In use with the U-19, U-37, U-569 and U-2536.

In use with the U-20.

In use with the U-23, called the "Froschkönig" (frog-king).

In use with the U-24 under the command of Oberleutnant Lenzmann.

In use with the U-24 (other command).

In use with the U-26, U-380, U-766 and U-850. Various shaped clovers were worn.

In use with the U-48 and U-564. At first this badge was worn, but later when Korvettenkapitän Suhren received the Knight's Cross, a badge was worn having the KC under the neck of the cat (between 1940 and 1941).

In use with the U-50 and was surely worn in 1940.

In use with the U-61, U-81, U-362, U-410, U-448, U-731, U-732 and U-734. This badge exists in various qualities of workmanship, and also with a different sword and ring.

In use with the U-62, U-152, U-225, U-277, U-419, U-472, U-539, U-596, U-761 and U-953. Several variations have been observed.

In use with the U-65. This badge, known as a "Jungvolk-Armscheibe," was worn in two variations by the crewmembers.

In use with the U-66 and U-181. It is known that the black cloth diamond, having the lion's head (Ritter Von Epp), was also worn. However, it cannot be verified if this was worn as a cap insigne.

This badge was probably worn by the crew of the U-67.

In use with the U-68 and U-843.

In use with the U-92, U-622, and U-2522.

In use with the U-93: the devil was painted red.

ECPA

In use with the U-71 and manufactured in brass by a crewman.

In use with the U-97, U-267, U-708, U-776 and U-3011. An insignia, shaped differently, was also used by the 5.U-Flottille.

In use with the U-74, the "Gau Essen" commemorative badge.

In use with the U-39, U-99, U-433, U-570 and U-1010. The horseshoe was normally fabricated in brass, but also painted examples may exist.

199

In use with the U-101, U-143, U-295, U-450, U-3001, U-3025, U-3501 and U-3517. The design varied greatly and was worn reversed as well.

In use with the U-106, normally fabricated in bronze.

In use with the U-107 and U-3040. Kessler, the commander of the U-107, was a passionate card player and authorized his men to wear this badge. This badge was possibly designed by a man called Helmut Witte.

In use with the U-108. This polar bear was fabricated of bronze.

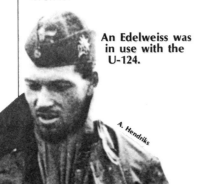

An Edelweiss was in use with the U-124.

A. Hendriks

In use with the U-161. The colors of this enameled badge are: white, water in Prussian blue, sail and boat in bottle-green, and border in black.

In use with the U-164, fabricated in brass, as well as in aluminum.

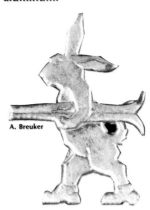

A. Breuker

Although this rabbit insigne was painted on the tower of the U-170, it was in fact worn by the crew of the U-171.

In use with the U-201. The commander was Kapitän-Leutnant Schnee (snow), thus a snowman with a broom (indicated a clean sweep of the target) and a Knight's Cross around his neck.

In use with the U-205. Kapitänleutnant Franz-Georg Reschke authorized his crew to wear the turtle, generally fabriced in brass.

In use with the U-211, U-214, U-411 and U-438. The U-214 crew may have worn this symbol for the city of Berlin, as well as the saw-fish (on opposite page). It is known that badges with various city crests were worn on other U-boats.

In use with the U-201 and U-847. Willi Lechtenbörger, chief engineer on both boats, wears a cloth version of the above badge on the side of his dark blue field cap.

In use with the U-228 and U-3028.

In use with the U-202. This type of badge is often found in bracelet form.

In use for the U-241, U-747 and U-1308.

In use with the U-203.

In use with the U-255 and U-3023. This fox was used by the crew under command of Reinhard. The shield was white, the fox head was red. It is also known that an enameled (3-colored badge) was manufactured. It was so popular with the crew that this badge was kept, even under other commanders.

In use with the U-270 and U-2525.

In use with the U-281, called U-Spinne, was fabriced aboard the boat and was authorized for wear by Kapitänleutnant Heinz Von Davidson.

In use with the U-282, designed after the name of the commander, Müller (Miller).

In use with the U-300.

O. Spronk

Hans Dietrich v. Tiesenhausen, commander of the U-331, wears an unofficial traditions badge in the shape of a snake on the side of his white top visored cap, called the Rheinschlange.

In use with the U-354, U-355, U-405, U-591, U-601, U-606, U-622 and U-1022. This badge is similar to that in use with the 11.U-Flottille, but the bear is looking to the right. Several variations of these two badges exist.

In use with the U-383. This badge was the insignia of the early youth organization "Freischar Junger Nation," also called "Bund der Freischaren" in Sudetenland. It is observed that other early youth badges were worn in the navy.

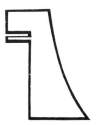

Probably in use with the U-404. This badge, fabricated in white sheet metal, was worn on the white top visored cap and the dark blue Bordmütze.

In use with the U-413. This badge was fabriced in brass and was highly detailed, authorized for wear by Kapitänleutnant Poel.

ECPA

In use for the U-437 and U-3049. This badge was worn by the crew of the U-437 in silvered metal (taken from the letterhead).

In use with the U-458.

In use with the U-475. The commander came from Düsseldorf. It is not known if this badge was ever worn on a cap.

In use with the U-481.

In use with the U-490, this badge, "fleiszige Biene," may have been worn, as it is in fact a cap insigne.

In use with the U-555.

Also in use with the U-555, the reason for changing insignia may have been because of a new commander.

O. Spronk

A member of the U-571 is wearing an unidentified badge on his blue top visored cap.

In use with the U-584.

A. Breuker

Bordmütze with insigne in use with the U-511. The U-211, U-513 and U857 also used the Viking ship but stylized differently.

In use with the U-586, U-1022, U-863 and U-2348. This badge exists in various styles. The crew for the U-586 also wore a shield in black. This shield, however, was in black, red and gold.

In use with the U-586 and also the U-2527.

Note: The eagle's head was worn after 1942.

In use with the U-591, but normally an eagle's head was worn by the crew of the U-591. Occasionally, this shield-formed badge may have been used.

In use with the U-592.

In use with the U-625. The color for the clover is green, the lightning is red, and the number may have been white.

In use with the U-636.

In use with the U-641. A badge shaped as shown was worn on the cap and the crew called it "U-Pan."

In use with the U-642, the crown was manufactured in brass.

In use with the U-672.

In use with the U-680.

Also in use with the crew of the U-680.

In use with the U-701.

In use with the U-704 and U-985.

In use with the U-759 and U-991.

In use with the U-763 and U-1195. The chief engineer of the U-763 came from Austria, and this may be the reason for using the coat-of-arms of Bludenz/Vorarlberg. The boat was named "U-Bludenz."

In use with the U-777. The brass badge consists of a 7 crossed with a torpedo, above a submarine and waves.

In use with the UD-5, the UD was a foreign boat, probably Dutch. This might have been the reason for a "Dutch" girl wearing wooden shoes.

In use with the U-802.

In use with the U-953 and U-3014.

In use with the U-968.

In use with the U-969, U-2537 and U-2546.

In use with the U-975, the old city crest for Chemnitz.

In use with the U-979.

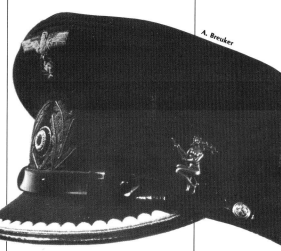

A. Breuker

In use with the U-1013 and U-1024. This "witch on a broom" badge is on the side of a blue top visored cap for the ranks of Leutnant to Kapitänleutnant. Several slight variations are known to exist.

In use with the U-1232.

In use with the U-2524.

In use with the U-3030. This insigne was designed by Dr. Hansmann, and the colors are black/white/red.

### Unidentified

Crewmembers of the U-552 wearing the so-called U-Adel-Heid.

### Notes:
1. The number of these badges produced is unknown, as some could have been worn by the entire crew or by only one crew-member.
2. Cap insignia illustrations by W. Saris.

ECPA

Badge for the U-704 or U-985.

Badge in use with U-454, the crest of Osnabrück.

## Navy Units wearing Field-Grey
## (Marineteile in Feldgrau)

As early as August 1919 there was a field-grey "Armeemütze" mentioned in the Marineverordnungsblatt.[59]

By 1921 official dress regulations authorized the wearing of two field-grey caps:

1. A field-grey visored cap like that used by the army, having a field-grey band and pipings. The visor and chin strap were of black leather. In the center of the cap band, the Reichsadlerkokarde was enclosed by a stamped yellow metal oakleaf wreath. A hand-embroidered oakleaf wreath could be worn on privately-purchased caps.

2. The second visored cap was like that above, but was of field-grey "Grundtuch," including the cloth-covered visor. No chin strap was worn on this cap.

A visorless cap in the form of a beret (Krätzchen) was worn during service at a post or during training.

[59]*MVBl. Nr. 264, August 1, 1919.*

A member of the II. Küstenwehrab-
teilung in 1925 wearing the field-grey
visored cap with old-style wreath and
the Reichsadlerkokarde.

Coastal artillery members
wearing the field-grey
"Krätzchen" with
Reichsadlerkokarde.

The Reichsadlerkokarde was replaced in 1933 by the black/white/red cockade. The national emblem was added to the cap top in 1934. In 1935 officers were authorized to wear silver cap cords (Kapitän zur See, to include Musikmeister) and the other insignia in matte-gold. Also the field-grey field cap (as worn by the army) was introduced at this time.

The field-grey uniform was worn by the following:

Marineartillerieabteilungen--Marineartillerielehrabteilungen;
Marineartillerieflakabteilungen--Flugmeldeabteilungen;
Marinenebelabteilungen--Küstenartillerievermessungskompanien;
Kanalwachabteilungen--Marinelandesschützenabteilungen;
Marinekraftfahrabteilungen--Motorisierte Nachrichtenabteilungen;
Marinebaubataillone--Transportbegleitkompanien;
Marinefreileitungsbaukompanien--Marlag und Milag Nord;
Wachkompanie Pilz--Landeseinheiten im südrussichen Raum.[60]

### Field-Grey Headdress (description from the 1938 regulations)

### Field Cap for Enlisted Men and Non-Commissioned Officers (Feldmütze)

A field-grey field cap was issued to navy units in 1935. The basic cut and flap angle were the same as the dark blue and white Bordmütze. The cap was constructed of field-grey "Blusentuch," a heavy fabric. A field-grey metal ventilation grommet was positioned at the forward portion of each side of the cap, just above the flap. A yellow Soutache was sewn at a 90 degree angle in the front center of the flap, in a manner so that the point reached the top of the flaps. The lower points of the Soutache reached the bottom of the flap. A cockade, machine-woven upon a square medium green backing for enlisted

R. Mundhenk

**Field-grey field cap with yellow Soutache. The national emblem is machine-woven yellow thread on field-grey.**

 [60]*MVBl. Nr. 204, April 3, 1943, pp. 271-272.*

men and non-commissioned officers, was sewn on a point within the Soutache (the two horizontal points touched the Soutache). Officers wore a bullion cockade. These caps were lined in field-grey twill, finished with a 3cm wide linen ribbon for stiffening purposes. The use of the Soutache was discontinued in November 1942.[61]

This war correspondent wears the field-grey field cap while filming the construction of coastal artillery positions.

The field-grey uniform in wear.

[61]*Schwert und Spaten. Nr. 11, November 30, 1942, p. 121; and Uniformen-Markt. Nr. 22, November 15, 1942, p. 170.*

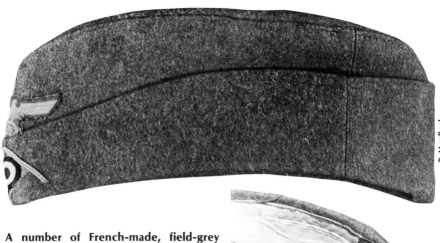

R. Mundhenk

A number of French-made, field-grey field caps have been observed with an altered rear portion. The French manufacturer, in a subtle act of resistance, reportedly produced a percentage of their order for headgear in a very small size so as to make them unuseable by their German occupiers. Upon receiving the produced caps, however, the Germans immediately discovered the ploy and returned the small sizes to be retailored to acceptable sizes. The reworked product is shown, above and at right.

**Note:**
The navy officers' field cap is often mistaken for an army generals' cap.

Oberleutnant Walter Ohmsen, Chief of Marine Battery "Marcouf," wears an officer's version of the field-grey field cap with gilt piping.

The yellow machine-woven, or yellow nylon or gilt bullion wire, national emblem was sewn to the front of the cap top, approximately 1.5cm below the top seam of the cap.[62] Officers wore a yellow or golden cord piping sewn around the flap.

The field-grey field cap with yellow Soutache. Note the traditions badge.

**Field-grey field caps being worn without the Soutache.**

[62]*Die Uniformen der deutschen Wehrmacht. E. Hettler, 1939, Nachtrag 1939-1940, p. 83.*

### Visored Cap, circa 1938

The field-grey naval visored cap for Portepeeoffiziere was a Klappmütze, but with no ventilation grommets on the underside of the cap top.

The height of the cap measured 11.8cm. The band (4.5cm wide) and its pipings, as well as the crown piping (2cm), were of dark bluish-green or field-grey cloth, the bottom edge of the band being field-grey (3cm).

The visor was black pliable leather, 27cm long, the widest portion of the front being 5cm, the underside of which was lacquered in black. Enlisted men wore a black leather chin strap, while officers to the rank of Kapitän zur See (including Musikmeister) wore silver cords in conjunction with matte gold insignia.[63] The NCO ranks of Fähnrich, Oberfähnrich and Marineunterärzte were permitted to wear silver cords on their Klappmützen after September 1938, instead of the black leather chin strap. Admirals wore the blue navy uniforms with gold cords and gold cap insignia (no decoration was worn on the visor). Administrative officials wore the national emblem and wreath em-

Field-grey visored cap for NCOs. Note political style national emblem.

John Coy

Field-grey visored cap with aluminum-colored cap cords.

J.R. Angolia

[63]*Bekleidungs- und Anzugsbestimmungen für die Kriegsmarine, (M.Dv.-260).* Berlin: 1935, pp. 59-64.

broidered in silver (all ranks had the option of wearing metal, instead of embroidered, insignia on their caps). Like regular officers, Beamte wore silver cords on the cap.

(Below) Two officers in the field-grey uniform. Note the man at left wears an early version of the cockade and wreath in gilt wire, while the man at right wears the standard version.

A Marineartillerie officer wearing the field-grey visored cap and a lightweight summer tunic.

French-made field-grey visored cap in the style of an army officer. Note sweat band marking at right.

Admiral's field-grey visored cap with yellow colored cap cords and yellow nylon insignia.

These caps were lined in Atlas or Atlasserge. The light-brown sweatband. 4.5cm wide, was made of either sheepskin or kid, was perforated at the front. Between this band and the interior of the cap band was glued a 15cm-long sponge, 2cm wide, to ease the weight of the cap on the wearer's forehead.

Note:

Plans existed for the development of a new style uniform, but with the onset of the war, they were shelved.

## Field Cap and Toque (Baschlikmütze/Kopfschützer)

The Baschlikmütze (similar to the M43 cap) in field-grey and the toque (Kopfschützer), also in field-grey, were only allowed to be worn during extremely cold weather, and then it was permitted only after orders were issued.[64]

The toque was tube-shaped and woven of pure wool tricot, having no seams. It was 40 to 42cm in length with a width of 24 to 26cm.[65]

## Field Cap (Einheitsfeldmütze)

Marine units wearing the field-grey uniform were authorized around 1943 to wear the "Feldmütze 42"*[66] during winter, and only after stocks of field caps were exhausted.[67]

*"Feldmütze 42" was the wording used in the MVBL, and not M43.

R. Mundhenk

Officer's field-grey M43 cap with yellow, machine-woven national emblem on a field-grey backing and gold twist cord around the crown.

J.R. Angolia

Enlisted rank's field-grey M43 cap.

---

[64]Ibid., p. 45.
[65]Ibid., 1938, Anhang H.
[66]Deutsche Uniformen Zeitschrift. Nr. 7, October 15, 1943.
[67]MVBl. Nr. 557, 1943.

An Einheitsfeldmütze with a white embroidered starfish on dark green. The
"Zeester" (starfish) was worn in the
Netherlands by the Marine-Küstenartillerie at Ijmuiden. The diameter of
the insignia is 38.5mm.

## Visored Cap for Navy Fortress Engineer Corps
## (Schirmmütze für Marinefestungspionierkorps)

A navy fortress engineer corps was created by decree on April 1, 1943. Navy
engineers wore a standard army visored cap piped in black (the only unit
within the Kriegsmarine to have a branch-of-service piping color). Gilt metal

An officer serving in the
Marinefestungspionier-
korps wearing the field-
grey visored cap piped in
black.

or embroidered navy insignia was worn on the cap. Enlisted ranks wore a black leather chin strap; officers wore silver cords.[68]

The Marine-Festungsbaubeamten wore the regular army-style visored cap with green piping until 1943 when the Marinefestungspionierwesens was incorporated into the navy. Aluminum cap cords and silver buttons were worn, as well as a matte-silver, navy-style wreath and national emblem, both on a dark bluish-green cloth backing. The leather visor was trimmed with leather, as were many navy caps, and the underside was also black. Other field-grey forms of headdress were worn by these engineer units.

### Tropical Helmet (Tropenhelm)

An article by Dr. phil. Wolfgang Janke, an authority in the Marineverwaltung, provided in 1941 a contemporary account of the developmental history of tropical helmet worn by the German Navy. The first helmet was designed in 1856, but to remain within the time-frame of this book, we will begin in 1902 when a new form of tropical headdress was designed. In 1910 a new helmet was designed by the Bortfeldt firm, located in Bremen, that was slightly smaller than the M-1902.

J. Zienert

These illustrations were made by Herbert Rothaengel and used for an article by Dr. phil. Wolfgang Janke in several magazines in 1941. The development of the naval tropical helmet is depicted. Nr. 9 is the 1930 Bortfeld type; Nr. 10 shows a sailor with the 1938 style made of artificial materials; Nr. 11 shows the M1940 in khaki; and Nr. 12 shows the M1940 in white with the large eagle on the front and no side shields.

A straw hat replaced the tropical helmet for a short time after February 1926. The Marineleitung of the Kriegsmarine of the Reichswehrministerium ordered that it could be worn by crew members while traveling in foreign countries/waters. The hat quickly proved impractical, and its use was abolished in October of that same year. Orders dated February 14, 1930 stated that the M-1902 was to be replaced by a new helmet, this one in the well-known English style. Again, the Bortfeldt firm was contracted to design and produce the Tropenhelm. Until stocks of this new helmet were ready, ships' commanders authorized the wearing of helmets bought mainly in Egypt at Port-Said.

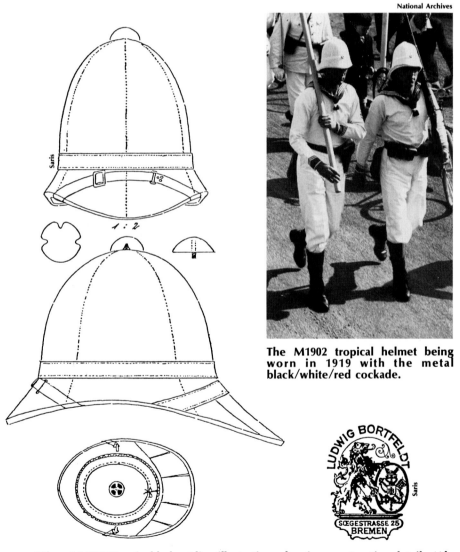

The M1902 tropical helmet being worn in 1919 with the metal black/white/red cockade.

(Above) M1902 tropical helmet line illustrations showing construction details. (Above right) Logo for the firm of Ludwig Bortfeldt.

(Above) M1902 white tropical helmet with Reichsadlerkokarde on a brown band, c. 1930. (Right) An officer wearing the tropical helmet with 0.8cm-wide gilt cords.

National Archives

In 1938 attempts at creating a helmet made of German substitute materials were made, but the end product proved to be too heavy. In the fall of 1939, with the given military situation, a tropical helmet became necessary, but all the designs attempted failed; even those made of natural cork or of pressed material were unsatisfactory.

Marineschule Muerwick

These navy pith helmets are worn with the same one-piece insignia as that utilized on the Matrosenmütze.

223

A memoir published on February 10, 1940 reflected the urgent need for a suitable sun helmet. The Berlin firms of C. Pose and Gustav Barre (the former foreman of the Bortfeldt company) were contracted each to develop two models of Tropenhelmen. The Pose firm would base its design on the old helmet, while the Barre company would create two new styles. The styles produced by the Barre firm were of two heights, the lowest one proved to be unpractical. The second helmet exceeded the first, meeting the standards not reached by the other model. The air circulation system from the Model-1902 was incorporated into this helmet.

Enough space was created by the sweatband/liner to prevent the head from touching the inside top of the helmet. It was attached to the inside of the helmet shell in a way that the liner was basically suspended by cotter pins, allowing air to circulate up through the vent in the top. The ventilation system in the top consisted of a rounded knob with four scalloped edges, which could be unscrewed to increase airflow.

The new canvas helmet had a brim that provided maximum protection from the sun, without reducing the wearer's visibility. The rear brim was a bit longer than the front, to provide additional protection for the neck. Tan leather trim on the brim and a tan leather chin strap were worn on the tan canvas model. The white helmet was edged in white leather with a white leather chin strap. The lower profile of this new helmet afforded better protection for the head than did the earlier helmets, which had been too tall and rigid.

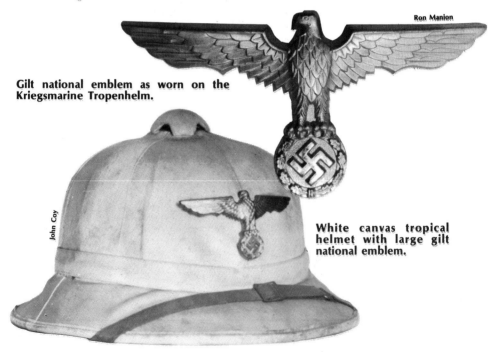

Ron Manion

Gilt national emblem as worn on the Kriegsmarine Tropenhelm.

John Coy

White canvas tropical helmet with large gilt national emblem.

The newly-designed helmet from the Barre company was officially commissioned by the naval high command on September 2, 1940. A helmet with a brown cover, as well as one in white, were issued simultaneously.[69]

Rank distinction introduced in 1934, was worn at least until 1940. Seamen from the ranks of Fähnrich and above wore a simple gilt brocade strip on the cap band, upon which was attached the Reichskokarde and, above this, the national emblem.

In 1934, Obermusikmeister (and after 1938, also Stabsmusikmeister), Musikmeister, Oberfeldwebel, Feldwebel, Oberfähnrich and Fähnrich wore a 0.4cm-wide gold braid. Officers wore a double gilt braid, 0.8cm wide. The remaining ranks at the Unteroffiziere and Mannschaften levels wore only the national cockade on the cap band. The national emblem was added to the helmet for all ranks by 1934.[70] When the braid was discarded, it was replaced by a large gilt or silver (representing administrative officials) national emblem positioned in the center of the helmet top (approximately 5cm above the helmet's cap band). The wearing of this eagle was short-lived, being replaced by a shield bearing the red/white/black national colors, secured to the wearer's right helmet side, and the Wehrmachtadler in gilt on the shield worn on the left side.

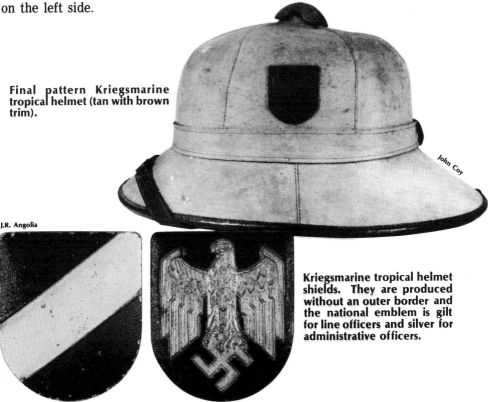

**Final pattern Kriegsmarine tropical helmet (tan with brown trim).**

J.R. Angolia

John Coy

**Kriegsmarine tropical helmet shields. They are produced without an outer border and the national emblem is gilt for line officers and silver for administrative officers.**

[69]*Uniformen-Markt. Nr. 9, May 1, 1941, several pages.*
[70]*Bekleidungs- und Anzugsbestimmungen für die Kriegsmarine, (M.Dv.-260). Berlin, 1938, p. 44.*

Final pattern Kriegsmarine tropical helmet with tan trim. Note that navy-issue helmets have a green lining.

Fralley

Interior photo showing manufacturer's name stamped on the leather sweat band.

By 1943 the tropical helmet was only utilized by units under the command of the admiralty in the Aegean Sea,[71] and did not see much use after this date.

## Headdress for Tropical Uniforms
## (Mützen zur Tropenkleidung)

Special uniforms were issued for wear by naval personnel in tropical areas. Caps with the blue or white top were also worn, mainly by officers, even after the creation of a tropical headdress.

### Visored Cap (Schirmmütze)

A khaki-colored visored cap of gabardine or cotton was first worn by navy personnel in Romania in 1942. The visor was covered in the same cloth, having a light brown leather chinstrap resting above. The strap was secured to the cap

The member of the 7. Marine-Kriegsberichter-Kompanie at far right wears the khaki visored cap described above but with cap cords.

---

[71]*MVBl. Nr. 204, April 3, 1943, p. 281.*

Khaki-colored visored cap with cloth covered visor and gold colored cap cords and insignia, for wear in tropical regions by regular naval officers. Administrative officials wore silver-grey insignia and aluminum cap cords.

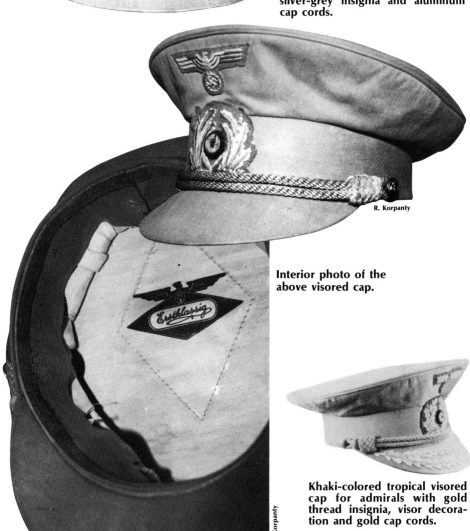

R. Korpanty

Interior photo of the above visored cap.

Khaki-colored tropical visored cap for admirals with gold thread insignia, visor decoration and gold cap cords.

R. Korpanty

228

It was not uncommon to see the standard naval visored cap worn with the tropical uniform. Knight's Cross holder Korvettenkapitän Wirich von Gartzen is shown at right.

Jim Jones

v. Hungen

NCO tropical visored cap (standard issue) with removable khaki top.

R. Mundhenk

John Coy

An administrative official wearing the khaki tropical uniform.

Yellow, machine-embroidered, cotton thread wreath on a medium brown backing and a standard Navy national emblem affixed to a similar colored material, for use on the khaki, tropical issue visored cap (officer).

John Coy

Administrative officials' cap insignia for wear on the khaki tropical cap. The example illustrated is embroidered grey thread on a medium brown backing. The cockade and wreath is padded and the national emblem backing is sewn over a cardboard stiffener.

band by a light brown button at each end of the strap. Enlisted men and NCOs wore a tan leather chin strap and officers wore braided aluminum or Celleon cap cords. Administrative officials wore aluminum cords as well. The difference between the two caps was the insignia: regular naval enlisted men, NCOs and officers wore yellow insignia, while Beamte wore silver-grey. The insignia (both the wreath/cockade and national emblem) were worked upon a khaki backing. Officers could wear a white top with this visored cap.[72] Metal insignia could also be worn.

A khaki-colored field cap (Einheitsfeldmütze or Baschlikmütze), having functional flaps secured in the front by two buttons, was introduced in 1943. A machine-woven yellow national emblem, also in metal, was worn above either a metal or machine-woven cockade, sewn to the front of the cap top. Officers; caps were piped in 0.4cm golden piping around the crown.

Officer's naval tropical cap with machine-woven national emblem and cockade on tan. A golden-yellow piping is sewn along the edge of the false turn-up with scallop.

Naval tropical cap with machine-woven yellow national emblem on tan. Exists with one or two vent holes per side.

[72]*Uniformen-Markt. Nr. 19, October 1, 1942, p. 146.*

231

Yellow on tan national emblem for use on the tropical issue field cap and tropical visored cap.

This young seaman wears a tropical visored cap with national emblem as above and a standard navy cockade on blue.

## Fur Caps

Fur caps were permitted to be worn in extremely cold weather. Blue or black leather caps were prominent with sheepskin front and ear/neck flaps. Caps were also worn similar to those used by other branches of the service.[73]

Kriegsmarine winter fur cap. This headgear was worn with or without insignia.

[73]*Ibid., Nr. 6, April 15, 1943, p. 42.*

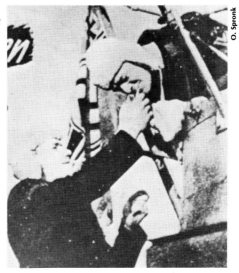

These crew members of a Kriegsmarine Schnellboot wear white fur caps.

O. Spronk

## Female Auxiliaries (Marinehelferinnen)

At the onset of war in 1939, the naval high command summoned women to replace men who were called to arms. Initially women wore the regular issued "Bürokleid" (special costume worn by office personnel). No cap was worn then.

J. Zienert

Marine-Helferinnen wearing the office-dress, as authorized in 1939.

Those naval assistants who were continuously employed outside of Germany were merged into units called "Marine-Helferinnenschaft" from July 1942.[74]

---

[74]Ibid., Nr. 15, August 1, 1942, p. 114.

The first dress regulations were authorized in August 1943 for those auxiliaries serving in the occupied eastern territories, as well as Norway and Finland. A dark blue garrison cap, shaped as for the familiar "Schiffchen" (like that worn by navy and air force members), was issued to the Helferinnen. A small machine-woven yellow national emblem was sewn above the flap in the center of the cap top. No cockade was worn. Often a signals "Blitz" in yellow upon a dark blue oval was sewn to the left upper side of the cap. Rank distinctions were shown by piping:

a. Marinevorhelferin — yellow piping around the upturn of the flap;
b. Marineoberhelferin — as above;
c. Marinehaupthelferin — as above;
d. Marineunterführerin — twisted black/golden cord;
e. Marineführerin — as above;
f. Marineoberführerin — as above;
g. Marinehauptführerin — as above;
h. Marinestabsführerin — golden cord;
i. Marineoberstabsführerin — as above.[75]

Marineschule Muerwick

**Members of the Marine-Helferinnenschaft stand as a guard of honor during the funeral of a deceased Marine-Helferin, Annemarie Henschel. Note the piped field caps.**

[75]*Deutsche Uniformen Zeitschrift. Nr. 7, October 15, 1943, p. 8.*

Dark blue field cap for female auxiliaries with yellow piping and yellow machine-woven national emblem.

O. Spronk

The Nachrichtenmädel above wears the army-style field-grey field cap according to April 3, 1943 regulations. She is welcoming a crewman of U-107. Note the deck of cards.

A mountain cap of "Sanitätsgrau" (the color of grey worn by the Red Cross) was also issued to Helferinnen, however no piping was worn on this cap. A small machine-woven national emblem was sewn to the front of the cap top. On April 3, 1943 the field-grey field cap was introduced for wear in the Marineverordnungsblatt. No information was given, however, for use by any special group of females. Marine-Kraftfahrerinnen (female marine drivers) were allowed to wear a black beret.[76]

---

[76]*MVBl. Nr. 204, April 3, 1943, p. 290.*

Male auxiliaries (Marinehelfer) wore the dark blue Bordmütze. Members of the Hitler Youth who joined the navy as Marinehelfer wore chiefly their HJ uniform cap. There existed, however, the possibility that they were supplied with navy headdress, such as the Bordmütze.[77]

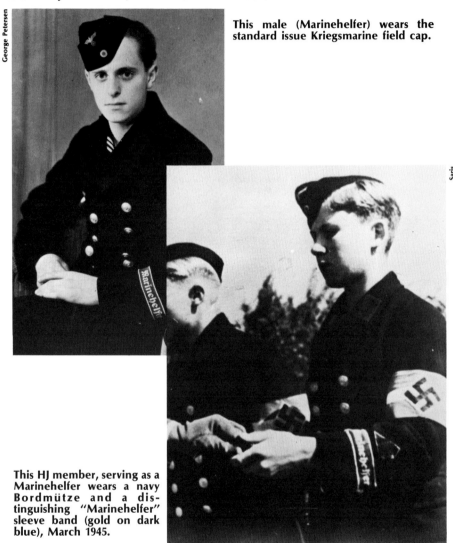

This male (Marinehelfer) wears the standard issue Kriegsmarine field cap.

This HJ member, serving as a Marinehelfer wears a navy Bordmütze and a distinguishing "Marinehelfer" sleeve band (gold on dark blue), March 1945.

## Heimatflakbatterien

According to regulations, civilians connected to naval anti-aircraft batteries protecting their home town could wear while on duty a field-grey field cap, mountain cap or the visored field cap. Officially, no national emblem was worn.[78]

---

[77]MVBl. Nr. 204, April 3, 1943, p. 289.
[78]Ibid., p. 291.

## Foreign Volunteers Serving in the Kriegsmarine
## (Freiwillige in der Kriegsmarine)

Foreign volunteers serving in the German Navy wore the standard authorized headdress with no specific badge to illustrate their status or nationality.

A navy volunteer from Belgium. Nothing on his uniform indicates his nationality.

## NS. Deutscher Marine-Bund (NSDMB)

After April 16, 1943, the veterans' organization NSDMB was no longer under the command of the NS-Reichskriegerbund, but was placed again under the command of the navy (as before 1938).[79] See chapter on veterans' organizations for cap information.

## Dress Regulations (Anzugsbestimmungen)

The following regulations were standard for the blue navy uniform:

a. Grosse Uniform: Initially, this dress was meant to only be worn when German ships visited foreign countries.[80] Officers were always to wear the fore-and-aft hat with this dress;

b. Dienstanzug: (Service Dress) Officers and Musikmeister, Oberfähnriche, & Marineunterärzte, as well as Oberfeldwebel and Fähnriche wore the blue

---

[79]NSDMB Bundesbefehl. Nr. 2/43, April 16, 1943, AM, A/Wehr. III, B-Nr. 2690.
[80]Bekleidungs- und Anzugsbestimmungen für die Kriegsmarine, (M.Dv.-260). Berlin, 1935, p. 11.

visored cap. Obermaate and cadets wore the blue Matrosenmütze. The white top could be worn from May 1 until September 30. Officers who were authorized could also wear the Matrosenmütze;

c. Ausgehanzug: (Walking-out dress). As with b., however, cadets wore only the blue Matrosenmütze;

d. Grosser Gesellschaftsanzug (Formal evening dress). Officers wore the blue visored cap. The hat was only worn when ordered for special occasions. The white top could be worn during the season: (Less formal evening dress) As with d., but no hat was worn;

f. Tropenanzug: (Tropical uniform). Officers wore the white visored cap or tropical helmet. Obermaate wore the white Matrosenmütze or Tropenhelm, as did enlisted ranks. Cadets wore the white visored cap or tropical helmet.

g. Sportanzug: (sports kit) No headdress.[81]

Note:
The authorized blue and white caps for officers and enlisted ranks were permitted to be worn with the parade-dress in the Spring of 1939.[82]

**Miscellaneous headgear being worn:**

Straw hats.

Schreiberobergefreiter Walther Gerhold, in a one-man submarine, wearing a cloth cap.

[81]Ibid., pp. 35-44.
[82]Uniformen-Markt. Nr. 9, May 1, 1939, p. 136.

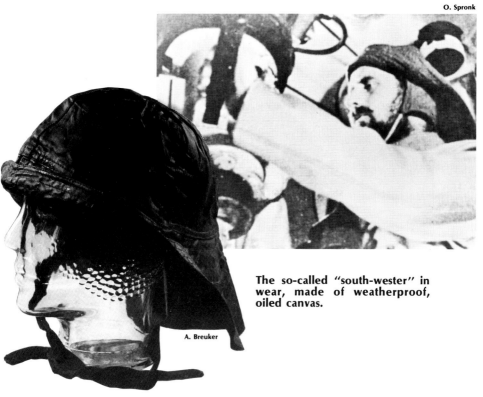

The so-called "south-wester" in wear, made of weatherproof, oiled canvas.

A. Breuker

J. Coy

A navy-issue Kopfhaube, made of medium grey material.

# 5

## REICHSLUFTWAFFE/LUFTWAFFE

When the allies ratified the Treaty of Versailles in 1919, it was ordered that the standing German flying units be disbanded along with the other branches of service. This was prior to the establishment of the army and navy as the new Reichswehr. There was no official airforce at this time.

Flight was still in its novelty stage, and interest in it as a sport remained. In the mid-1920's amateur and professional pilots founded aero clubs, such as the Deutscher Fliegerbund:[1] within the Reichsheer and Reichsmarine flying units did exist, as well as the "schwarze Luftwaffe" (see chapter on air organizations in Vol. II). It was not long, though, before the value of the airplane as an offensive and defensive weapon was realized, meriting that a distinct branch of service be formed. Since an airforce was forbidden by the treaty, it was necessary to disguise it. In 1933 work began in earnest, and an infant airforce was created, masked as the Deutsche Luftsport Verband. Uniforms were designed for the DLV which would be the models for those worn by members of the forthcoming Luftwaffe. The uniforms were designed so no additional costs or alterations would be incurred once the period of deception had passed.

The Reichsluftwaffe became the third branch of service within the Reichswehr by decree of the Führer on February 26, 1935, but the official creation date was March 1, 1935.

### Visored Cap (Schirmmütze)

Initially, in 1935, the DLV visored cap was worn by Luftwaffe personnel.[2] Officer's caps were piped in aluminum around the crown and the top and bottom of the cap band. General rank's caps were piped as above but in gold, with gold insignia. The DLV cap for enlisted men was piped in grey-blue. In March 1935 an order was issued authorizing the branch-of-service piping (Waffen-

---

[1]*Das Dritte Reich, Blätter für Freiheit und Gemeinschaft. Bund Oberland e.V. Nürnberg. 1928, p. 159.*

[2]*Luftwaffe-Verordnungsblatt (LVBl.). Nr. 303. June 14, 1935. p. 144*

farbe) around the cap top, effective in November of that year.[3] In August 1935 an order authorized additional 2 or 3mm color piping around the top and bottom of the mohair cap band.[4] In late 1935, when stocks permitted, modified caps were distributed for wear with the walking-out dress.[5] The old-style DLV/Reichsluftwaffe caps were permitted a wear-out period until April 1936, but by this date stocks of the new caps were available for issue or purchase.

These early piped caps were initially worn with metal DLV insignia as stocks of the newly designed Luftwaffe insignia were not always available. For an example of this cap see the DLV chapter in Volume II of this series.

The basic construction of the Model 1935 visored cap (Klappmütze -- name used in early regulations) worn by enlisted men, non-commissioned officers and officers involved several different parts. The top, or "Deckel," for enlisted men and NCOs was of grey-blue (Fliegerblau) Grundtuch, a standard wool material as used in uniforms. This material was for issued caps, but private-purchase caps could be bought in basic wool, doeskin, or a material called "Strichtuch," which were of finer quality and were normally worn with a private-purchase uniform for walking-out dress. Officers' and generals' visored caps were usually of doeskin or tricot.

Tim Knight

The "Tellerform" visored cap in wear by an officer.

**(Right) A DLV officer wearing a white top visored cap. Note that the DLV uniform and cap is like those of the Luftwaffe. A metal DLV winged wreath/cockade and a hand-embroidered national emblem on blue are worn on the cap.**

George Petersen

[3]Ibid. Nr. 80, March 25, 1935, pp. 34-35.
[4]Ibid. Nr. 514, August 15. 1935, p. 250.
[5]Ibid. Nr. 733, October 15, 1935, p. 341.

**Deutschlands größte Uniformmützenfabrik**

# PETER KÜPPER

Wuppertal-Ronsdorf ✦ liefert UNIFORMMÜTZEN aller Art

Jede

Peküro-Mütze

verkörpert
Qualität u.
Fortschritt

Stirndruckfreie Schirmbefestigung

Deutsches Reichs - Patent
Nr. 538 943

This advertisement shows a Luftwaffe officer's visored cap made by the firm of Peter Kupper, with its "Peküro" trademark. This company produced many officer and EM/NCO private-purchase caps.

The cap top, with its four under panels, consisted of a felt inner lining sewn between the outer cap cloth and inner lining. Furthermore, a 3mm galvanized steel wire was sewn into and under the top piping seam to retain the semi-oval shape of the cap. This wire was often removed or bent by the owner to give the cap a more relaxed appearance. The top was usually saddle-shaped, or "Sattelform." Enlisted and, initially, some officer caps had a low, saucer-shaped "Tellerform" top. Without a doubt the Sattelform top was the most popular of the two types. To retain the cap's Sattelform, a 4.5cm wide linen stiffener was glued or riveted at the front of the cap top between a corrugated metal stiffener (mounted in the front center of the cap). The front and part of the cap sides were padded with gauze and wadding. These measures were not only taken to retain the crisp shape of the cap top, but also to make certain that the peak of the top was supported adequately, allowing it to slant properly from front to back. The top and the four panels were sewn to a band made of 4.3cm wide black all-cotton mohair Tresse, under which was a 1mm thick lacquered molded cardboard strip, which supported the band and some of the weight of the top. The completed cap band, that is, one with top and bottom piping and a bottom edging, 2 or 3mm, in fliegergrau material, measured 4.9cm wide.

The visored caps worn by enlisted men and NCOs were normally lined in Havanna-brown (rust) watered cotton moiré. Officers' caps were lined in golden-yellow, white or blue satin (the color of the lining for both enlisted men and officers' caps could vary if the cap was purchased privately). A celluloid sweatshield was sewn onto the top lining, measuring 15.5cm in length, 13.5cm in width. To accommodate a tag printed with the owner's name, a small, three-sided rectangular "pocket" was sewn near the front end of the shield (this feature was usually incorporated into the visored caps worn by virtually every other military, para-military, or political organization). The cap size, manufacturer's name and the year of issue (Lieferjahr) was printed onto the lining under the shield, or impressed onto the shield itself. A 5cm wide sheepskin sweatband was sewn to the bottom interior edge. The front portion of it was perforated in many cases. The wearer's battalion or regiment number(s) were often found stamped in black ink on the reverse of the sweatband on issue caps. This practice was discontinued, however, during the war for security reasons. Officers frequently elected to affix their initials in thin metal letters to the sweatband. A 5mm gummed pad was glued to the front underside of the cap band, between it and the sweatband. This aided in absorbing the weight from the wearer's forehead (thus, the manufacturer's marking, "Stirndruckfrei," usually found pressed onto the sweatband). The ends of the sweatband were usually joined together at the rear of the cap by a silk bow or a simple "x"stitch.

A black visor was sewn below the bottom edge of the cap band at a 35 degree angle. In 1935 it was available in two materials: black grained leather, 3mm thick (reportedly abolished in 1937), or in black Vulkanfiber, 1.2mm thick. Regulations state that the visor was always black on both the obverse and reverse, however, the obverse of many leather visors are covered in green leather with a fine checkered pattern. The visor made of Vulkanfiber was covered on the inside with black grained artificial leather, and was finished with a 3mm black lacquered canvas strip, machine-sewn to the leading edge. The visor worn on Luftwaffe caps expressly lacked the raised rim normally found along the edge of most visored caps. It should be noted, however, that caps exist without the visor edging. The leather visor was finished with a 3mm wide black leather machine-sewn edging. Some visors produced late in the war were made of pressed black lacquered cardboard, or other "Ersatz" materials.

P. Pauwels

(Left) This Luftwaffe NCO wears a red piped (Flak) visored cap, in "Sattelform." Note the army-style rectangular buckles on his chinstrap. (Above) Visored cap as at left but worn by an enlisted man.

## Chinstrap and Cords

Enlisted men and non-commissioned officers wore a 1.5cm wide black, three-part, leather chinstrap, having an oval black laquered buckle positioned midway on each side. Although the oval buckles were specifically for the Luftwaffe, caps can be found with army rectangular buckles as well as SS/DAF styles on various forms of black leather chinstraps. Caps were not issued or purchased with these variations, but were changed to suit the wearer's taste, or were replacements for damaged chinstraps. The strap had a 1.5cm slit at each end, through which fitted black laquered buttons, which were sew-on or a split prong model and normally had a diameter of 1cm (smaller dimensions can be found on private purchase caps).

Flak enlisted man's visored cap with first pattern national emblem. The sweat diamond is marked with the maker's name and year of issue (Lieferjahr), 1938. Note oval buckles on chinstrap.

Officers (Leutnant through Oberst) wore aluminum twisted cap cords, usually with a 5mm thickness (some firms made 6mm cords). Officers could wear cords of silver or late in the war, white nylon cords. At the end of each cord was a slide normally made of aluminum, covered with the same material as that of the cap cords, which allowed the cords to be adjusted. At the end of each cord was a loop, 3cm in length (of the same material as the rest of the cord), which fitted over side buttons. Of-

Unteroffizier (Fahnrich) Werner Rohde wears a non-regulation black leather chin strap normally found on veterans' visored caps. The photo is dated 1943.

ficers wore sew-on or split prong buttons (Neusilber until 1935, when changed to aluminum[6] (late war types could be grey metal)). The diameter of these buttons was normally 7mm, but size variations exist. General officers wore gilt cap cords[7] and side buttons. During the war, Celleon or gold-colored artificial silk cords were also worn.

The dashing Oberst Werner Mölders is shown wearing the basic Luftwaffe officers' visored cap with twisted aluminum cap cords.

Generalfeldmarschall Albert Kesselring wears a fine example of a general officers' visored cap with twisted gilt cap cords.

---

[6]*LVBl. Nr. 846, November 18, 1935. p. 405.*
[7]*Anzugordnung für die Luftwaffe (L.Dv. 422). Abschnitt A. Berlin, November 27, 1935, pp. 12-13.*

Aspirant officers with the rank of Oberfähnrich and Unterarzt were permitted to wear officers' aluminum cap cords and hand-embroidered wire insignia on their Waffenfarbe-piped visored caps.[8] It should be noted that metal insignia were also used by these ranks. The above applied to both the grey-blue and white top visored caps.

(Above) Medical officer aspirant (Unterarzt) wearing a non-regulation visored cap with dark blue piping around the crown and aluminum piping on top and bottom of cap band. (Below) Medical officer aspirant visored cap with all dark blue piping and hand-embroidered insignia.

NCOs who were aspirant officers were entitled to wear aluminum cap cords and officers' insignia on their visored cap. Their caps were piped in appropriate Waffenfarbe.

[8]LVBl. Nr. 193, May 2, 1935, p. 91.

The Luftwaffe visored cap was slightly modified in 1937, but this pertained mainly to the new insignia[9] and substituted materials. Due to the war economy, it was ordered in 1943 that the national emblem and winged wreath/cockade for all ranks, including officers and generals, were to be made of stamped metal, instead of being hand-embroidered.[10] But with sufficient stocks of hand-embroidered insignia already on hand, there was probably more than enough to fill demands for the remainder of the war.

## Insignia

Although the fliegergrau[11] color of the DLV visored cap remained, the insignia was replaced by a distinct national emblem worn on the cap top, and a winged wreath and national cockade on the cap band.

### Cockade and Wreath (Flügel mit Kokarde)

The cap band insignia, consisting of a cockade and winged wreath stamped from a common piece of metal (aluminum or light metal), was introduced with the initial Luftwaffe visored cap in 1935. The black/white/red cockade, measuring 24.5mm in diameter, resembled a cockade made of several parts. The national cockade was segmented into four sections: The outer aluminum or light metal ring was 3.5mm wide, followed by a painted or black lacquered ring 2.5mm wide. The next ring was light metal or aluminum, and encircled the red painted "bull's eye" of the cockade center, 4.5mm in diameter. All of these rings were finished with a clockwise twisted rope or pointed design. Each of the cockade sections were encompassed by a 0.5mm wide twisted or pointed simulated aluminum rope design. These sizes varied slightly, however, from manufacturer to manufacturer.

### Winged Wreath (Enlisted Ranks)

The cockade was enclosed by a lightweight metal oakleaf wreath consisting of five leaves and two acords on each side. The wreath was joined at the bottom center by a simple band with a vertical row of beads. The wreath was flanked on each side by a wing segmented into four sections, having the detail

Enlisted ranks' metal wreath and cockade.

---

[9]Anzugordnung für die Luftwaffe (L.Dv. 422). Abschnitt A. Berlin, April 1, 1937, pp. 12-14.

[10]Uniformen-Markt (UM). Nr. 6, March 15, 1943, p. 44.

[11]Handbuch der neuzeitlichen Wehrwissenschaften, Dritter Band. 2: Die Luftwaffe. Berlin, 1939, pp. 410-411.

of simulated embroidery.[12] The wingspan of the winged wreath/cockade varied from 12.6cm, produced by the F.W. Assmann firm in 1940.[13] The early version of the winged wreath/cockade produced by Assmann (ca. 1935) had a width of 13.3cm. In 1937 the Wilhelm Deumer firm produced a winged wreath/cockade with a width of 14.5cm.[14] The approximate height of all such wreaths was 3.9cm. The metal winged wreath/cockade insignia was slightly vaulted to conform with the curvature of the cap band. It was affixed to the band by two metal (aluminum or brass) prongs, which pushed through the cap band and were flattened on the inside.

Author's Collection

This Feldwebel wears an enlisted grade Luftwaffe visored cap with a first pattern national emblem and the metal winged wreath.

## Winged Wreath (Officers)

Officers wore the same style of winged wreath and cockade, but their insignia was made of hand-embroidered aluminum wire, worked upon a black

Officers' hand-embroidered wreath and cockade.

---

[12]*Anzugordnung für die Luftwaffe (L.Dv. 422). Abschnitt A. Berlin, November 27, 1935, p. 123.*

[13]*F.W. Assmann Katalog. Ausgabe 1936, p. 16 & Ausgabe 1940, p. 16c.*

[14]*Wilhelm Deumer Katalog. Ausgabe 1937, p. A6.*

cloth blacking. Early styles were smaller in size with cockades of black/silver/red hand-embroidery. Since the silver wire tended to tarnish dark, aluminum was a popular alternative. Aluminum wire winged wreaths with metal cockades were also available. Officers could purchase any style they preferred. Officers with the rank of Leutnant to Oberst wore the aluminum wire winged wreath, and generals wore the winged wreath of hand-embroidered gilt wire or Celleon/nylon. Regardless of rank, the national cockade was always black/white/red. The winged wreath/cockade insigne was sewn directly to the cap band. The metal winged wreath/cockade was not normally worn by officers, but could be by personal choice or as a replacement if no hand-embroidered styles were available.

Flak Major Schroeder wearing a Luftwaffe visored cap with early insignia and cap cords removed. Some officers preferred to remove the cap cords while in the field to make them less conspicuous.

Hauptmann Josef Prentl, battery chief of Flak-Rgt. 29 (mot) and a Knight's Cross holder, wearing the metal national emblem and winged wreath/cockade on his visored cap.

George Petersen

George Petersen

An early pattern, officer's hand-embroidered winged wreath with black/silver/red cockade (note tarnished silver), and early pattern national emblem.

A hand-embroidered aluminum wire winged wreath with metal cockade, and a national emblem with early turned-down tail.

Standard hand-embroidered aluminum wire winged wreath/cockade with a slight down-swept curve of the wings, and a typical hand-embroidered national emblem.

The most commonly encountered Luftwaffe officer's, hand-embroidered aluminum wire winged wreath/cockade (note flat base on backing and straight wings), with wartime pattern national emblem. These particular examples are on dark green wool backings for use on the Luftwaffe forestry visored cap.

Gold nylon wreath/cockade/wing insigne for wear by ranks of Generalmajor through Generalfeldmarschall. Note that this particular piece features a cockade with a ventilated center of wire mesh, a technique most often found on visored caps manufactured by "Erel."

## Winged Wreath for Reserve Officers

Luftwaffe reserve officers wore the standard embroidered wreath/cockade on the band of their caps, but with the addition of a bright aluminum Maltese cross[15] worn in the center of the red "bull's eye."* The use of this special cockade was discontinued at the same time as it was in the army and navy (June 1936).

Aluminum wire cap band insigne for reserve officers' visored caps. The Reichskokarde replaced the cockade with the traditional Maltese cross in 1936.

*Outside ring was 3mm, middle ring was 3mm, and inside ring was 2mm. The red field in the center was painted and had a diameter of 11.5mm: the elevated, pressed cross was 10mm.

---

[15]*LVBl. Nr. 177, May 13, 1935, p. 85.*

A Luftwaffe reserve officer wears the Maltese cross over the red field of the cockade.

A. Breuker

## National Emblem (Hoheitszeichen)

### Enlisted Men

The model 1935 Luftwaffe national emblem was made of light metal or aluminum. Two brass or aluminum prongs were attached to its reverse to attach the emblem to the cap top. This national symbol featured an eagle in descent, clutching in its left talon a canted swastika. The right talon was raised; the tail feathers were downswept.[16] The official wingspan size of the eagle was 5.5cm. The height was 3.5cm.[17] It should be noted, however, that sizes varied slightly from manufacturer to manufacturer. It should also be noted that civilians employed by the Luftwaffe were forbidden to wear the national emblem of that service (LVBl, Nr. 562, August 27, 1935, p. 269).

In 1937 a new larger and more refined national emblem was introduced to the cap top. The wingspan of the model 1937 eagle was 6.7cm.[18] The height remained 3.5cm. There was a greater space between the wings and the tail feathers were outswept. Also, the swastika was thinner.

---

[16]*Anzugordnung für die Luftwaffe (L.Dv. 422). Abschnitt A. Berlin, November 27, 1935, Enlage VI, p. 152*

[17]*Katalog Gebr. Gloerfeld. Ausgabe 1936, p. 6.*

[18]*Anzugordnung für die Luftwaffe (L.Dv. 422). Abschnitt A. Berlin, April 1, 1937, Anhang V, p. 173.*

First pattern national emblem.          Second pattern.

A Luftwaffe metal national emblem after its first step of production. Once the planchet was stamped, it was cut-out and back prongs/pins were attached.

A Luftwaffe Unteroffizier wearing the visored cap with metal winged wreath and second pattern national emblem.

253

Confusion within the tailoring industry arose in 1937 concerning the new national emblem. Several trade magazines maintained that the style of the eagle had not been changed.[19] Finally, though, official regulations established the new national emblem as instituted on April 1, 1937.

Several finishes, from matte to a high silver polish, were available for the eagle. It was strictly forbidden for enlisted men to wear bullion, instead of metal, cap insignia.[20]

### National Emblem for Officers

Officer ranks of Leutnant through Oberst wore the national emblem in hand-embroidered aluminum wire on a cloth backing of assorted shades of grey-blue. Wire versions of both the 1935 and 1937 national emblems were produced in many variations and were sewn to the cap top. Metal national emblems were commonly worn on the white top cap, and on rare occasions on the grey-blue cap according to the wearer's preference. The officer aspirant ranks of Oberfähnrich, Unterarzt, Stabsmusikmeister, Obermusikmeister and Musikmeister were also permitted to wear the national emblem (as well as the winged wreath) in hand-embroidered form.[21]

Heinz J. Nowarra

Author's Collection

**Luftwaffe officer's visored cap with an early pattern national emblem.**

**Note that Oberleutnant Dähue wears a national emblem on a triangle rather than the close-cropped backing usually encountered.**

---

[19]*Rundschau-Deutsches Schneiderfachblatt. Nr. 32, August 7, 1937, p. 1135.*
[20]*LVBl. Nr. 197, May 20, 1935, p. 93.*
[21]*Anzugordnung für die Luftwaffe (L.Dv. 422). Abschnitt A, Berlin, November 27, 1935, pp. 12-13.*

A Luftwaffe officer's visored cap with early pattern insignia (note silver on cockade), soft bendable visor, and wire stiffener removed from the top. The Luftwaffe had no version of the army "crusher" field cap, so this example was not uncommon among some aircrews or ground field units.

(Left) Leutnant Georg Ackermann of 5/KG 53 "Legion Condor" and a Knight's Cross holder is shown wearing a Luftwaffe visored cap with hand-embroidered winged wreath/cockade and a metal national emblem. This photo was taken in 1945 after being awarded the Knight's Cross.

Luftwaffe officer's visored cap with hand-embroidered winged wreath/metal cockade, and standard wartime national emblem.

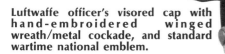

A cardboard template (Unterlage) used as a guide for the hand-embroidery of a Luftwaffe officer's national emblem.

255

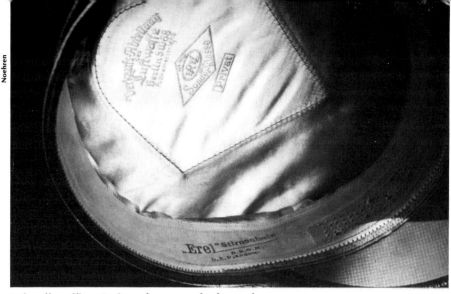

Luftwaffe officers' visored cap made by Erel. Note sweat diamond and sweat band markings.

(Above) Luftwaffe officer's visored cap with a field-grey wool top, instead of the normal grey-blue. The wool under the cap band is also field-grey, and the piping is dull grey. Standard hand-embroidered insignia is sewn on. The specific use of this cap is not known.

This Luftwaffe officer has removed the metal wire support from the cap top to give it a more "jaunty" look.

Saris

**Members of Aufklärungsgruppe 10 "Tannenberg" wear the first and second pattern national emblems in Poland, 1939.**

The ranks of Generalmajor through Generalfeldmarschall and Reichsmarschall wore the national emblem embroidered in gold wire or Celleon/nylon on a blue-grey backing.

General officers' visored cap with hand-embroidered, gilt wire insignia.

George Petersen

General officer's visored cap with gold-colored hand-embroidered Celleon/nylon insignia, piping and cap cords. Note the different shades of Celleon thread used. The cap is made by Erel.

## Summer Visored Cap (Sommermütze)

Instituted for wear by all ranks during the period of April 1 through October 1,[22] the summer visored cap was constructed to accommodate a white removable top. The visor and the mohair cap band constituted the "body" of the summer cap. The wearer's branch-of-service piping was worn above and below the edge of the band. The edge (approximately 3mm) below the bottom piping was covered in the normal fliegergrau material. A reinforced edge was affixed to the upper side of the cap band to hold the bottom edge of the white top in place. This top was piped around the crown seam in 2mm white material with an inner white cord for shape. The form was basically flexible, since no metal cap wire was sewn into the top. The only stiffeners used were cloth-covered metal supports or leather reinforcement pieces mounted vertically from the center of the band, extending up into the front of the cap top. Some caps employed a padded section sewn around the front top of the band as support for the cap top front. These summer caps were equipped with a permanent white top lining that was sewn to the cap band interior and could not be removed. Normally a sweatshield was sewn to the white cotton lining.

Helga Sichermann-Spielhagen

This signals Obergefreiter wears the Sommermütze for enlisted ranks.

A. Breuker

An enlisted rank's Sommermütze with yellow piping.

[22]*Anzugordnung für die Luftwaffe (L.Dv. 422). Abschnitt B, Berlin, April 1, 1935,* p. 19.

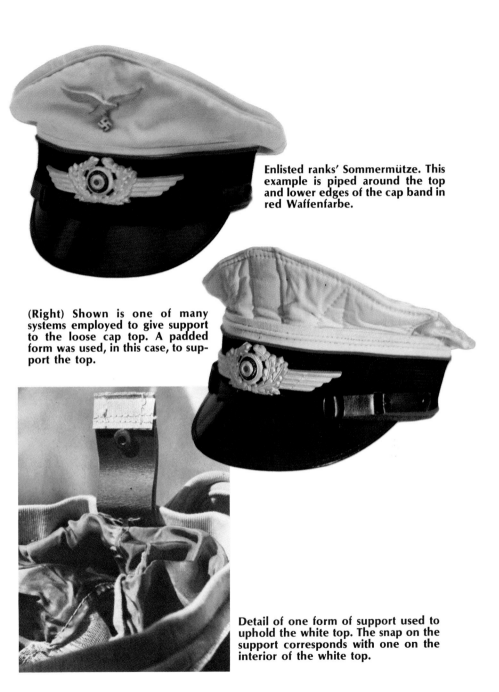

Enlisted ranks' Sommermütze. This example is piped around the top and lower edges of the cap band in red Waffenfarbe.

(Right) Shown is one of many systems employed to give support to the loose cap top. A padded form was used, in this case, to support the top.

Detail of one form of support used to uphold the white top. The snap on the support corresponds with one on the interior of the white top.

Officers' Sommermütze with metal first pattern national emblem and first style white top.

A. Breuker

The white top visored cap as worn by an administrative official.

Author's Collection

Ron Kwan

Officer's white top visored cap with second pattern national emblem.

The white top visored cap as worn by Luftwaffe officers below the rank of general.

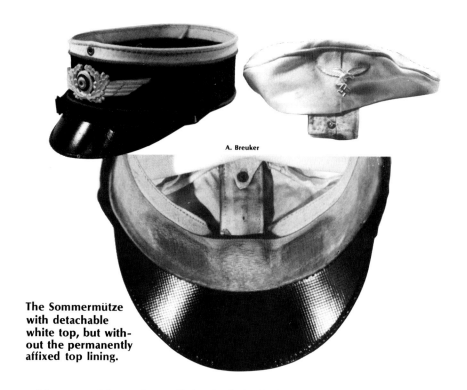

A. Breuker

The Sommermütze with detachable white top, but without the permanently affixed top lining.

The normal type of wreath/cockade insignia was positioned in the center of the cap band and, according to rank, the chinstrap or cords were worn. Enlisted and officer ranks[23] below General der Flieger were to wear the national emblem in stamped metal. However, by and large, the officer ranks elected to wear the national emblem embroidered in silver upon a white, often reinforced, piece of cloth. General ranks wore the national emblem embroidered in gilt wire. Usually two snaps were sewn to the reverse of the insignia and on the cap top to allow it to be removed while the top was being laundered. This cap was slightly modified in 1937.

George Petersen

George Petersen

First and second pattern Luftwaffe officer's national emblem on white for use on the white top visored cap. These could be sewn to a metal plate with two or three attachment prongs (as shown). Versions also exist with small loops for attachment with metal rings, as used on summer tunic buttons. Others were sewn directly to the cap top.

[23]*Ibid. Abschnitt A, Berlin, November 27, 1935, pp. 14-15.*

This Luftwaffe Hauptmann wears an early style white top visored cap with first pattern national emblem and early pattern winged wreath/cockade.

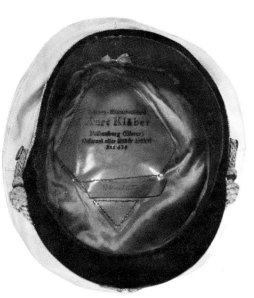

Interior view of a white top officer's visored cap.

General officer's national emblems hand-embroidered on white for the white top visored cap. (Top row) Metal back plate (front view); early style national emblem in gold wire on illustrated metal plate; (bottom row) Celleon/nylon embroidered version; and a later style national emblem in gold wire on heavy white wool.

263

Generalleutnant von Roques wears the early style white top cap with first pattern national emblem in metal.

Excellent example of a white top visored cap worn by Luftwaffe generals. Note the delicate detail of the second pattern national emblem.

Generalmajor Aschenbrenner wearing the white top visored cap with hand-embroidered national emblem.

## Special Visored Cap for Reichsmarschall Hermann Göring

On July 19, 1940, Hitler bestowed the unique rank of "Reichsmarschall" upon his commander of the airforce, Hermann Göring. Göring, being the great admirer of uniforms and regalia that he was, immediately designed a uniform befitting this new rank. In August 1940 he made his first appearance wearing the new uniform and visored cap. The visored cap exhibited the finest workmanship of the industry. It was manufactured by the Robert Lubstein firm of Berlin. The insignia design was beautifully executed by two men by the names of Tröltsch and Hanselmann, also from Berlin.

The cap top was made of the finest quality light-grey (hellgrau) material. The band was made of light-grey velvet, and totally surrounded by a laurel leaf decoration (Lorbeerranke).

All the insignia was made of real gold wire embroidery. It was especially noted in the trade magazines of that period that the insignia was embroidered in "Blankgold," a shining, glittering gold. The national emblem of the Luftwaffe was hand-embroidered directly to the cloth of the cap top. Its wingspan was considerably wider than the second model Luftwaffe eagle. A wire black/white (silver)/red cockade, surrounded by a gold wire laurel leaf wreath, flanked by wings segmented into four sections, along with the previously mentioned laurel leaf band decoration were hand-embroidered directly to the velvet cap band. The cap was piped around the crown and above and below the band in gold cord. Gold cap cords were secured to the visored cap by two gilt pebbled buttons. The visor was of black leather, and it appears from period film footage that it was slightly longer than normal visors. The creation of this unique visored cap was widely advertised in period trade magazines, such as the popular "Uniformen-Markt."[24]

From photographs and surviving caps it is known that Göring wore other Luftwaffe caps with different styles, some of which are illustrated.

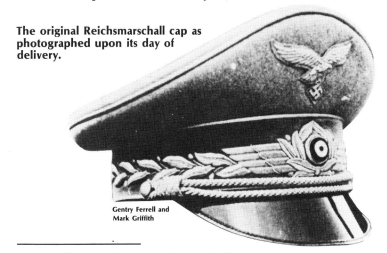

The original Reichsmarschall cap as photographed upon its day of delivery.

Gentry Ferrell and Mark Griffith

---

[24]UM. Nr. 17, September 1, 1940 (also, supplements and announcements published in August, November and December of the same year), and Schwert und Spaten. Nr. 8, August 1940, pp. 108-109 (also, an announcement in July 1940).

Göring's preoccupation with uniforms is well-reflected in this unique visored cap. The cap top is light grey; the cap band is mouse-grey velvet. The national emblem, wreath and laurel leaf decoration around the band are embroidered directly onto the cap material.

Interior view of a Reichsmarschall's cap.

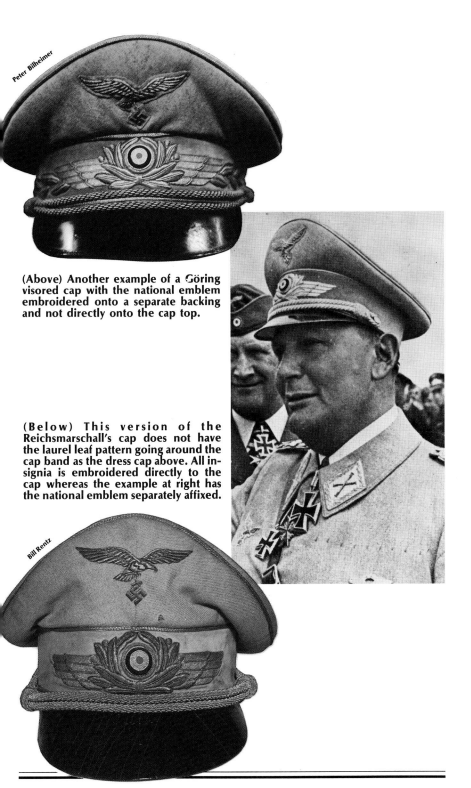

Peter Bilheimer

(Above) Another example of a Göring visored cap with the national emblem embroidered onto a separate backing and not directly onto the cap top.

(Below) This version of the Reichsmarschall's cap does not have the laurel leaf pattern going around the cap band as the dress cap above. All insignia is embroidered directly to the cap whereas the example at right has the national emblem separately affixed.

Bill Rentz

## Luftwaffe Administrative Officials (Wehrmachtbeamte der Luftwaffe)

Administrative officials serving in the airforce wore the regular Luftwaffe officer's visored cap. NCOs and persons without officer status wore the enlisted visored cap piped in dark green.[25] Officials of officer's rank had aluminum piping and officials of general's rank had gilt piping.

A rare example of a visored cap piped in dark green for Wehrmachtbeamtem that did not have officer status.

## Specialist Officers (Sonderführer)
## Wartime Officials (Beamte auf Kriegsdauer)

Sonderführer and Beamte auf Kriegsdauer wore the Luftwaffe officer visored cap. These officials wore silver or aluminum piping around the flap of the field cap, whereas lower officials (assistants) did not.[26]

Sonderführer, Offiziere auf Kriegsdauer, Offiziere der Reserve and Landwehr, as well as Wehrmachtbeamte der Luftwaffe wore the regular pattern visored cap worn by Luftwaffe officers.

Author's Collection

(Left) This Wehrmachtbeamter a. Kr. (rank as Oberfeldwebel) wears the green piped visored cap as that for Wehrmachtbeamte illustrated above.

### Luftwaffe Clergy (Militärseelsorge bei der Luftwaffe)

No official Luftwaffe clergy uniform distinction or unit was devised. Normally, navy or army clergy ministered to the Luftwaffe. The first Luftwaffe regulations (1935) mentioned that clergy wore the traditional black coat and felt hat or top hat.[27]

### Luftwaffe Forestry Officials (Forstbeamte der Luftwaffe)

Luftwaffe forestry officials wore special uniforms, like those worn by army forestry officials.

The visored cap was green, having a dark green cap band and piping and a black visor. Ranks through Unterförster wore the black leather chinstrap, while higher officials wore silver cords. The rank of Oberlandforstmeister wore gilt cords.[28] Standard Luftwaffe insignia was utilized on these visored caps. Silver or gilt metal buttons secured officers cap cords, but green matte

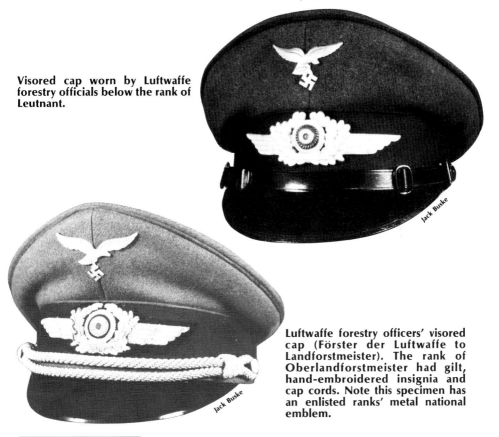

Visored cap worn by Luftwaffe forestry officials below the rank of Leutnant.

Luftwaffe forestry officers' visored cap (Förster der Luftwaffe to Landforstmeister). The rank of Oberlandforstmeister had gilt, hand-embroidered insignia and cap cords. Note this specimen has an enlisted ranks' metal national emblem.

[25]*Anzugordnung für die Luftwaffe (L.Dv. 422). Abschnitt A, Berlin, November 27, 1935, p. 99.*

[26]*UM. Nr. 1, January 1, 1940, p. 2.*

[27]*LVBl. Nr. 174, March 28, 1935, p. 82, and Nr. 461, July 31, 1935, p. 231.*

[28]*Hettler, Uniformen der Deutschen Wehrmacht, mit Nachtrag, 1939-1940, p. XLVII.*

buttons were worn on the enlisted visored caps.[29] On some occasions the Luftwaffe national emblem was embroidered upon a green cloth backing in aluminum interwoven with green thread.

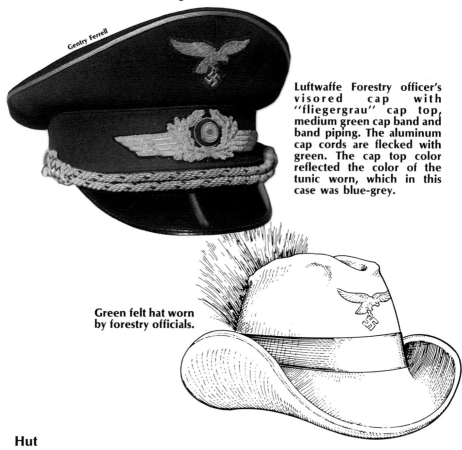

Gentry Ferrell

Luftwaffe Forestry officer's visored cap with "fliegergrau" cap top, medium green cap band and band piping. The aluminum cap cords are flecked with green. The cap top color reflected the color of the tunic worn, which in this case was blue-grey.

Green felt hat worn by forestry officials.

## Hut

A green felt fedora with a darker green band and brim edging was worn for a time. It resembled the basic Hut worn by state forestry officials, but the Luftwaffe national emblem was worn in the center of the front, above the hat band.[30]

## Visored Field Cap (Baschlikmütze)

Similar to a mountain cap, the Baschlikmütze was made of grey-green material. An embroidered Luftwaffe national emblem was sewn to the cap top. A cloth cockade was stitched to the center of the flaps.[31]

Enlisted ranks wore a dark green field cap in Schiffschen form with the national emblem and cockade machine-embroidered on a dark green backing.

---

[29]*Handbuch der neuzeitlichen Wehrwissenschaften, Dritter Band. 2: Die Luftwaffe. Berlin, 1939, p. 417.*

[30]*UM. Jahrgang 1940, p. 63, (also Nr. 18, September 15, 1940, p. 139).*

[31]*E. Hettler, Uniformen der Deutschen Wehrmacht, mit Nachtrag 1939/1940, p. XLVII.*

It is possible that officer-quality field caps were also worn, but no known examples have been encountered as of this writing.

Luftwaffe forestry enlisted rank's Schiffschen in dark green with insignia machine-embroidered on dark green.

George Petersen

A visored field cap made of lightweight material was also available for wear. No cords or chinstrap was worn on this cap and the insignia was embroidered. The visor was fabricated of soft, flexible leather.

### Experimental Airforce Units (Prüfungslager der Luftwaffe)

Persons serving in these special units wore, from 1937 onward, the regular airforce uniform. One outstanding feature of their visored cap was that all the pipings were in the same "fliegergrau" color as the cap top. No branch-of-service pipings were worn.[32]

### Generalluftzeugmeister

The technical offices, including the offices for testing (Erprobungsstellen der Luftwaffe) and supply (Nachschubamt) were directly under the jurisdiction of the Generalluftzeugmeister (called "Luftzeugmeister" until 1941).[33] The Generalluftzeugmeister was responsible for promotions and transfers, and also for ordering of spare parts, raw materials, and consumer goods.[34] The Generalluftzeugmeister also cooperated closely with the Seenotdienst (Sea

O. Spronk

Udet in his rank of Luftzeugmeister wearing the standard white top visored cap. The special cogwheel cap insigne was not introduced until a few years later.

---

[32]*Der Dienstunterricht in der Luftwaffe. Jahrgang 1941, Berlin, p. 71.*
[33]*Luftfahrt-Taschenkalender, 1943, p. 19.*
[34]*LVBl. Nr. 238, May 20, 1935, p. 110.*

Emergency Service) in supplying life-buoys at sea (Köhlers Flieger-Kalender, 1942, p. 143).

Prior to the progression of the war, Generalluftzeugmeister personnel wore the basic Luftwaffe officers' visored cap. As more and more civilians were engaged in the Generalluftzeugmeister, a new national emblem was ordered for them in 1941. It consisted of a lightweight metal silver cogwheel, superimposed with the Luftwaffe national emblem (wingspan approximately 6.5cm). This new emblem was affixed to the cap top,[35] replacing the former Luftwaffe eagle. On rare occasions, the new national emblem was constructed of hand-embroidered silver wire upon a grey-blue cloth backing. Only officer visored caps were noted, having a silver wire winged wreath/cockade worn in conjunction with a silver metal cogwheel and eagle. A white removable top was available for wear during the summer months. No photographs of this visored cap being worn have been found.

Author's Collection

Civilian Technicians' visored cap. Regulations indicated that if the cap band insigne was embroidered, the cap top insigne should also be embroidered (except on white top caps).

White top Generalluftzeug-meister visored cap for summer wear. This specimen was manufactured late in the war as its visor is made of lacquered cardboard.

Author's Collection

[35]UM. July 15, 1941.

Generalluftzeugmeister visored cap with hand-embroidered cogwheel and national emblem.

## Truppensonderdienst der Luftwaffe

Luftwaffe officers in the TSD (Verwaltungsdienst) wore the basic airforce visored cap.[36]

## Cap Band (Mützenband)

Colored cap bands were worn on several occasions over the regular mohair cap band. Umpires (Schiedsrichter), runway officials (Startleiter), and persons assigned duties during field exercises wore a white cotton band, 4cm wide. The length of this band was approximately 75cm. The band was held in place by clamps. One end of the band had a matte white stainless buckle, measuring 4.7cm.[37]

A yellow-to-red reversible band was also worn during field maneuvers, yellow indicating soldiers who were put out of action during the war games. Red indicated the "Rote Partei," or the mock enemy.[38]

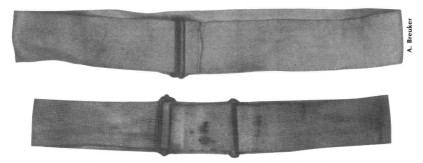

Two variations of the white Luftwaffe cap band.

---

[36]*Deutsche Uniformen-Zeitschrift (DUZ). Nr. 7, July 1944, p. 2.*
[37]*Anzugordnung für die Luftwaffe (L.Dv. 422). Abschnitt A, Berlin, November 27, 1935, p. 94.*
[38]*Ibid., Abschnitt B, Berlin 1935, p. 25.*

These bands could also be worn around the visorless field cap, covering the flaps.[39]

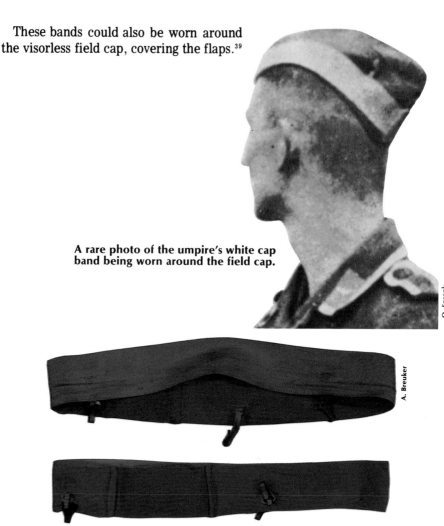

A rare photo of the umpire's white cap band being worn around the field cap.

O. Spronk

A. Breuker

The yellow/red cap band (top). The cap band on bottom is with the red side out.

### Traditions Badges (Erinnerungsabzeichen)

The wearing of insignia of any style as a traditions badge (Geschwader- u. Staffelabzeichen) on Luftwaffe caps was not permitted (Uniformen- Markt. Nr. 7, April 1, 1942, p. 50).

Two exceptions to this order were the standard army mountain troops' Edelweiss which was sometimes worn by Luftwaffe troops on the left side of their mountain cap, who were assigned to mountain duty as weather specialists, aircraft warning service personnel, etc. The most commonly worn traditions badge was the "Division Meindl" badge in Russia in 1943. This badge was the trademark of General Meindl and he and some of his officers

[39]*Anzugordnung für die Luftwaffe (L.Dv. 422). Abschnitt A. Berlin, November 27, 1935, p. 94.*

wore it on the side of their M43 field caps. Meindl has also been observed wearing this badge while at Normandy in 1944, as well as General Schimpf, CO of the 3rd Parachute Division at Normandy.

**This Luftwaffe Obergefreiter wears the army mountain troops' Edelweiss on the left side of his mountain cap.**

George Petersen

v. Hungen

**"Division Meindl" badge.**

George Petersen

**General Schimpf wearing the "Meindl" badge in Normandy, 1944.**

275

### Visorless Field Cap (Fliegermütze)

This field cap was developed for the DLV in 1933, and its form was carried over by the Luftwaffe in 1935. The Fliegermütze was worn by all ranks and was made of grey-blue material. Enlisted men and NCOs wore the cap in wool (Grundtuch), and officers and generals in doeskin or tricot material. Privately purchased caps by enlisted men/NCOs can be found of officer-quality material, while officer's versions can be upgraded enlisted rank's caps.

The shape of the cap was known as Schiffchenform, having gently sloping side panels. The front and rear of the cap were approximately 9.5cm high, being approximately 11cm in the middle of the cap (the size of the flap measuring about 5cm high at the front and back, and 7.5cm in the middle). The front center of the flap was tacked to the body by two stitches.

Field caps for enlisted men and NCOs were lined in grey-blue twill, as were some officer models. Private purchase EM/NCO caps and officer's caps were normally lined in satin-type lining. Variations, however, can be found in all models, depending on the manufacturer. The cap size was stamped in black ink on the lining, as well as the manufacturer's name in many cases. Early issue caps also had the oweners unit stamped inside. Later issue caps normally have a RBN manufacturer's code stamp. Additionally, some officer's models have a front half or full leather sweatband.

The national emblem, worn by all ranks, was sewn to the center of the cap front. The early issue caps retained the DLV eagle, with or without the cockade, and was eventually replaced by the Luftwaffe eagle as stocks became

(Left) The first Luftwaffe EM/NCOs continued to wear the DLV field cap. This airman is shown wearing the cap with only the eagle. The photo is dated 1935. (Right) This Luftwaffe Unteroffizier wears the cap with the DLV national emblem and the national colors cockade. Note the mixture of DLV and early Luftwaffe insignia being worn. This was a normal practice during the first months of the Luftwaffe's existence until sufficient stocks of Luftwaffe insignia became available.

available. Enlisted ranks wore an eagle embroidered in grey cotton thread upon a grey-blue backing.[40] Senior officer candidates (Oberfähnrich, etc.) and officers (Leutnant to Oberst) wore the enlisted rank's eagle, or more commonly, a hand-embroidered aluminum wire national emblem. The wingspan of the early national emblem measured approximately 5.5cm, but this was changed to 6.7cm in 1937.[41] It should be noted that many variations exist, depending upon the manufacturer or time period. Later war specimens were produced on a thin cloth backing, and machine-woven examples exist but were rarely observed being worn.

George Petersen

Illustrated are most of the known variations of the Luftwaffe EM/NCO national emblem used on the field cap. They range from machine-embroidery on grey-blue wool to the late war versions on thin cotton. A machine-woven example is at the lower left.

---

[40]*Anzugordnung für die Luftwaffe (L.Dv. 422). Abschnitt A. Berlin, November 27, 1935, p. 123.*
[41]*LVBl. Nr. 225, May 16, 1935, p. 102.*

Issue EM/NCO caps were unpiped, but for a short period of time (dates unknown) piped versions were produced and worn. In these cases, the branch color (Waffenfarbe) was sewn to the leading edge of the flap. In a privately published insignia and uniform booklet (dated 1942) a red piped field cap is illustrated, but little is known about this model field cap. Illustrated below are variations of the piped field cap.

George Petersen

EM/NCO field caps with colored piping (Waffenfarbe) on the leading edge of the flap. The far left and far right examples are made of officer quality material and the center three are issue caps made of wool. Piping colors are (from left to right) green, white, yellow, red and brown. All have the twisted cord piping except the center cap which is piped in yellow wool.

P. Pauwels

P. Pauwels

Excellent study of the Fliegermütze in wear, front and side views.

This enlisted ranks' field cap exhibits the typical machine-embroidered national emblem and cockade.

The Luftwaffe field cap for enlisted men and non-commissioned officers is shown being worn.

The manufacturer's stamp and date of manufacture is shown inside the enlisted rank's field cap at right. The owner's name tag is sewn in.

Senior officer candidates (Oberfähnrich, etc.) and officers (Leutnant to Oberst) wore a 3mm aluminum piping sewn to the leading edge of the cap flap. Normal cap piping or twisted cord as worn on the uniform collar was utilized. It should be noted that some officers wore EM/NCO caps which had been upgraded to officer status. General officers wore caps piped with gilt cord, with the national emblem in gilt (normally in hand-embroidered wire or of yellow nylon thread).

Officer's field cap with hand-embroidered national emblem in aluminum wire and an EM/NCO style machine-enbroidered cockade.

Officer's field cap with both insignia of the EM/NCO machine-embroidered style.

George Petersen

George Petersen

George Petersen

Luftwaffe non-regulation officer's field cap, in the style of the army M38 officer's cap with aluminum piping around the top and on the front scallop of the flap. Note the hand-embroidered aluminum wire national emblem and cockade.

Author's Collection

George Petersen

Two versions of the officer's national emblem in hand-embroidered aluminum wire for the Fliegermütze.

J.R. Angolia

George Petersen

Generalmajor Theo Osterkamp as commander of a Jagdgeschwader wearing a field cap with twisted gilt cord piping, a hand-embroidered national emblem and a padded EM/NCO cockade.

Officers of a bomber unit on the channel coast in 1940, during the early stages of the battle of Britain. All are wearing the field cap with EM/NCO insignia.

General officer's field cap with gilt piping and hand-embroidered gilt wire national emblem and aluminum wire cockade.

George Petersen

George Petersen

General officer's national emblems for the field cap. The version at top is hand-embroidered gilt wire and the one at right is of yellow Celleon/nylon.

All ranks wore the national cockade, which was introduced in May 1935, on the front center of the cap flap. Enlisted ranks wore the cockade, machine-embroidered in black/white/red thread. Machine-woven (BeVo) cockades also were produced but are normally found only on the M43 field cap. Officer candidates, officers and generals wore the cockade hand-embroidered in aluminum wire. The outer black ring (4mm) was enclosed on both sides by a narrow twisted aluminum wire, followed by an aluminum, hand-embroidered wire ring (4mm) with a narrow twisted aluminum wire inner border, enclosing a red wool center (4mm). Officers and generals have also been observed wearing the EM/NCO style of national cockade.

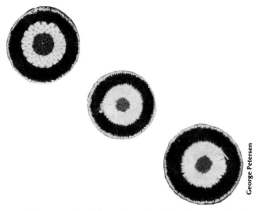

George Petersen

Basic patterns of the machine-embroidered national colors cockade worn on the field cap, which range from the "padded" style to the late war "flat" style.

(Above) Officers' field cap with hand-embroidered aluminum insignia and aluminum cord piping.

Luftwaffe reserve officers wore the Maltese cross cockade in the center of the cap flap for a brief period of time.[42] The 8mm red field had a 7mm metal cross, and the total diameter was 22mm (LVBl, Nr. 326, June 21, 1935, p. 149).

## Black Visorless Field Cap (Arbeitsmütze)

Luftwaffe mechanics and ground crews (fitters, machinists, bomb loaders, etc.) wore a black twill field cap similar in form to the grey-blue Fliegermütze. The cap was actually available in both a black twill and a cream colored twill to match the color of the work/fatigue uniform of the Luftwaffe.

(Above) A black cotton twill version of the work cap. (Right) A cream-colored version of the work cap with white on black national emblem. No cream-colored backed national emblem is known to exist.

---

[42]LVBl. Nr. 326, June 21, 1935, p. 149.

The cap was slightly smaller than its grey-blue counterpart, measuring 9cm in the front and rear, and 10.7cm in the center.[43] These caps were lined with either a black or cream cotton, and in some cases, a grey cotton. Similar size/manufacturer/unit stamps as in the grey-blue Fliegermütze were utilized. For unknown purposes, padded linings were also available for use.

The only insigne worn on this cap was the machine-embroidered white on black national emblem. Flakartillerie personnel (probably others as well) were allowed to wear this cap during training courses.[44]

The early (1935) and later (1937) national emblems for wear on the work cap (machine-embroidered white on black). The bottom example (1937) is unfinished with white thread line for trimming.

The black Arbeitsmütze being worn by ground personnel.

---

[43]*Anzugordnung für die Luftwaffe (L.Dv. 422). Abschnitt A. Berlin, 1935, Anhang I: Sonderbekleidung, p. 59.*

[44]*Besondere Luftwaffe-Bestimmungen. Nr. 149, April 8, 1938, p. 82.*

## Visored Field Caps (Bergmütze and Feldmütze)

A grey-blue mountain style cap was officially introduced in 1937, and was meant to be worn only in sports and skiing activities.[45] In 1939, this same cap was issued to Flak and signals units stationed in mountain areas while on aircraft spotting duty, weather service, etc. It was made of standard grey-blue wool, and had a short cloth visor similar to the army's Bergmütze. The normal machine-embroidered Luftwaffe national emblem and cockade were worn on the cap with one small metal button holding the front flap in position. Officers' models had a 3mm aluminum piping around the crown.

EM/NCO Bergmütze with short visor, single grey-blue button, and machine-embroidered national emblem and cockade (dated 1942).

A single-button Bergmütze with small grey-blue button being worn by a Luftwaffe Unteroffizier of flying troops.

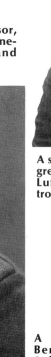

A single-button version of the Bergmütze being worn by this Stabsgefreiter of construction troops in a Luftschutz school. Note the large aluminum-colored button.

[45]*Anzugordnung für die Luftwaffe (L.Dv. 422). Abschnitt A. Berlin, April 1, 1937,* p. 62.

Officer's grey-blue doeskin Bergmütze with small, single aluminum button, aluminum piping and hand-embroidered aluminum wire national emblem/cockade.

*George Petersen*

*George Petersen via Alfred Otte*

Zahlmeister (Paymaster) Alfred Otte, an administrative official in officer rank from the "General Göring" Regiment, wearing the officer's Bergmütze with aluminum piping and small single aluminum button.

In 1942/1943 the Luftwaffe adopted this style of visored field cap for use in its field divisions, parachute units and by other ground-based personnel. Early issue caps had a short visor and one metal flap button (small or large size, as

Standard M43 cap for enlisted men and NCOs.

*Anthony Jessen*

well as a single plastic button), and were similar to the pre-war mountain caps. When the army adopted the Einheitsmütze (M43) as its standard field cap, the Luftwaffe did so as well. The new cap featured a two-button flap and a higher peak. It should be noted that both the one and two button models were produced throughout the late war years.

EM/NCO caps were not piped, whereas senior officer candidates, administration officials of officer rank, and officers with the rank of Leutnant to Oberst wore a 3mm aluminum piping around the crown of their caps. General officers' caps were piped in gold or yellow Celleon. EM/NCO caps had grey-blue pebbled metal or plastic flap buttons, officers' versions had silver buttons,[46] and generals had gilt buttons.

**Generalleutnant Hermann Plocher wearing a M43 cap with gilt buttons and piping.**

**Luftwaffe officer's M43 cap with aluminum buttons and piping.**

John Coy

**Officer's Bergmütze with single large button closure, aluminum piping, and two-piece EM/NCO insignia.**

Noehren

---

Fine quality, doeskin M43 cap for general officers with gilt piping, hand-embroidered gilt wire national emblem, hand-embroidered cockade, and two small gilt flap buttons.

George Petersen

Early issue caps were made of quality wool and retained their shape but late war versions were made of thin wool with poor quality lining and had no shape. Variations exist as it was common to see private-purchase caps worn which had been produced in Germany as well as any of the occupied countries. For example, Luftwaffe M43 caps manufactured in Italy, were sometimes constructed of Italian air force, grey-blue wool. Some caps have half or full leather sweatbands.

The visored caps (commonly called M43 caps) were lined in either grey cotton or a grey-blue silk-like material. The cap size was stamped inside. Early issue caps also had a manufacturer's stamp while later issues normally carried the manufacturer's RBN number.

The national emblem and cockade could be affixed separately or, later, could be combined on a grey-blue trapezoid-shaped backing. Officers wore either hand-embroidered aluminum wire insignia or the standard EM/NCO pattern, according to personal preference. When the two-button model cap was worn, the flap normally covered the national cockade with only the national emblem showing.

Anthony Jessen

John Coy

(Left) Enlisted ranks' M43 cap with one-piece insigne (see above).

George Petersen

Detailed photo of the national emblem and cockade as worn on the Bergmütze and M43 cap. At left is a 1935 style national emblem and machine-woven cockade; and at right is a 1937 style national emblem and "padded" machine-embroidered cockade. Any combination of insignia can be found as existing stocks of insignia were utilized at either the factory or as replacements at the unit level.

On rare occasions some officers and generals wore the appropriate aluminum or gilt cap cords on their M43 caps. The most commonly observed example is that of General Meindl, who wore gilt cap cords while commanding "Division Meindl" in Russia in 1942/1943, and later at Normandy as commander of the II. Fallschirmkorps.

George Petersen

Generalleutnant Meindl is shown wearing a single-button EM/NCO wool Bergmütze with gilt cap cords and side buttons added. He also wears the traditions badge of the Luftwaffe "Division Meindl" on the left side of his cap. He is decorating paratroopers at the Normandy front in 1944 as commander of the II. Fallschirmkorps.

Generalkommissar Alfred Frauenfeld is at left and a Luftwaffe officer wearing a mountain cap with cap cords is at right.

Field caps constructed of camouflage material were popular with combat troops in field divisions, paratrooper units, and other ground units. They could be either one or two-button versions with fold-down flaps, or could be like the tropical field cap without buttons or fold-down flaps. The most commonly encountered caps are made from "splinter" camouflage material to match the shelter-quarter or jump smock. Italian camouflage material was also widely used in the Italian theater, or by troops on any front who had at one time been stationed there. To date, no "water" pattern camouflage caps have been observed.

M43 style cap made of "splinter" pattern camouflage material. This version has turn-down flaps, two small plastic flap buttons, and a standard machine-embroidered national emblem.

Paratroop General Ramcke wears a M43-style cap made of Italian camouflage material.

Combined Luftwaffe M43 cap insignia in trapezoid form exist on a field-grey backing and are believed to have been worn on field-grey M43 caps (standard army models) by Luftwaffe Sturmgeschütz crews who wore the field-grey field dress of armor design. It was also probably worn with the short, field-grey M44 jacket which was used by the Luftwaffe in limited numbers.

## Crash Helmet (Sturzhelm)

Luftwaffe motorcyclists were equipped in 1935 with a black cowhide oval helmet. No special insignia was worn. It consisted of six leather parts sewn together. The edges were piped in the same material and stuffed with felt. Twelve metal air vents were positioned around the edges with four extra screened vents (14mm in diameter) being inserted on each side of it.

A black leather visor was sewn to the front of the helmet, being 4.5cm at its widest part. A 1.6cm wide leather chinstrap was attached to the helmet, and could be removed by unsnapping it. The chinstrap had two metal slides to adjust it for a proper fit.

A sheepskin sweat band was sewn onto a 2cm wide leather strap. The helmet was lined in black cotton stuffed with wadding and gauze.

The neck protection flap was made from cowhide and was attached to the helmet by two metal snaps, 13mm in diameter. Two leather flaps covered the wearer's ears. A smaller flap unsnapped on the ear flaps, to allow the cyclist better hearing.[47]

The use of this helmet was discontinued by an order issued April 1, 1938. The standard Luftwaffe steel helmet was to be worn thereafter by motorcyclists.[48]

George Petersen

The pre-war motorcyclist helmet is use by a courier of a flak unit. Note that the license plate on his BMW motorcycle has been obliterated for security reasons.

---

[47]*Anzugordnung für die Luftwaffe. Anhang I: Sonderbekleidung. Berlin, 1935,* pp. 72-74.

[48]*Besondere Luftwaffe-Bestimmungen. Nr. 179, May 23, 1938, p. 105.*

Luftwaffe motorcyclist protective helmet. This style helmet was used by the Luftwaffe as well as the army and police. Luftwaffe-issue helmets will, however, be marked with "L.B.A." (Luftwaffe Bekleidungs-Amt - Luftwaffe Clothing Office) and a date of manufacture. This particular helmet is marked "L.B.A.37." Since this was a pre-war piece of headgear, it is not uncommon to see unit markings inside.

## Tropical Headdress

Tropical uniforms and headdress worn by the first Luftwaffe personnel in North Africa were taken from existing army stocks and were olive-green in color. Period photos show that it was not uncommon for Luftwaffe enlisted ranks and officers to stitch the Luftwaffe national emblem directly over the army pattern on the jacket and cap, to replace the army pattern, or to simply continue wearing the army national emblems.

In early 1941 the khaki-brown, Luftwaffe issue tropical clothing was introduced. According to the "Uniformen-Markt," this new color was already in use by other foreign armies, and was to become the distinguishing mark for Luftwaffe tropical clothing.[49]

A tropical version of the field cap (Fliegermütze) was worn by all ranks. It was made of khaki-brown cotton material, and was lined in either red or tan cloth. Manufacturer's name, cap size, or later, a RBN number were stamped on the lining. The standard 1937 style Luftwaffe national emblem was worn on the field cap, normally machine-embroidered on a khaki background. This insigne was either trimmed around the edge, folded in a triangular form, or folded in a triangular form with the top portion turned under the eagle's wings. This pattern was worn on both the EM/NCO and officer caps. The national cockade was normally machine-embroidered in a "padded" or "flat"

---

[49]UM, Nr. 13, July 1, 1941, p. 121.

This Flak Oberleutnant wears the army olive-green uniform. Only his collar insignia and Flakkampfabzeichen indicate he is a member of the Luftwaffe.

O. Spronk

EM/NCO tropical Fliegermütze with standard machine-embroidered national emblem and cockade.

George Petersen

Interior view of an EM/NCO tropical Fliegermütze with tan lining, showing various markings often encountered.

293

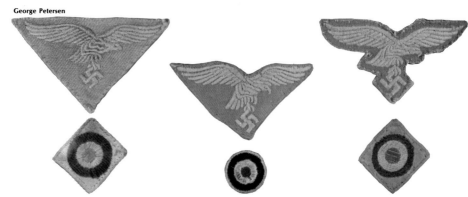

Basic patterns of machine-embroidered national emblems as worn on the tropical field cap, the M43, and the tropical visored cap. Also shown are two basic forms of the machine-embroidered cockade and a machine-woven version at far right.

This Luftwaffe Gefreiter wears the tropical Fliegermütze in a "jaunty" manner.

style, and could have the underlay folded under to form a diamond shape. Machine-woven cockades were manufactured, but were used mainly on M43 style caps.

Senior officer candidates (Oberfähnrich), administrative officials in officer rank, and officers with the rank of Leutnant to Oberst wore a 3mm aluminum piping around the top of the cap flap. Officers were authorized to wear a hand-embroidered aluminum wire national emblem and cockade on khaki, but this practice was uncommon, as it was more efficient to have cloth insignia for wear in the field and for cleaning purposes. General officers wore gilt or Celleon insignia and piping.

A grey-blue cotton version of the tropical Fliegermütze was also worn in tropical areas. This cap matched the blue cotton tropical uniform and the blue cloth-covered tropical helmet.

Officer's tropical Fliegermütze with aluminum piping and EM/NCO pattern machine-embroidered insignia.

Knight's Cross holder Oberleutnant Freytag, a well-known fighter pilot in the Mediterranean theater, is shown wearing the officer's tropical Fliegermütze. The photo is dated 1942.

The grey-blue cotton tropical Fliegermütze, dated 1942, with normal machine-embroidered cap insignia.

295

A khaki-brown M43 style cap was worn by all ranks stationed in tropical areas. This cap was similar to the army style but the crown was normally not as high. It had non-functional side flaps and no buttons. The lining was either of red or tan cloth and carried the manufacturer and cap size stamp, or the RBN number. Sometimes only the cap size was stamped on the lining. The insignia for this cap was the same as for the Fliegermütze, and could be in any combination of national emblem and cockade style.

Helga Sichermann-Spielhagen

George Petersen

(Left) Luftwaffe tropical EM/NCO M43 style cap being worn with standard machine-embroidered insignia. (Right) Tropical M43 style cap being worn with a padded national colors cockade and a metal national emblem as worn on the tropical helmet (note eagle faces to wearer's right).

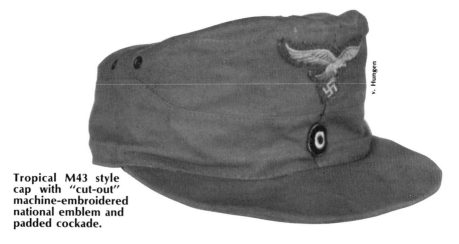

v. Hungen

Tropical M43 style cap with "cut-out" machine-embroidered national emblem and padded cockade.

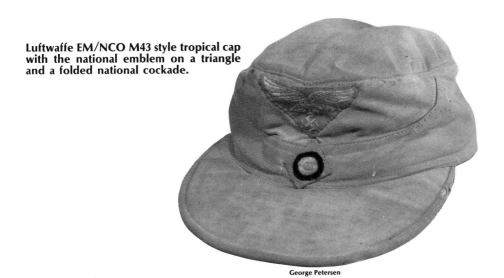

Luftwaffe EM/NCO M43 style tropical cap with the national emblem on a triangle and a folded national cockade.

George Petersen

Senior officer candidates, administrative officials in officer rank, and all officer grades wore aluminum piping around the crown of the cap and many times on the front scallop. It was common to upgrade an EM/NCO cap to officer grade by adding a 3mm twisted aluminum cord to the crown of the cap. Officers could wear either machine-embroidered or hand-embroidered insignia. General officers wore the visored field cap with a gilt or Celleon national emblem and piping.

George Petersen

George Petersen

(Above) Luftwaffe officer's M43 style tropical cap with aluminum piping around the crown and front scallop, and machine-embroidered insignia. (Left) This Luftwaffe Hauptmann is wearing an officer's tropical M43 style cap with hand-embroidered aluminum wire national emblem on a khaki backing and a padded cockade.

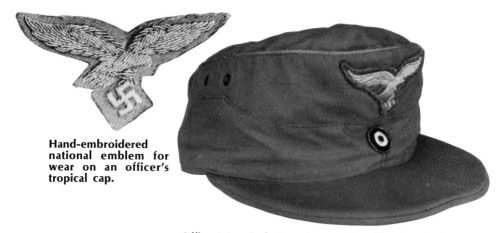

Hand-embroidered national emblem for wear on an officer's tropical cap.

Officer's tropical visored cap with enlisted ranks' insignia. Note that this cap does not have the aluminum piping around the front scallop.

George Petersen

A Luftwaffe officer in charge of a mixed service film unit, wearing a tropical officer's M43 style cap with a metal national emblem from a tropical helmet and a padded national cockade.

Hauptmann Hans v. Teusen, a Knight's Cross holder from Fsch.-Jäg.Rgt. 2, wears the officer's tropical visored cap with twisted aluminum cord piping around the crown.

The tropical field visored cap (Tropenschirmmütze) was introduced for wear by all ranks in 1942. The cap top, cap band and visor were made of khaki-brown cotton with the band being semi-stiff to give the cap shape. Air vents (small open or large screened) are found on each side of the cap top underside. It is similar to the Kriegsmarine model but has a larger visor and was issued with a neck flap (Nackenschutz). The neck flap was attached to the cap by three metal or plastic buttons at the rear base of the cap band, and was designed to protect the wearer from exposure to the sun but was unpopular and often discarded. The cap has a red lining and is marked with the manufacturer's name and cap size, or RBN number. EM/NCO models were issued with a soft thin leather chinstrap (black outside, tan inside) with two black painted adjustment buckles. The side buttons were either metal or plastic.

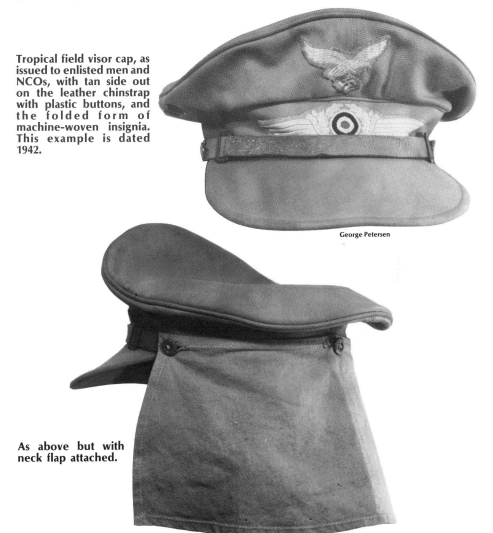

Tropical field visor cap, as issued to enlisted men and NCOs, with tan side out on the leather chinstrap with plastic buttons, and the folded form of machine-woven insignia. This example is dated 1942.

George Petersen

As above but with neck flap attached.

George Petersen

The Luftwaffe tropical visor cap shown at right is with machine-embroidered national emblem and padded cockade. The thin leather chinstrap is shown with correct side out (black).

George Petersen

The Generalmajor (far left), wearing the sleeve patch for Sonderverband 287/288, and the Oberstleutnant are both wearing officers' versions of the tropical visor cap. The Generalmajor's cap has hand-embroidered insignia and the Oberstleutnant's cap has standard machine-woven insignia.

Tropical visor cap with officer's twisted aluminum cap cords, machine-embroidered national emblem, and a padded cockade.

Richard Long

The insignia worn on this cap consisted of a machine-woven national emblem and winged wreath/cockade. The backing was either folded underneath to conform to the outline of the woven insignia or folded in a block form (in a triangular form for the national emblem). Optional insignia worn could consist of a standard machine-embroidered national emblem and cockade of any style.

Machine-woven national emblem and winged wreath/cockade as worn on the tropical visor cap. The edges of these examples have been folded under before being sewn on.

As above, but the national emblem is unfolded as it would come off a roll of insignia, and the winged wreath/cockade has had its edges folded under to conform to the insigne's outline.

The true officer's model of this tropical visored cap has 3mm aluminum piping around the top and bottom of the cap band. It was originally issued with machine-woven insignia of flat aluminum wire, but was worn with other combinations. At this writing it has not been determined if the officer's model was issued with a twisted aluminum cap cord or the thin leather style chinstrap. According to period photos, officers preferred to wear the aluminum cap cords. It was common for an officer to take an EM/NCO model and add aluminum cap cords, and even aluminum side buttons. Period photos also show general officers wearing this cap with hand-embroidered insignia, and assuming that standard German practice was followed, the piping and insignia were probably gilt.

George Petersen via Jim Peterson

A true issue officer's tropical visor cap, with aluminum piping and machine-woven flat aluminum wire insignia. The twisted aluminum cap cords are only pinned on the cap and it is, therefore, uncertain which model chinstrap was issued with the officer's model.

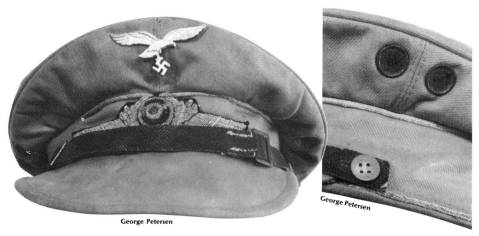

George Petersen

George Petersen

(Above left) An issue officer's tropical visor cap with aluminum piping. At some time the wearer has replaced the original insignia with a metal EM/NCO visored cap national emblem and an officer's hand-embroidered winged wreath/cockade. The chinstrap is the thin leather version. (Above) Detailed photo of the 3mm aluminum piping around the cap crown and on the top and bottom of the cap band, as well as the screened vents.

## Tropical Helmet (Tropenhelm)

The first tropical helmets worn by Luftwaffe personnel were the army olive-green model, with army side shields, which were all that was available early in the North African campaign. In 1941 the Luftwaffe developed and issued its own tropical helmet, made of khaki-brown colored canvas, and similar in design to that of the army. It was lined in red or tan cloth with the manufacturer's name, and later the RBN number, stamped on the lining. The helmet size was stamped under the sweatband. The most common color encountered is the khaki-brown version, but a light olive-green helmet was also produced and issued. Additionally, a blue cotton canvas model was produced for wear with the tropical blue uniform.

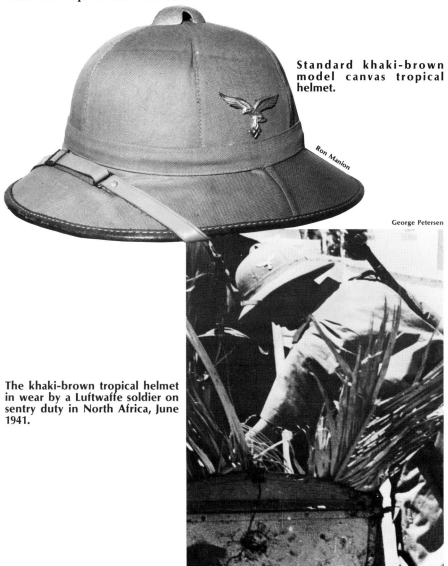

Standard khaki-brown model canvas tropical helmet.

Ron Manion

George Petersen

The khaki-brown tropical helmet in wear by a Luftwaffe soldier on sentry duty in North Africa, June 1941.

303

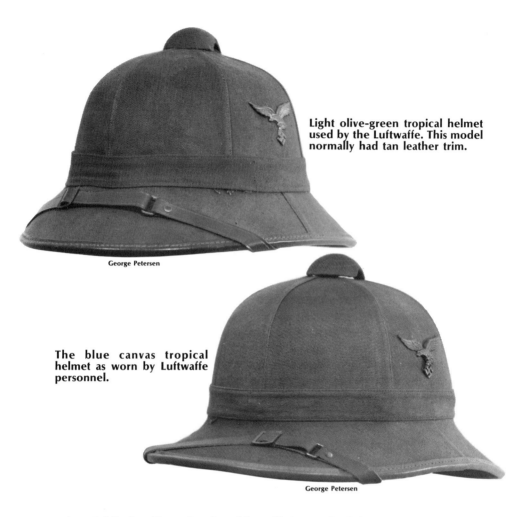

Light olive-green tropical helmet used by the Luftwaffe. This model normally had tan leather trim.

George Petersen

The blue canvas tropical helmet as worn by Luftwaffe personnel.

George Petersen

A metal Luftwaffe national emblem (flying to the left) was worn on the left side of the tropical helmet and a red/white/black national colors shield was on the right. Early production metal helmet insignia were made of stamped brass and later versions were made of light metal.

George Petersen

Metal national colors shield and Luftwaffe national emblem, facing left, for use on the tropical helmet. The above insignia are stamped brass.

It was a common practice to utilize captured tropical helmets. Paratroopers on Crete wore British models, and captured stocks of Dutch and French helmets also saw considerable use by German forces. Also, any style of army or navy tropical helmet acquired by a Luftwaffe individual or unit was worn, normally with the proper Luftwaffe national emblem added. Additionally, officers could wear private-purchase models.

It should be noted that tropical helmets were not always practical in the field and were not made available to every unit in tropical areas. Thus, many soldiers wore the cloth field cap instead.

Generalmajor Stefan Fröhlich wears a private-purchase tropical helmet without insignia.

Captured stocks of Dutch-style tropical helmets are distributed by a Luftwaffe Flak NCO, on the Mediterranean coast in June 1943. Normally no insignia was worn on these helmets and were mainly used on garrison duty.

### Head Protector (Kopfschützer)

The form and shape of the Kopfschützer like that worn in the army and navy was of grey-blue material (a blend of wool and worsted tricot). It was meant to be worn while on guard duty since 1935.[50] From 1937 it was to be used by mechanics. This head protector measured 41cm in length, 25cm in width.

### Southwester (Südwester)

The Southwester was introduced to the Luftwaffe for duties in bad weather on airfields and for wear by crews of ships serving with the Luftwaffe in 1935. It was made of black Öltuch, or oil cloth (also, coated canvas or tarpaulin). The cap consisted of a four-part hood with a wide-stitched brim, stuffed with gauze and a doubled, sewn together, neck protector. The crown portion was lined with wool or other materials. Two long (25cm) cloth laces were sewn below the brim.[51] They were tied in a bow under the wearer's chin.

The color of the Southwester was changed from green to grey in 1937, and its use was extended to mechanics and ground personnel on airfields.

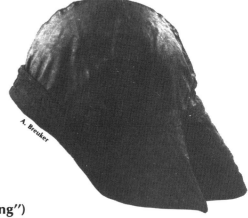

### Regiment "General Göring" (later Division "Hermann Göring")

On September 24, 1935 the Landespolizeigruppe "General Göring" was renamed Regiment "General Göring," and from that point on was part of the Luftwaffe.

The field-grey Landespolizei uniforms were worn until approximately March 1936, the visored cap having the standard Luftwaffe metal insignia. LPG "General Göring" officers wore the early style, hand-embroidered national emblem and winged wreath/cockade. After that, regular Luftwaffe uniforms were worn by the new regiment. The grey-blue enlisted ranks' visored cap was piped in the basic white branch-of-service color around the crown and above and below the black mohair band. Regiment "General Göring" officers wore the basic Luftwaffe officers' visored cap. In general, it can be said that all forms of Luftwaffe headdress were worn by members of this regiment and later the Division "Hermann Göring."

---

[50]*Anzugordnung für die Luftwaffe (L.Dv. 422). Abschnitt B. Berlin 1935, p. 51.*
[51]*Ibid. Anhang I: Sonderbekleidung, p. 64.*

This member of LPG "General Göring" wears the green Schutzpolizei uniform with proper insignia, late 1935.

This photo was taken shortly after LPG "General Göring" was transferred into the Luftwaffe on September 23, 1935. Members continued to wear their Landespolizei uniform for six months but with the addition of a Luftwaffe breast eagle and Luftwaffe cap insignia.

George Petersen via Alfred Otte

Enlisted men/NCOs of LPG "General Göring," with Oberleutnant Weidermann of the 1st Company, in 1935. Note the early Luftwaffe hand-embroidered national emblem and winged wreath on the officer's cap.

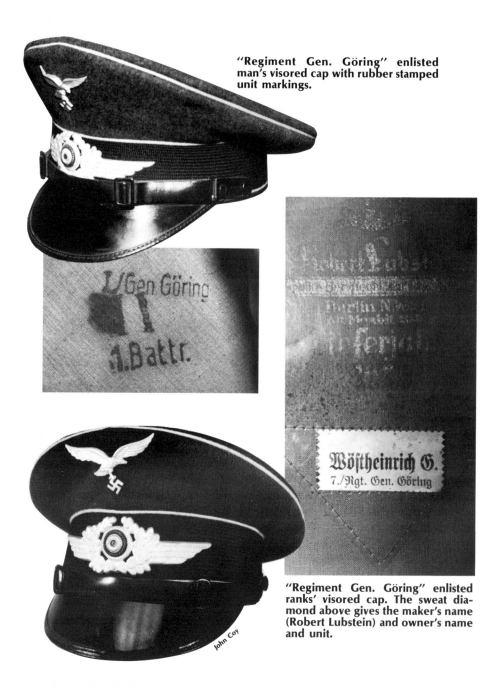

"Regiment Gen. Göring" enlisted man's visored cap with rubber stamped unit markings.

"Regiment Gen. Göring" enlisted ranks' visored cap. The sweat diamond above gives the maker's name (Robert Lubstein) and owner's name and unit.

In April 1938 the black Panzer beret (Schutzmütze) was introduced for use within the Luftwaffe, to be worn by crews of armored vehicles, armored reconnaissance cars, and tank crews of Regiment "General Göring."[52] The standard army model was utilized with the addition of Luftwaffe insignia. It is believed that the Luftwaffe national emblem, machine-embroidered on black,

[52]*Besondere Luftwaffe-Bestimmungen. Nr. 161, April 23, 1938, p. 97.*

and the national colors cockade, also on a black backing, were used, but to date no close-up photos of the beret in wear have been discovered. The use of this beret was discontinued in January 1941.

George Petersen via Alfred Otte

7.5cm Pz.Kpfw. IVs of Regiment "General Göring" at Berlin-Reinickendorf in 1939. Note that the tank crews are wearing the Panzer beret.

The black wool M43 cap was introduced for wear by tank or armored vehicle crews in the mid-war years, and was identical in design to the grey-blue models. Officers' versions had 3mm aluminum piping around the crown of the cap. Aluminum or grey-blue flap buttons have been observed on the black M43 cap. Normally, only a size stamp can be found on the lining.

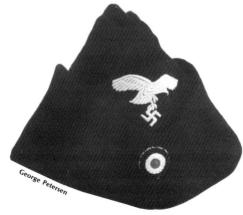

George Petersen

George Petersen

Black Panzer EM/NCO Fliegermütze. Both emblems are machine-embroidered on black.

Officer's black Panzer Fliegermütze with hand-embroidered aluminum wire insignia.

Gefreiter Horst Flemming, 14./Sturmgesch. Art. Rgt. HG, wears a black wool field cap with black-backed national emblem (Italy, 1943).

Horst Flemming

George Petersen

This "Hermann Göring" Division member and Knight's Cross holder wears a black wool field cap with grey-blue backed national emblem and cockade. Note the white Soutache.

A black Fliegermütze was also worn by armored vehicle crews of all ranks. Enlisted men and NCOs wore a black wool cap with a machine-embroidered or machine-woven national emblem and a cockade, both on a black backing. It should be noted that cockades on a grey-blue backing have also been observed being worn. Officer's models were piped with a 3mm aluminum cord around the flaps, and carried either EM/NCO or hand-embroidered aluminum wire insignia on a black backing.

Luftwaffe enlisted rank's M43 cap in black for tank crews.

Basic Panzer headgear as used by "Hermann Göring" Division tank crews. At left is Major Rossmann, commander of the Fsch.Pz.Rgt. "Hermann Göring," wearing a black M43 officer's cap with one-piece insignia on a grey-blue trapezoid backing. The officer in the center wears a black officer's Fliegermütze and an assault gun jacket. The NCO at right wears an EM/NCO black Fliegermütze (Russia, late 1944).

Officer's black M43 cap with aluminum piping and buttons, machine-embroidered on black EM/NCO national emblem and a hand-embroidered cockade.

311

### Flying Helmets (Fliegerkopfhaube)

Several types of flying helmets were worn by Luftwaffe flight personnel; unlined models for summer use, fleece or fur-lined models for winter use, with and without earphones, and with or without oxygen mask fittings. Their useage was based upon the type of aircraft flown and the weather conditions. Special models also existed for test pilots at aircraft factories, as well as for aircraft commanders.

The following descriptions of early summer and winter issue flying helmets are from official Luftwaffe regulations,[53] but apply to later models as well.

### Summer Flying Helmets

The helmet was manufactured in medium-brown linen material. The interior lining was "Stahlgrau," or "steel grey," a dark grey satin (Satinella). The upper edge of the helmet was to rest 1cm above the wearer's eyebrows. The helmet was constructed of five parts sewn together with ribbon and edged on the inside with the same material. The corners at the front of the forehead had a small piece of leather for padding. A rubber strip of padding filled with wool (1cm high and 1.5cm long) was first glued, then sewn across the forehead section of the helmet, to ease the weight of the cap on the wearer's brow. The locking chinstrap was made of calves' leather and was 16mm wide. The right strap measured approximately 16cm in length, the left strap was 18cm. Both straps were backed with kidskin and between the calf and kidskin was a linen cloth. The straps were pressed with 14 holes, being 1cm apart. A 5cm long piece of lamb's fleece was glued on the right strap, and a loop was attached. The straps could be fastened by a small buckle.

Loops with snap buttons, measuring 1.8cm wide by 8.5cm long, were sewn around the helmet (cloth or leather type) to hold the goggles strap in place. Two hooks and a leather loop (1.8cm wide by 6cm long) were positioned so that an oxygen mask could be attached to the helmet.

There are two basic models of the summer flying helmet, the first being the Model FK 34 (Fliegerkopfhaube für Sommer ohne FT-Gerät, FK 34), which had no provisions for radio receivers or transmitting microphones. This model was used in training gliders and aircraft without radio equipment, such as training biplanes.

Model FK 34 summer flying helmet without earphone mountings.

J.R. Angolia

A similar helmet was used including the earphone mountings, a throat microphone, and provisions for an oxygen mask (Fliegerkopfhaube für Sommer mit FT-Gerät). The early style helmet for use in aircraft with radio and oxygen equipment was the Model LKp S-53 and can be identified by oval, molded plastic earphone mountings on each side, and no depression for the goggles strap. The microphone and radio receiver equipment for this model and Model LKp S-100 were assigned assorted LN (Luftnachrichten - air signals) stock numbers, plus a basic Luftwaffe stock number of FL 31218.

This Ju 88 pilot is shown wearing the Model LKp S-53 summer flying helmet.

Joe Stone

George Petersen

Model LKp S-53 summer flying helmet showing the oval plastic earphone mountings, throat microphones, and oxygen mask top and side provisions.

The later version of this flying helmet was similar in design but the smooth oval earphone mountings were replaced with leather-covered mountings which had a depression between the raised ear portion and the top of the mounting, which held the goggles strap in place. These models, referred to as LKp S-100 and LKp S-101, were the standard summer flying helmets for the duration of the war. Another variation of this model had no catch on the front top of the helmet for the oxygen mask.

---

[53]*Anzugordnung für die Luftwaffe. (L.Dv. 422.), Abschnitt, Anhang I: Sonderbekleidung, Berlin, 1935, pp. 13-25.*

The LKp S-100 summer flying helmet above is a later version with depressions on the upper portion of the earphone mountings for retaining the goggles strap.

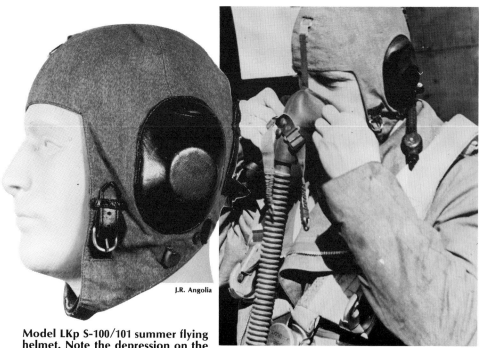

J.R. Angolia

Model LKp S-100/101 summer flying helmet. Note the depression on the side of the earphone mountings to hold the goggles strap.

The oxygen mask is being attached to this Model LKp S-100/101 flying helmet.

A special model for aircraft commanders (Fliegerkopfhaube mit FT für Kommandanten - für Sommer), known as the LKp S-54 and a variation LKp S-53, were also used. It had additional internal features which allowed the wearer to have aircraft to ground communications as well as normal useage.[54]

The remaining style of the summer flying helmet was the net top version, the Model LKp N-101 (Netzkopfhaube). This helmet had a thin mesh net top with leather side cups to hold the radio receivers. The throat microphone consisted of two oval pods; the signals equipment number for this helmet was LN 26670.

On each side of the helmet was a metal retaining knob for attaching the double-strap oxygen mask. One side of the mask was fitted with a quick-release mechanism and it should be noted that this helmet did not have a chinstrap.

Two variations exist of the net top helmet. The first has a short neck cord (5cm long) with plug, which was favored by fighter pilots because it could be easily disconnected when bailing out of their aircraft. This short cord version usually was trimmed in light brown leather. The second variation has a long cord with plug and was used by bomber and other aircraft crews. This helmet was trimmed in dark brown leather.

Side view of the Model LKp N-101 flying helmet with light brown leather trim and 5cm long plug-in cord. Note single aluminum side attachment for the oxygen mask.

---

[54]*Besondere Luftwaffe-Bestimmungen. May 26, 1941.*

The Model LKp N-101 summer net helmet is worn in this pilot's graduation photo. Note the light brown leather trim.

Side view of the Model LKp N-101 with dark brown leather trim and long plug-in cord. Note the goggles (Blendschutzbrille) are held in place by the back loops and depressions on the earphone mountings.

This LKp N-101 net top summer flying helmet was a favorite with fighter pilots. Versions exist with either light or dark brown leather trim.

A special version of the net top helmet was also produced with only cross straps on the top and no netting. These cross straps bore size markings and were used to properly fit the helmet to the wearer.

Other variations of the summer flying helmet exist which were not standard Luftwaffe issue but were worn by personal choice or because of a lack of normal issue equipment. The variations included civilian models, and foreign models such as Italian, Finnish, captured Russian, etc. Additional models, such as that illustrated below, were believed used by test pilots at aircraft factories. The helmet shown is medium blue in color, has the early style (oval) plastic earphone mountings, and a cloth chinstrap with concealed throat microphones. It has a long plug-in cord and the "Siemens" firm label.

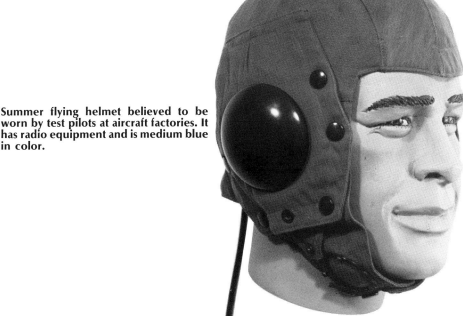

Summer flying helmet believed to be worn by test pilots at aircraft factories. It has radio equipment and is medium blue in color.

George Petersen

## Winter Flying Helmets

As with the summer flying helmets, there were two basic versions of the winter model. The winter flying helmet without radio equipment (Fliegerkopfhaube für Winter ohne FT-Gerät) was known as the FK 33. This model came in various shades of brown kid leather and was normally fleece-lined for warmth. Variations exist with fur lining and have been observed in black or grey leather. These winter models also came with and without the provisions for the oxygen mask. These helmets, without radio equipment, were used in training gliders as well as training aircraft without radios. During the war they were also utilized for warmth by ground personnel assigned to flying units.

Model FF 33 winter flying helmet being worn without radio equipment.

The winter flying helmet with radio equipment (Fliegerkopfhaube für Winter mit FT-Gerät) was known as the LKp S-53 and was assigned the Luftwaffe stock number (Anforderungsnummer) of FL 31219 on October 4, 1937. The early models used oval plastic earphone mountings, and later models had the leather mountings with depressions for the goggles strap. All models had provisions for the oxygen mask.

The special helmet for aircraft commanders (Fliegerkopfhaube für Kommandanten für Winter), was as for the summer model and was designated LKp W-54.

The Model LKp S-53 being worn.

A LKp S-53 fleece-lined winter flying helmet, this one being of black leather.

A Model LKp S-53 flying helmet with oxygen mask. Note the metal wire loop on front of helmet for oxygen mask attachment.

An example of a non-standard winter flying helmet being worn in 1936/37. This model is fleece-lined and has no provisions for radio equipment.

A special cloth cover was manufactured for wear over all models of the flying helmet and was used by crews flying over water. There were at least two different models and came in both white and yellow. They were developed to assist in spotting downed aircrew members in water.

Bomber pilot Hauptmann Werner Baumbach, an oakleaves holder (and later swords), wearing the cover for the flying helmet. This model covers the side of the helmet and is the one most commonly seen.

George Petersen

George Petersen

This Me-109 fighter pilot of the Pik As-Jagdgeschwader wears another version of the flying helmet cover, which only covers the top of the helmet.

## Flight Protection Helmets

The need for aircrew protection from Flak shrapnel became necessary shortly after the start of the war, especially with the ever increasing raids over England.

The first temporary flight protection helmet was the standard M35 Luftwaffe steel helmet. It was worn directly over the flying helmet, and if the fit was not proper, the liner was removed. Examples exist with the sides flared out to accomodate the earphones.

This Oberfeldwebel in a bomber cockpit wears the normal steel helmet over his summer flying helmet.

The first specifically designed flight protection helmet was the Model SSK 90, and was officially adopted for use by the Luftwaffe on May 8, 1941. The most distinctive feature of this helmet was the grab-roll, or comb, attached to the front. The helmet was constructed of dark brown leather covering a 1mm chromium nickel-steel crown. It was manufactured solely by the Siemens company. The helmet had cut-outs on each side to accomodate the earphones of whatever flying helmet it was worn over. Because the SSK 90 was heavy and uncomfortable, it became unpopular with the aircrews and saw only limited useage. It was deemed "unacceptable for service at the front" on May 26, 1941.[55] Although the time of officially sanctioned use was extremely short, the SSK 90 surely saw use before the introductory date and after the date of suggested withdrawal. In postwar publications this flight protection helmet was referred to as a jet pilot's helmet, which was incorrect.

---

[55]*Ibid.*

**Side and rear view of the Fliegerstahlhelm SSK 90.**

**Interior view of the SSK 90 showing the manufac-
turer's label.**

Several other models were produced, in limited quantities, in an attempt to develope a lighter-weight, serviceable flight protection helmet, but little information is known about them. Two of the more commonly seen are illustrated below. The first example is a lightweight, all steel model with a leather liner designed to fit over the normal flying helmet, and had cut-outs on both sides to accomodate the earphones. Two thin cord chinstraps held the helmet in place. A Luftwaffe steel helmet decal was positioned on the front of this flying protection helmet, and a Siemens company decal has also been observed on some. Other examples of this helmet have unit insignia painted on them, such as the "Dutch shoe" emblem used by the ZG 26 "Horst Wessel."[56]

George Petersen

The SSK 90 flight protection helmet worn by a bomber crew over their winter flying helmets.

George Petersen

The lightweight, all steel flight protection helmet with standard helmet decal on the front.

The second example is a steel helmet with a thick leather covering, a sloping neck protector and no chinstrap. It also has side cut-outs for the earphones of the normal flying helmet. The illustrated example has a hand-embroidered aluminum wire breast eagle sewn to the front.

George Petersen

The leather-covered steel flight protection helmet with an officer's hand-embroidered breast eagle on the front.

### Air Inspection (Reichsluftaufsichtsdienst)

Since April 1934 the Luftaufsicht had been a part of the Reichsluftfahrtverwaltung, serving to enforce the air traffic laws and proper flight operations.[57] In December 1935 the re-appointed Reichsluftaufsichtsdienst became a part of the Luftwaffe.

RLA personnel wore the basic Luftwaffe uniform. The visored cap featured the Luftwaffe insignia. Since they were considered officials, officers wore dark green cap piping, while the lower ranks wore light green. Before 1935 the regular DLV uniform was worn. Obermeister and Meister wore aluminum cap cords. Hand-embroidered insignia was permitted to be worn on the band and cap top.[58] The visorless field cap (Fliegermütze) was the same that was worn by Luftwaffe officers.

O. Spronk

This Reichsluftaufsichtdienst member is shown in early 1935. His uniform is that of the Deutscher Luftsport-Verband but with light green Waffenfarbe.

---

[57]Westarpscher Taschenkalender für die Luftwaffe, 1940-1941. pp. 274-277.
[58]Anzugordnung für die Luftwaffe (L.Dv. 422). Abschnitt A. Berlin, November 27, 1935, p. 110.

**Airforce Fire Brigades**
**(Fliegerhorstfeuerwehren, including Feuerschutzbeamte der Luftwaffe)**

These fire brigades serving on military or civilian air fields were divided as follows:

I: Ziviles Stammpersonal--civilian workers, mainly sent from the Deutsche Arbeits-Front;

Löschkommandos--firefighters, made up of Luftwaffe enlisted men detached from their normal duties;

II: Feuerschutzbeamte--Fire protection officials.

Created officially in 1935, the Fliegerhorstfeuerwehren had existed since 1934. Their duty was to protect airfields and technical installations.

I: Civilians wore a dark blue visored cap (Klappmütze (LVBl. Nr. 770, October 21, 1935, p. 362)) with a black cloth cap band. The crown and top and bottom band pipings were crimson. The chinstrap was black leather and the visor was made of black Vulkanfiber. Higher ranking civilians, for example, Löschmeister and Oberfeuerwerker, wore aluminum cords. They could also wear silver wire hand-embroidered or machine-woven insignia.[59]

Visored cap for wear by civil firemen of the Fliegerhorstfeuerwehr (air field fire department).

An aluminum or aluminum-colored national emblem was positioned in the center of the cap top. Below this, in the center of the cap band, was worn the insigne in bright aluminum metal for civil employees. This insigne featured a raised canted swastika upon a pebbled field surrounded by a circle of oakleaves. Stylized wings (with a wing span of approximately 10.9cm and a wreath height of 2.9cm--sizes vary slightly), divided into four sections, extended from each side of the circle. This band insigne was secured to the cap

---

[59]*Westarpscher Taschenkalender für die Luftwaffe, 1940-1941. P. 1189.*

band by two prongs pushed through and flattened on the underside of the cap. This cap insignia (national emblem and winged wreath/swastika) was instituted in December 1934.[60] It was available with a matte finish, or in a polished or unpolished finish.

Early style national emblem.

George Petersen

George Petersen

(Top illustrations) Matte-grey national emblems and winged wreath. (Bottom) Aluminum colored insignia.

George Petersen

Uniformed civilian personnel wearing the above insignia on their dark blue visored cap. The man, second from left, is a Feuerschutzbeamte and wears the standard Feuerschutz insignia.

[60]L.D.M. 9056/34, D. IV. 3a, December 13, 1934.

George Petersen

Hand-embroidered officer's winged wreath.

A black twill field cap worn with the working dress, was shaped like a regular airforce field cap, however a smaller eagle in matte-grey machine embroidery was worn on the top.

Hall

J.R. Angolia

Löschkommandos were not permitted to wear the civilian fire uniform, but had to wear the standard Luftwaffe dress.[61] Civilians could, however, wear it while on fire or guard duty, or during training exercises.

II: Higher ranking Feuerschutzbeamte wore the Luftwaffe officials' uniform, lower ranking personnel such as Hauptbrandmeister, Brandmeister and Unterbrandmeister wore the dark blue visored cap with a black band, chin strap and visor. Their caps were piped around the crown and above and below the cap band in crimson. An aluminum or light metal Luftwaffe eagle was worn in the center of the cap top. The standard Luftwaffe winged/wreath and cockade was worn on the band. Brandmeister and Hauptbrandmeister were permitted to wear the insignia in hand-embroidery, as well as silver cap cords above the visor.[62]

From November 1940 a new color uniform was ordered, instead of the dark blue one. At this time the visored cap for the Feuerschutzbeamte in higher ranks was introduced in grey-blue and as worn by the Wehrmachtbeamten of the airforce. This transition was to take place as soon as possible (Der Schneidermeister-Der Uniformschneider, Nr. 49, December 8, 1940, p. 667).

These officials were also permitted to wear the black field cap since 1937 (UM Nr. 9, May 1, 1937, p. 131).

[61]*UM. Nr. 8, April 15, 1937, p. 128.*
[62]*Anzugordnung für die Luftwaffe (L.Dv. 422). Abschnitt A. Berlin, Neudruck April 1, 1937, p. 127.*

Candidates for a career as Feuerschutzbeamte wore the visored cap as worn by the "Löschmeister" of the "Ziviles Stammpersonal."

Visored cap worn by members of the Feuerschutzbeamte of the Fliegerhorstfeuerwehr. The cap is dark blue with a black ribbed mohair cap band and is piped in crimson.

Helga Sichermann-Spielhagen

William J. Floyd

(Far left) Note the uniform worn by this Feuerschutzbeamte of the air field fire department, April 20, 1939.

## Female Communication Auxiliaries
## (Luftwaffe-Nachrichtenhelferinnen)

Prior to the war, the Flugmeldehelferinnenschaft was created within the Luftwaffe. These female aids were the first Nachrichtenhelferinnen used

G. Rudloff

Various forms of dress for female members of the Flugmeldedienstpersonal (1940).

328

within the armed forces. The positive result of their service was instrumental in the creation of female auxiliary units in the other branches of service, such as the weather service (Wetterdienst), etc. These units were consolidated into the Luftwaffe-Helferinnenschaft.[63]

Ron Manion

(Above) Flugmeldedienstpersonal field cap. Note the golden-brown piping and the absence of a cockade.

Lower ranking Helferin wearing the field cap without piping.

Field cap without piping for lower ranking personnel.

George Petersen

Dresses were created in 1940 for the Flugmeldedienstpersonal and these females, in service as telephone operators, wore a grey-blue cap, Schiffchen-form, while on duty.[64] Since the fall of 1940 all females wore the Luftwaffe national emblem machine-embroidered in matte grey thread upon a grey-blue backing. The flap was piped in 3mm golden-brown piping.[65]

In June 1940 a grey-blue, cloth-covered, visored field cap (in the mountain cap style) with functional flaps was issued to Führerinnen (female leaders) of the Luftnachrichtenhelferinnen. A matte-grey machine-woven national emblem was sewn to the center of the cap top. The top was piped in 3mm golden brown cord.[66]

---

[63]DUZ. Nr. 3, 1944, p. 2.
[64]UM. July 15, 1940, p. 106.
[65]Ibid. Nr. 24, December 15, 1940, p. 196.
[66]Ibid. Nr. 17, September 1, 1941. p. 171.

Three Luftwaffe Helferinnen in France, 1943.

Officer ranked females wore a piped field cap with a shiny artificial silk national emblem sewn to the front of the cap above the flap. Lower ranks wore no piping. Their national emblem was machine-sewn of matte artificial silk.[67] These female auxiliaries were stationed in countries such as Norway, Denmark, the Netherlands and Belgium.

Dark blue field caps were also worn, but with the national emblem positioned in the front-center of the flap instead of on the top. It appears that this version was worn exclusively by females in the medical services.

A rare photo of the dark blue field cap and uniform being worn. This female is serving in the Sanitätsdienst as a hospital orderly.

In the fall of 1942 a large brimmed felt hat with narrow hat band was created for Nachrichtenhelferinnen in Mediterranean areas (UM. Nr. 23, December 1, 1942, p. 178). No insignia was worn with this hat. Confusion arose concerning the color of this hat and its manner of wear. The tailors' magazine "Uniformen-Markt" had incorrectly described it as grey-blue but it was to be bright-blue, and it was to be worn with the dress and not the "costume" (office dress). They later apologized explaining that at the time of the photo session no manikin with correct dress was available (Ibid., Nr. 4, February 15, 1943, P. 26).

Large brimmed felt hat created for the Nachrichtenhelferrinnen in Mediterranean areas, as discussed above.

It is believed that in 1944 a grey-blue version was introduced and did not have time to be covered by regulation as this style of hat was abolished in June 1944 (DUZ. Nr. 6, June 20, 1944, p.8).

### Female Anti-Aircraft Units (Flakwaffenhelferinnenkorps)

Females serving in the Flakwaffenhelferinnenkorps since fall 1943 were mainly volunteers and considered employees of the airforce (Gefolgschaftsmitglieder der Luftwaffe). Their duties were serving as searchlight crews, using listening devices and radio or telegraphy aggregates of ground batteries within the territory of war in the homeland.

A grey-blue visorless field cap, a grey-blue mountain cap (Bergmütze) with functional flaps secured by a single button were worn by these auxiliaries, as well as the M-1943 cap. The national emblem was machine-sewn in either matte or shiny artificial silk, depending on the wearer's rank. Flakwaffenführerinnen wore a 3mm wide silver or aluminum piping around the flap of the visorless field cap.[68]

[67]DUZ. Nr. 3, 1944, p. 2.
[68]DUZ. Nr. 7, July 1944, pp. 4-5.

Members of the Flakwaffenhelferinnenkorps wearing the single button M43 style cap.

George Petersen

M43 style cap as worn by Flakwaffenhelferinnenkorps members.

### Flak Auxiliaries (Flakhelfer)

Flakhelfer were members of the Hitler-Jugend called up to assist anti-aircraft battery crews as well as the Luftschutz during the war. The normal HJ headdress was worn,[69] or Luftwaffe issue caps.

Luftwaffenhelfer which also came from the HJ (mainly the Flieger- and Motor-HJ) were organized to accelerate them into Luftwaffe personnel. They were instructed in ground and anti-aircraft defense. Sometimes a visorless field cap was worn, but the black HJ visored field cap with the HJ diamond in the center of the cap top or a field-grey type was worn while on duty. The Luftwaffe national emblem was generally worn with the field-grey version. The HJ badge could be either metal or cloth.[70] (Flak- as well as Luftwaffenhelfer will be discussed in detail in the Hitler Youth chapter.)

[69]DUZ. Nr. 9, September 1944, p. 7.
[70]DUZ. Nr. 3, June 20, 1943, p. 10.

(Left) A young Flakhelfer being instructed by a Luftwaffe NCO. Note the unique leather chin strap added to the youth's cap. (Below) Three very young Flakhelfer POWs.

## Home Guard Anti-Aircraft (Heimatflak)

The home guard defense units, made up of civilians, wore the standard grey, or on some occasions, black, working cap in the Schiffchenform. These so-called Flakwehrmänner often wore the Luftwaffe national emblem and cockade on this cap, but it was not officially sanctioned.

## Fliegerisch tätigen Angestellten der Luftwaffe

This group of civilian specialists was active in training and instruction, and were, in most cases, experienced pilots and wireless operators on loan from Lufthansa. Their navy blue uniform was to be worn on special occasions and never on duty.

The visored cap resembled that worn by the merchant marine and was made from navy blue doeskin. The cap band was black mohair.

A special insigne measured 14.5cm wide. It consisted of a large canted swastika resting on outstretched wings. Two oakleaf sprigs were positioned at the bottom of the insigne. This emblem exists in two metal variations:

Metal insigne in either gilt or aluminum.

333

Flugbetriebsleiter, as well as his deputy (Stellvertreter), Fliegerkapitän and Flugzeugführer wore a gilt metal or hand-embroidered insigne.

Bordfunker and others wore an aluminum metal or hand-embroidered insigne. The embroidered specimens were on a dark blue backing.

George Petersen

(Above) Cap for higher grades with gilt wire insigne and gilt/black cap cords. A similar visored cap is worn at right.

George Petersen

Hand-embroidered gilt wire wings with aluminum swastika.

George Petersen

Hand-embroidered aluminum wire wings with gilt swastika.

George Petersen

Helga Sichermann-Spielhagen

Saris

The leader of Air Signals Station Zwischenahn (left) wears the uniform of the Fliegerisch tätig Angestellte der Luftwaffe. Note that his cap insignia is hand-embroidered wire, while the official from a Flugsicherungsschiff (facing camera) wears a metal version.

The following cap cords were worn:

| | |
|---|---|
| Flugbetriebsleiter, Stellvertreter as well as Fliegerkapitän | gold cords, alternating in black. |
| Flugzeugführer | black cords, alternating in gold. |
| Funker | aluminum cords, interwoven with black. |
| Other employees | blue cords[71] |

Occasionally the insignia described above was also worn by members of the Luftdienstverband. This organization was a Luftwaffe unit and was in charge of assisting in the docking of the enormous "flying boats." It is known that such a unit was stationed at Bad Zwischenahn. They were also in charge of the towing of air targets.

---

[71]*Rundschau-Deutsches Schneiderfachblatt. Nr. 27, July 3, 1937, pp. 953-954.*

## Seefliegerhorstflugsicherung

With the rebirth of the Luftwaffe, a first world war tradition was carried on, the "Marinefliegersoldat" (naval pilots) were re-introduced around mid-1937. They were also called "Seeflieger."

This section came under the command of the Luftwaffe inspection and was abbreviated as "S.Fl.H.F.S."[72] Their purpose was to guard Germany's coastal borders, to reconnoiter and to escort and warn ships and boats.[73] These pilots wore Luftwaffe uniforms when not on duty.[74] They were stationed ashore or aboard ships.[75]

The ship crews for these Flugsicherungsschiffe (ships in service of the Luftwaffe)[76] and for the other connected section, the Seenotdienst (air-sea rescue),[77] had to be trained in naval skills in the navy or by their civil profession.

Special uniforms and headdress were created for these ship's crews. The visored caps were of the merchant marine style. The insigne has a swastika surmounting two crossed anchors with scalloped wings on each side. This insigne exists in metal as well as machine-woven or hand-embroidered wire on a dark blue backing: silver for ship's technical personnel, wireless officers and administrative officials; gold for deck personnel. Employees also wore a white top visored cap similar to that of the navy. The cap cords, however, may have been structured in the style of the "fliegerisch tätigen Angestellten der Luftwaffe" as reflected in period photos. In this case the ranks were:

| | |
|---|---|
| Kapitän | gold cords, alternating in black; |
| Steuerleute u. Bootsmänner | black cords, interwoven with gold; |
| Maschinisten u. Funker | aluminum cords, interwoven with black; |
| Other employees | a black leather chinstrap. |

George Petersen

White top visored cap for personnel of Flugsicherungsschiffe.

[72]*Besondere Luftwaffe-Bestimmungen. Nr. 118. August 24, 1937, p. 64.*
[73]*Kyffhäuser-Kalender des Dt. Reichskriegerbundes. 1938, pp. 71-73.*
[74]*Der Schneidermeister-Der Uniformschneider. Nr. 31, 1940, p. 436.*
[75]*Die deutsche Luftwaffe. Stuttgart, 1937, pp. 6-7.*
[76]*UM. 1938, p. 171.*
[77]*Köhlers Flieger-Kalender, 1942. pp. 140-143.*

Ron Manion

S.Fl.H.F.S. metal visored cap insigne. Note the fine feather detail. In gilt metal for deck personnel and in aluminum for machine crews.

O. Spronk

George Petersen

Yellow and white colors as above, but in machine-embroidered thread. The insigne at left is for the dark blue field cap.

George Petersen

Personnel of Flugsicherungsschiffe wearing both the white and blue top visored cap. These caps were also worn by members of the Seenotdienst (air-sea rescue).

Excellent photo of members of the Flugsicherungsschiffe wearing their special visored cap with various cap cords and chin straps. It was also worn by members of the Seenotdienst (Air-Sea Rescue), see below.

### Civilian Drivers (Zivilkraftfahrer der Luftwaffe)

Civilian drivers wore a black visored cap in the style of that worn by army drivers. The Luftwaffe national emblem and winged-wreath/cockade were worn on this cap. During rides which were top secret or particularly sensitive the insignia could be removed by the driver.[78] A crash helmet was available for wear until 1938. This dress was permitted for wear only by employees involved in driving individuals. Drivers of motor-trucks and motorcycles were not allowed to wear this special visored cap (UM., Nr. 5, March 1, 1940, p. 34).

### Doormen and Elevator Operators (Pförtner u. Fahrstuhlführer)

Regulations dated 1936 show that a uniform was created for civil guards acting as doormen and elevator operators of the Reichsluftfahrtministerium and Luftflottenkommando-buildings.

The old DLV uniform, as worn until December 1935, could still be used. However, no insignia was allowed to be worn then.[79] These persons were mainly used to guard munition stores and building construction sites.

In 1937 doormen connected to Luftkreis- and Luftgaukommando, as well as Fliegerdivisionen buildings were allowed to wear the same uniform.[80]

The visored cap worn by all grades was made of grey-blue material with a 4.5cm wide cap band. The cap was piped (2mm) around the top and above and below the cap band in mignorette-green (Reichsluftfahrtministerium) or bordeaux red (official Luftwaffe buildings). A black cord or leather chinstrap was secured above the black Vulkanfiber or leather visor.

**Visored cap with bordeaux red cap band and piping worn by civilian employees serving as doormen or elevator operators at Luftwaffe buildings.**

---

[78]LVBl. Nr. 545, August 24, 1935, p. 545.
[79]Ibid. Nr. 890, November 19, 1935, p. 420.
[80]UM. Nr. 15, August 1, 1939, p. 240.

The insigne worn by civilian firemen was worn on the cap band. A small aluminum national emblem was affixed to the cap top. Before January 1938 this cap and insignia was also permitted for wear by other civilian employees of the Luftwaffe, at which time this was abolished (UM., Nr. 4, February 15, 1938, p. 52). After this date the cap and insignia was only authorized for wear by:

Ziviles Stammpersonal der Fliegerhorstfeuerwehren;
Pförtner u. Fahrstuhlführer des RLM;
Pförtner bei den Luftkreiskommandos;
Wächter u. Pförtner bei Dienststellen.

Assistant of the Reichsluftfahrtverwaltung (technical or other employees) and also Werkführer and Beamtenanwärter (called Versorgungsanwärter-supporting candidates) wore a similar visored cap with a leather chinstrap. Specifics of this cap are not known.

Note:<br>
A visored cap exists, identical to the cap for employees in<br>
official Luftwaffe buildings with Bordeaux-red piping and<br>
cap band, but with a pinkish-red piping and cap band.<br>
Purpose unknown.

George Petersen

The man at left is a factory official (Werkmeister) working with a Luftwaffe engineer on aircraft testing. Note he is wearing an enlisted ranks' national emblem on his worker's cap, which was against Luftwaffe regulations.

George Peteresn

Unidentified, Luftwaffe-related individual wearing a unique visored cap. He was possibly associated with a watch service of some sort. Note that the style of the wreath/cockade is identical to that of a Luftwaffe officer, but without the wings on either side.

### Fur Caps (Pelzmützen)

Various patterns of fur caps were issued to Luftwaffe personnel serving in cold climates or during the winter season. Metal as well as cloth Luftwaffe insignia were worn on the various forms of headdress. It should be noted that captured caps, especially Russian, were widely used.

One example of the many forms of fur caps worn in cold climates by Luftwaffe personnel.

A high-quality version of the winter fur cap with aluminum wire officer's national emblem, first pattern.

Len Champion

Another example of a Luftwaffe winter cap with both the national emblem and cockade affixed.

George Petersen

Assorted models of the winter fur cap in wear.

John Coy

Excellent example of a white leather
Pelzmütze with fur ear flaps.

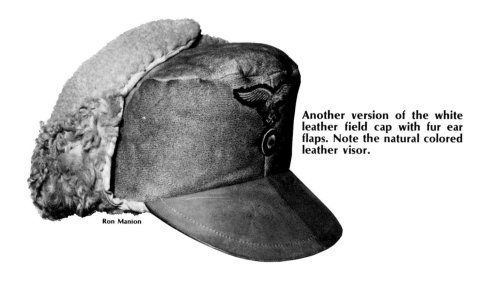

Another version of the white leather field cap with fur ear flaps. Note the natural colored leather visor.

Ron Manion

### Freiwillig in der Luftwaffe

During the war foreign volunteers served in the Luftwaffe, both in flying and Flak units. The regular Luftwaffe, grey-blue field cap was worn, as were the mountain cap and M43 cap.

For example, the "Flämische Flakbrigade" was officially instituted on July 2, 1944. They were to protect the Flemish coastal areas as well as their home cities. Members of this unit were classified as "Wehrmachtangehörige." As the war progressed they were transferred to Germany where they saw heavy combat.

J. Vincx

Members of the Flämische Flakbrigade in November 1944 at Philippsburg. From left to right: J. Maes, F. Wabbes, R. Lenoir and M. Popelier. Regular field and mountain-style caps are being worn.

Flying units from Croatia, Latvia, Estonia, Spain, etc., wore the standard Luftwaffe uniform and headgear with little or no additional cap insignia. An exception to this was the Russian flying unit, "Fliegerstaffel Ost," in which some members wore an oval in their national colors directly over the cockade on the M43 cap and the Luftwaffe visored cap.

## Waffenfarben--1935

| | |
|---|---|
| Reichsluftfahrtministerium | black |
| Fliegertruppe | golden-yellow |
| Flak-Artillerie | red |
| Luftnachrichtentruppe | bright brown |
| Sanitätdienst | dark blue |
| Luftaufsichtsbeamte | bright green[81] |

## Waffenfarben--1935-1937

| | |
|---|---|
| Generale | gold |
| RLM u. unmittelbar unterstellte Dienststellen | black |
| Exceptions: | |
| a. Medizinalabt. des RLM; | dark blue |
| b. Kommando der Fliegererprobungsstellen u. Fliegererprobungsstelle Travemünde | golden-yellow |
| Kommandobehörden u. Stäbe, oberer Führer | branch-of-service color |
| Fliegertruppe | golden-yellow |
| Flakartillerie, Festungsflakartillerie | bright red |
| Luftnachrichtentruppe | light brown, changed in 1937 to golden-brown |
| Sanitätsoffiziere, S-U-Offiziere, usw. | dark blue |
| Offiziere (W) bei sämtlichen Dienststellen | branch-of-service |
| Feuerwerker bei sämtlichen Dienststellen | branch-of-service |
| Luftzeugämter, Luftzeugnebenämter, Lufthauptmunitionsanstalten u. Luftmunitionsanstalten | branch-of-service |
| Luftaufsicht (Reichsluftaufsicht) | light green |
| Luftwaffenreserve | light blue |
| Offiziere (E), Sanitätsoffiziere (E), Offiziere (WE u. LaE), Reserveoffiziere | as active officers |

---

[81]*LVBl. Nr. 80, March 25, 1935, pp. 34-35.*

Schools:
- a. Luftkriegsakademie — golden-yellow
- b. Lufttechnische Akademie — golden-yellow
- c. Flakartillerieschule — bright red
- d. Luftnachrichtenschule — light brown
- e. Reichsschule für Luftaufsicht — light green
- f. Luftkriegsschule, Luftwaffesportschule — golden-yellow

| | |
|---|---|
| Wehrmachtbeamte der Luftwaffe | dark green |
| Wehrmachtbeamte im RLA | light or dark green[82] |
| Wirtschaftsinspekteure | branch-of-service[83] |

These colors did not change, but others were added:

| | |
|---|---|
| Reichsluftfahrministerium | branch-of-service since 1941 |

Aussenstellen RLM u. Dienststellen;
- a. Flugbereitschaft, Hauptbild- u. Hauptfilmstelle — golden-yellow
- b. Nachrichtenabteilung — golden-brown
- c. Others in the RLM — branch-of-service

| | |
|---|---|
| Luftwaffengruppenkommandos, Luftgaukommandos | golden-yellow |
| Flieger-Divisionskommandeuren | golden-yellow |
| Höhere Kommandeuren der Flak. Abt. | bright red |
| Kommandeur der LW-Lehr-Division | branch-of-service for the "Waffengattung" |
| Generalstabsoffiziere | crimson |
| Regiment General Göring | white |
| Wachbataillon der Luftwaffe Berlin | golden-yellow |
| Lehrtruppe der Luftwaffe | branch-of-service |
| Aufklärungsgruppe Jöterbog, Lehrstaffel See | golden-yellow |
| Offiziere (W), Feuerwerker einschl. RLM | bright red |

---

[82]*LVBl. Nr. 423, July 23, 1935, p. 191.*
[83]*Ibid. Nr. 614, September 11, 1935, p. 289.*

| | |
|---|---|
| Nachschubdienststellen | golden-yellow |
| Militär-F Übungsstelle (abolished in 1941) | golden-yellow |
| Offiziere u. San. Offiziere z.D., Offiziere des Beurlaubtenstandes | orange, thereafter branch-of-service color |
| Reichsanstalt für Luftschutz | bright red |
| Ingenieurkorps, Nautikerkorps der Luftwaffe | pink[84] |
| Luftwaffe-Baukompanie (added in 1940) | black[85] |
| Flieger Waffentechnische Schulen | golden-yellow |
| Flak Waffentechnische Schulen | bright red[86] |

## Dress Regulations (Anzugordnung)

| | |
|---|---|
| Flugdienstanzug (fliegendes Personal) | visorless field cap |
| Anzug für Sonderdienst | flight helmet |
| a-planmässige Ausstattung | visorless field cap |
| b-zugelassenen Abweichung | head protector |
| c-Flakartillerie | working cap |
| Feldanzug | visorless field cap, during the first years of the war by signal and flight units; thereafter a steel helmet |
| Dienstanzug u. Wachanzug (kleiner Dienstanzug) | field or visored cap (with white top, if desired) |
| Meldeanzug | visored cap |
| Paradeanzug | steel helmet or field cap |
| Ausgehanzug | visored cap or white visored cap from April 1 through September 30. |
| Gesellschaftsanzug, grosser kleiner | both as Ausgehanzug |
| Sportanzug | Bergmütze when ordered[87] |

---

[84]*Handbuch der neuzeitlichen Wehrwissenschaften, dritter Band. 2: Die Luftwaffe. Berlin, 1939, pp. 412-414.*
[85]*UM. Nr. 2, January 15, 1940, p. 10.*
[86]*Ibid. Date and page number unknown.*
[87]*Der Dienstunterricht in der Luftwaffe. Jahrgang 1941, Berlin, pp. 48-55.*

The Flieger-Technische Vorschule of the Luftwaffe will be covered in the Hitler Youth chapter although they were technically Luftwaffe.

The NSKK-Motorgruppe Luftwaffe, Transportkorps Speer and affiliated organizations will be discussed in their respective chapters.

## Glossary of Terms

Baskenmütze - Beret-type cap
Bergmütze - Mountain cap
Bootsform - Boat-shaped field or garrison cap
Bordmütze - Side cap
Dienstmütze - Service Cap
Einheitsfeldmütze - General-issue field cap (M43)
Feldmütze - Field or garrison cap
Filzmütze - Felt hat
Fliegermütze - Garrison cap
Kepi - "Coffee can" style cap
Klappmütze - Uniform cap with sloping top and grommets on underside of cap
    top
Kokarde - A rosette of state or national colors
Lagermütze - Garrison cap
Landesfarben - State colors
Landeskokarde - Cockade in state colors
Mannschaftsmütze - Enlisted man's nat
Matrosenmütze - Brimless cap (Donald Duck style)
Mützenband - Cap band
Pelzmützen - Fur cap
Sattleform - Saddle-shape
Schachthut - Tube-shaped cap
Schiffchen - Garrison cap, boat-shaped
Schimütze - Ski cap
Schirmmütze - Visored uniform or service cap
Schnüre - Piping
Schutzmütze - Panzer beret
Seglermütze - Yachtman's cap
Soutache - Inverted "V" in Waffenfarbe on field caps
Sternen - Pips
Stumpenhut - Brimmed hat
Sturzhelm - Crash helmet
Tellerform - Saucer shape
Tropenhelm - Tropical helmet
Tresse - Braid of varying widths
Tuchmütze - Cloth kepistyle cap
Waffenfarbe - Branch of service color
Weiche - Semi-stiff
Weissebezug - White cover
Zweispitzhut - "Fore and Aft hat"